100 YEARS OF
COWBOY STORIES

Edited by
TED STONE

LONE
PINE

The Publisher
Lone Pine Publishing

206, 10426 - 81 Ave.	202A, 110 Seymour Street	16149 Redmond Way, #180
Edmonton, Alberta	Vancouver, British Columbia	Redmond, Washington
Canada T6E 1X5	Canada V6B 3N3	USA 98052

This book is a co-publication with Red Deer College Press of Red Deer, Alberta.

Canadian Cataloguing in Publication Data

Main entry under title:
100 years of cowboy stories

ISBN 1-55105-054-4

1. Cowboys—Canada—Fiction. 2. Short stories, Canadian (English)—20th century.
I. Stone, Ted, 1947– II. Title: One hundred years of cowboy stories.
PS8323.C68O53 1994a   C813'.0108352636   C95-910050-4 PR9197.35.C68O53
1994a

The publisher gratefully acknowledges the assistance of Alberta Community Development and the Department of Canadian Heritage, the support of the Canada/Alberta Agreement on the cultural industries, and the financial support provided by the Alberta Foundation for the Arts.

Cover Art and Design by Kurt Hafso.
Text Design by Dennis Johnson.
Printed and bound in Canada by Parkland ColorPress.

ACKNOWLEDGMENTS

"The Cattle Rustlers" by Stewart Edward White, from *Arizona Nights*, The McClure Company, © 1907.

"On the Brazos and Wichita" by Andy Adams, from *The Log of a Cowboy*, Houghton Mifflin and Company, © 1903.

"Beyond the Desert" from *Beyond the Desert* by Eugene Manlove Rhodes, The McClure Company, © 1914.

"Longrope's Last Guard" from *Trails Plowed Under* by Charles M. Russell, © 1927 by Doubleday, a division of Bantam Doubleday Dell Publishing Group, Inc. Used by permission of Doubleday, a division of Bantam Doubleday Dell Publishing Group, Inc.

"Trail Fever" by S. Omar Barker, © 1956, used by permission of Robert Phillips for the estate of S. Omar Barker.

"The Girl in the Humbert," © 1939 by Mari Sandoz, © renewed 1966 by Caroline Pifer. Reprinted by permission of McIntosh and Otis, Inc.

"Carrion Spring" from *Collected Stories of Wallace Stegner* by Wallace Stegner, © 1990 by Wallace Stegner. Reprinted by permission of Random House, Inc.

"Open Winter" by H.L. Davis, from *Team Bells Woke Me and Other Stories*, William Morrow & Company, © 1939. Used by permission of Elizabeth T. Hobson.

"A Day with a Deer, a Bear, and Norah Smith," from *Smith and Other Events* by Paul St. Pierre, © 1985, published by Douglas & McIntyre. Reprinted by permission.

"The Horsebreaker" from *Up Where I Used to Live* by Max Schott, © 1978, University of Illinois Press. Used by permission of University of Illinois Press and Max Schott.

"Cowboys Are My Weakness" is reprinted from *Cowboys Are My Weakness, Stories by Pam Houston*, by permission of W.W. Norton & Company, Inc., © 1992 by Pam Houston.

~ CONTENTS ~

100 YEARS OF
COWBOY STORIES

INTRODUCTION

Ted Stone

UNTIL THE 1890s, the lives of cowboys and ranchers were generally thought unfit material for literature. Even in the Dime Novel adventure stories popular at the time, cowboys were usually little more than Western backdrops for the plainsmen, detectives and outlaws who were the real heroes of the stories.

By the nineties, the life of the old-time cowboy was already disappearing. Homesteaders had divided much of the West into small farms. Ranchers large and small were obliged to fence off huge areas of the remaining ranges. In 1892, though, Owen Wister, in *Harper's* magazine, published "Hank's Woman"—the first serious attempt at a literary story in the genre, and cowboy stories, in a variety of brands, have been with us ever since.

Wister, a Philadeplphia lawyer, wrote "Hank's Woman" following an evening with Teddy Roosevelt. Both men had spent time in the West, and that night over dinner at an exclusive men's club, both lamented the fact that there hadn't yet been credible fiction written about ranchers and cowboys. After their conversation, Wister went home and began working on "Hank's Woman." A decade later, the cowboy hero of the story became the title character in his famous novel, *The Virginian*.

The tremendous success of *The Virginian* encouraged more cowboy fiction. Ironically, one of *The Virginian*'s most lasting legacies came when Zane Grey took the character Wister created and began using him as the model for the protagonists of his own Western novels and stories. Grey's stories, in turn, have furnished the template for formula Western novels, television shows and movies ever since.

It has been these popular formula Westerns, in the tradition of the Dime Novels that preceded them, that have generally accounted for the low opinion accorded "cowboy stories," and to some extent, Western writing generally. But the literature of the North American West is both greater and older than formula Westerns and Dime Novels.

Stories of the frontier have always been popular with eastern readers— initially with readers back in Europe, and then, as the frontier moved west, in the eastern areas of this continent. The humorous yarns of Mark Twain and Bret Harte, the Leatherstocking tales of James Fennimore Cooper, earlier legends about Daniel Boone, Davy Crockett and Mike Fink all, for a time, and in differing degrees, captured the imagination of easterners.

Succeeding types of stories enjoyed short-term popularity before being pushed aside by new frontier adventures. Legends of early frontiersmen crossing the eastern mountains were followed by the tales of new pioneers pushing still farther West. The stories of fur traders and mountain men, such as Washington Irving's *Astoria* and *The Adventures of Captain Bonneville,* were followed by tales of new migrants crossing the mountains and settling the far West. In a few more years, Harte and Twain came along with tales of the California mining camps.

Cowboy stories began appearing when the Old West was already coming to an end, when the North American frontier had virtually disappeared. By the time large numbers of readers had discovered the Virginian and other fictional cowboys, the Twentieth Century had arrived. Perhaps that, at least partly, explains why, of all our frontier heroes, the cowboy has been the most lasting. He is, simply, the last one.

The special place the cowboy fills in the North American imagination, though, is something more complicated and meaningful than simply an accident of timing. Cowboy stories have been too much a part of our culture these last hundred years to think otherwise. To a surprising extent, people of the Twentieth Century, with urban lives dominated by science and technology, have continued to be fascinated by visions of the Nineteenth Century cowboy.

For several generations now, North Americans have grown up with Western novels and movies and, for nearly fifty years, Westerns on television. In 1959, which might have been the popular peak for TV Westerns, there were at least thirty-five Western shows airing on the three American networks. Eight out of the top ten shows that year were Westerns.

This century has also seen the sale of millions of copies of Western novels. Louis L'amour's novels alone have sold 150 million copies. Zane

Grey's have sold even more. Only some of these books, movies and television shows have been specifically about cowboys or ranchers, but in large measure, it has been the image of the cowboy that has come to define the standard Western hero, no matter what his occupation. If the character has the right amount of grit, he is, or is as good as, a cowboy.

No matter what the reality might have been, the cowboy has become the North American knight on horseback, a knight who lived his life, in the public mind at least, in unfettered freedom—beyond the reach of law and other impediments of civilization. In some ways, the imagined life of the cowboy is the original North American dream, a life of spiritual and moral rejuvenation in a new place unspoiled by the civilization of the East.

For nearly a century, our vision of the cowboy has dominated what we imagine the Old West to have been. Even though Western stories, both in popular and serious fiction, are more likely to be about other Westerners (homesteaders, lawmen, trappers, miners, prospectors, Indians, immigrants, soldiers, contemporary Westerners, etc.) than cowboys or ranchers, the cowboy story is still what most of us think of when we think of Western stories. Even when the cowboy isn't there, we measure the Western story with a cowboy yardstick. The fictional cowboy on horseback, armed with his six-shooter, has become an almost mythical figure, and as such, the most important North American literary character since Huckleberry Finn.

Yet, surprisingly, although there have been dozens of anthologies of Western stories, cowboy stories have been the focus of only a few. More often, they have played slight roles, sometimes being overlooked entirely, as if their inclusion would diminish the worth of the collection.

But cowboy stories don't have to be formula shoot-'em-ups. Throughout this century, there have been cowboy stories with vistas and insights that range well beyond anything imagined by Owen Wister. Over the years, Western writers of the cattle country have continued to search for the elusive qualities of story, myth, legend and truth that go into the making of any literature.

No editor can hope to include every story of merit in the hundred years or so that cowboy stories have been with us, or even give examples of all the different kinds of stories that have been written about ranchers and cowboys—or the mythology that has developed around them. What

I've tried to do instead is gather a sample of those stories, from the earliest to the most recent.

While every anthology must benefit and suffer from the biases of its editor, most of the stories in this collection have been selected for reasons that go beyond personal favorites. "Hank's Woman," for instance, I selected in large measure because of its role in the history of the genre and the creation of the archetypal cowboy hero. Other stories, like Andy Adams' "On the Brazos and Wichita," I've chosen because of the accurate accounting they give of old-time cowboy life.

I've presented the collection chronologically, but the chronology is sometimes based on date of publication, sometimes on subject matter. This was done with the notion that one story flowed more naturally to the next in this order rather than some other. Certainly, something of the changing nature of the cowboy story can be seen as the stories unfold.

The first three stories in the collection are by outsiders, writers who observed the West with an outsider's curiosity and enthusiasm. Of the three, Stephen Crane's tale, "Twelve O'Clock," brings the strongest notion of realism to the telling. In the next few stories—"The Cattle Rustlers" by Stewart Edward White, "Beyond the Desert" by Eugene Manlove Rhodes, "Longrope's Last Guard" by the Western artist Charles M. Russell and Andy Adams' "On the Brazos and Wichita" —the Old West is depicted with an insider's knowledge and perspective, and the stories give a somewhat more realistic and detailed account of that life than even Crane presents.

It's interesting that, although Wister's Virginian is a cowboy, the reader never sees him at work, not in the story, not in the novel. Wister was too busy making the Virginian measure up to his romantic notions of the cowboy West to worry much about presenting the mundane affairs of raising cattle. That job was left to writers such as Russell and Adams, who were once cowboys themselves.

"The Girl in the Humbert," by Mari Sandoz, and "Carrion Spring," by Wallace Stegner, are tales of a changing West by writers born after the days of the open range, whose lives and words have bridged the gap between that time and now. Stegner and Sandoz look at the beginnings of modern ranching with conflicting emotions ranging from admiration to dismay. Their contemporary, S. Omar Barker, in "Trail Fever," on the other hand, looks back to the original days of the cowboy with a mixture of realism, nostalgia and humor.

Barker wrote for magazines during a time when popular periodicals offered a ready market for Western stories. Like H.L. Davis' "Open Winter," though, Barker's stories rise above the formula plots and cardboard characters generally associated with the short story magazines of the day. "Trail Fever" and "Open Winter" take what appears to be a well-worn topic and turn it to artful storytelling.

Finally, we have the three most recent stories. Paul St. Pierre gives the reader a glimpse at life, only a few years past, in one of the most remote outposts of old-style ranching on the continent. Max Schott takes a contemporary rancher off the ranch and, in the process, shows that being a rancher is as much a matter of character as occupation. Pam Houston, in the final story of the collection, looks at the myth of the cowboy from the point of view of a contemporary woman.

It's noteworthy that Houston's story, published exactly one hundred years after "Hank's Woman," is, in most respects, the antithesis of Wister's story and the novel he developed from it. Where Wister's fondness for the Virginian colors everything he has to say about the cowboy, the heart of Houston's narrator has been captured, she discovers, more by the cowboy ideal—the cowboy ideal Wister helped to create—than the cowboy himself. Where the woman in Wister's story is there solely to illuminate the Virginian, the cowboy in Houston's story illuminates the woman.

On one level, Houston's heroine simply fell for some of the same romantic notions about cowboys and ranch life that Wister did. They're fantasies most of us have harbored at one time or another. There's something noble and appealing about life on a ranch, even to city folks who will never get any closer to a real ranch than a good book.

Tales of the cattle country attract a wide range of readers, but it's the people who live on ranches who make these stories a living part of our collective literature. People in the cattle-raising areas of the West have maintained a cultural identity that many of their fellow Westerners have lost. It's this cultural separateness, more than anything else, that suggests people will still be writing and reading cowboy stories for another hundred years.

—TED STONE
June, 1994

HANK'S WOMAN

Owen Wister

I

Many fish were still in the pool; and though luck seemed to have left me, still I stood at the end of the point, casting and casting my vain line, while the Virginian lay and watched. Noonday's extreme brightness had left the river and the plain in cooling shadow, but spread and glowed over the yet undimmed mountains. Westward, the Tetons lifted their peaks pale and keen as steel through the high, radiant air. Deep down between the blue gashes of their cañons the sun sank long shafts of light, and the glazed laps of their snow-fields shone separate and white upon their lofty vastness, like handkerchiefs laid out to dry. Opposite, above the valley, rose that other range, the Continental Divide, not sharp, but long and ample. It was bare in some high places, and below these it stretched everywhere, high and low, in brown and yellow parks, or in purple miles of pine a world of serene undulations, a great sweet country of silence.

A passing band of antelope stood herded suddenly together at sight of us; then a little breeze blew for a moment from us to them, and they drifted like phantoms away, and were lost in the levels of the sage-brush.

"If humans could do like that," said the Virginian, watching them go.

"Run, you mean?" said I.

"Tell a foe by the smell of him," explained the cow-puncher; "at fifty yards—or a mile."

"Yes," I said; "men would be hard to catch."

"A woman needs it most," he murmured. He lay down again in his lounging sprawl, with his grave eyes intently fixed upon my fly-casting.

The gradual day mounted up the hills farther from the floor of earth. Warm airs eddied in its wake slowly, stirring the scents of the plain together. I looked at the Southerner; and there was no guessing what his thoughts might be at work upon behind that drowsy glance. Then for a moment a trout rose, but only to look and whip down again into the pool that wedged its calm into the riffle from below.

"Second thoughts," mused the Virginian; and as the trout came no more, "Second thoughts," he repeated; "and even a fish will have them sooner than folks has them in this mighty hasty country." And he rolled over into a new position of ease.

At whom or what was he aiming these shafts of truth? Or did he moralize merely because health and the weather had steeped him in that serenity which lifts us among the spheres? Well, sometimes he went on from these beginnings and told me wonderful things.

"I reckon," said he, presently, "that knowing when to change your mind would be pretty near knowledge enough for plain people."

Since my acquaintance with him—this was the second summer of it—I had come to understand him enough to know that he was unfathomable. Still, for a moment it crossed my thoughts that perhaps now he was discoursing about himself. He had allowed a jealous foreman to fall out with him at Sunk Creek ranch in the spring, during Judge Henry's absence. The man, having a brief authority, parted with him. The Southerner had chosen that this should be the means of ultimately getting the foreman dismissed and himself recalled. It was strategic. As he put it to me: "When I am gone, it will be right easy for the Judge to see which of us two he wants. And I'll not have done any talking." All of which duly befell in the autumn as he had planned: the foreman was sent off, his assistant promoted, and the Virginian again hired. But this was meanwhile. He was indulging himself in a several months' drifting, and while thus drifting he had written to me. That is how we two came to be on our way from the railroad to hunt the elk and the mountain-sheep, and were pausing to fish where Buffalo Fork joins its waters with Snake River. In those days the antelope still ran there in hundreds, the Yellowstone Park was a new thing, and mankind lived very far away. Since meeting me with the horses in Idaho the Virginian had been silent, even for him. So now I stood casting my fly, and trusting that he was not troubled with second thoughts over his strategy.

"Have yu' studied much about marriage?" he now inquired. His serious eyes met mine as he lay stretched along the ground.

"Not much," I said; "not very much."

"Let's swim," he said. "They have changed their minds."

Forthwith we shook off our boots and dropped our few clothes, and heedless of what fish we might now drive away, we went into the cool, slow, deep breadth of backwater which the bend makes just there. As he came up near me, shaking his head of black hair, the cowpuncher was smiling a little.

"Not that any number of baths," he remarked, "would conceal a man's objectionableness from an antelope—not even a she-one."

Then he went under water, and came up again a long way off.

We dried before the fire, without haste. To need no clothes is better than purple and fine linen. Then he tossed the flap-jacks, and I served the trout, and after this we lay on our backs upon a buffalo-hide to smoke and watch the Tetons grow more solemn, as the large stars opened out over the sky.

"I don't care if I never go home," said I.

The Virginian nodded. "It gives all the peace o' being asleep with all the pleasure o' feeling the widest kind of awake," said he. "Yu' might say the whole year's strength flows hearty in every waggle of your thumb." We lay still for a while. "How many things surprise yu' any more?" he next asked.

I began considering; but his silence had at length worked round to speech.

"Inventions, of course," said he, "these hyeh telephones an' truck yu' see so much about in the papers—but I ain't speaking o' such things of the brain. It is just the common things I mean. The things that a livin', noticin' man is liable to see and maybe sample for himself. How many o' them kind can surprise yu' still?"

I still considered.

"Most everything surprised me onced," the cow-puncher continued, in his gentle Southern voice. "I must have been a mighty green boy. Till I was fourteen or fifteen I expect I was astonished by ten o'clock every morning. But a man begins to ketch on to folks and things after a while. I don't consideh that when—that afteh a man is, say twenty-five, it is creditable he should get astonished too easy. And so yu've not examined yourself that-a-way?"

I had not.

"Well, there's two things anyway—I know them for sure—that I expect will always get me—don't care if I live to thirty-five, or forty-five, or eighty. And one's the ways lightning can strike." He paused. Then he got up and kicked the fire, and stood by it, staring at me. "And the other is the people that other people will marry."

He stopped again; and I said nothing.

"The people that other people will marry," he repeated. "That will surprise me till I die."

"If my sympathy—" I began.

But the brief sound that he gave was answer enough, and more than enough cure for my levity.

"No," said he, reflectively; "not any such thing as a fam'ly for me, yet. Never, it may be. Not till I can't help it. And *that* woman has not come along so far. But I have been sorry for a woman lately. I keep thinking what she will do. For she will have to do something. Do yu' know Austrians? Are they quick in their feelings, like I-talians? Or are they apt to be sluggish, same as Norwegians and them other Dutch-speakin' races?"

I told him what little I knew about Austrians.

"This woman is the first I have ever saw of 'em," he continued. "Of course men will stampede into marriage in this hyeh Western country, where a woman is a scanty thing. It ain't what Hank has done that surprises me. And it is not on him that the sorrow will fall. For she is good. She is very good. Do yu' remember little black Hank? From Texas he claims he is. He was working on the main ditch over at Sunk Creek last summer when that Em'ly hen was around. Well, seh, yu' would not have pleasured in his company. And this year Hank is placer-mining on Galena Creek, where we'll likely go for sheep. There's Honey Wiggin and a young fello' named Lin McLean, and some others along with the outfit. But Hank's woman will not look at any of them, though the McLean boy is a likely hand. I have seen that; for I have done a right smart o' business that-a-way myself, here and there. She will mend their clothes for them, and she will cook lunches for them any time o' day, and her conduct gave them hopes at the start. But I reckon Austrians have good religion."

"No better than Americans," said I.

But the Virginian shook his head. "Better'n what I've saw any Americans have. Of course I am not judging a whole nation by one citizen, and especially her a woman. And of course in them big Austrian towns the folks has shook their virtuous sayin's loose from their daily doin's, same as we have. I expect selling yourself brings the quickest returns to man or woman all the world over. But I am speakin' not of towns, but of the back country, where folks don't just merely arrive on the cyars, but come into the world the natural way, and grow up slow. Onced a week anyway they see the bunch of old grave-stones that marks their fam'ly. Their blood and name are knowed about in the neighborhood, and it's not often one of such will sell themselves. But their religion ain't to them like this woman's. They can be rip-snortin' or'n'ary in ways. Now she is getting naught but hindrance and temptation and meanness from her husband and every livin' thing around her—yet she keeps right along, nor does she mostly bear any signs in her face. She has cert'nly come from where they are used to believing in God and a hereafter mighty hard, and all day long. She has got one o' them crucifixes, and Hank can't make her quit prayin' to it. But what is she going to do?"

"He will probably leave her," I said.

"Yes," said the Virginian—"leave her. Alone; her money all spent; knowin' maybe twenty words of English; and thousands of miles away from everything she can understand. For our words and ways is all alike strange to her."

"Then why did he want such a person?" I exclaimed.

There was surprise in the grave glance which the cow-puncher gave me. "Why, any man would," he answered. "I wanted her myself, till I found she was good."

I looked at this son of the wilderness, standing thoughtful and splendid by the fire, and unconscious of his own religion that had unexpectedly shone forth in these last words. But I said nothing; for words too intimate, especially words of esteem, put him invariably to silence.

"I had forgot to mention her looks to yu'." he pursued, simply. "She is fit for a man." He stopped again.

"Then there was her wages that Hank saw paid to her," he resumed. "And so marriage was but a little thing to Hank—agaynst such a heap of advantages. As for her idea in takin' such as him—maybe it was that he was small and she was big; tall and big. Or maybe it was just his white teeth. Them ridiculous reasons will bring a woman to a man, haven't yu' noticed? But maybe it was just her sorrowful, helpless state, left stranded as she was, and him keeping himself near her and sober for a week.

"I had been seein' this hyeh Yellowstone Park, takin' in its geysers, and this and that, for my enjoyment; and when I found what they claimed about its strange sights to be pretty near so, I landed up at Galena Creek to watch the boys prospectin'. Honey Wiggin, yu' know, and McLean, and the rest. And so they got me to go down with Hank to Gardner for flour and sugar and truck, which we had to wait for. We lay around the Mammoth Springs and Gardner for three days, playin' cyards with friends. And I got plumb inter-ested in them tourists. For I had partly forgot about Eastern people. And hyeh they came fresh every day to remind a man of the great size of his country. Most always they would talk to yu' if yu' gave 'em the chance; and I did. I have come mighty nigh regrettin' that I did not keep a tally of the questions them folks asked me. And as they seemed genu-winely anxious to believe anything at all, and the worser the thing the believinger they'd grow, why I—well, there's times when I have got to lie to keep in good health.

"So I fooled and I fooled. And one noon I was on the front poach of the big hotel they have opened at the Mammoth Springs for tourists, and the hotel kid, bein' on the watchout, he sees the dust comin' up the hill, and he yells out, 'Stage!'

"Yu've not saw that hotel yet, seh? Well, when the kid says 'Stage,' the consequences is most sudden. About as con-spicuous, yu' may say, as when Old Faithful Geyser lets loose. Yu' see, one batch o' tourists pulls out right after breakfast for Norris Basin, leavin' things empty and yawnin'. By noon the whole hotel outfit has been slumberin' in its chairs steady for three hours. Maybe yu' might hear a fly buzz, but maybe not. Everything's liable to be restin', barrin' the kid. He's a-watchin' out. Then he sees the dust, and he says 'Stage!' and it touches the folks off like a hot pokeh. The Syndicate manager he lopes to a lookin'-glass, and then orga-nizes himself behind the book; and the young photograph chap bounces out o' his private door like one o' them cuckoo-clocks; and the fossil man claws his specimens and curiosities into shape, and the porters line up same as parade, and away goes the piano and fiddles up-stairs. It is mighty con-spicuous. So Hank he come runnin' out from somewheres too, and the stage drives up.

"Then out gets a tall woman, and I noticed her yello' hair. She was kind o' dumb-eyed, yet fine to see. I reckon Hank noticed her too, right away. And right away her trouble begins. For she was a lady's maid, and her lady was out of the stage and roundin' her up quick. And it's 'Where have you put the keys, Willomene?' The lady was rich and stinkin' lookin', and had come from New Yawk in her husband's private cyar.

"Well, Willomene fussed around in her pockets, and them keys was not there. So she started explaining in tanglefoot English to her lady how her lady must have took them from her before leavin' the cyar. But the lady seemed to relish hustlin' herself into a rage. She got tolerable con-spicu-ous, too. And after a heap o' words, 'You are discharged,' she says; and off she struts. Soon her husband came out to Willomene, still standin' like statuary, and he pays her a good sum of cash, and he goes away, and she keeps a standing yet for a spell. Then all of a sudden she says something I reckon was 'O, Jesus,' and sits down and starts a cryin'.

"I would like to have given her comfort. But we all stood around on the hotel poach, and the right thing would not come into my haid. Then the baggage-wagon came in from Cinnabar, and they had picked the keys up on the road between Cinnabar and Gardner. So the lady and her toilet was res-cued, but that did no good to Willomene. They stood her trunk down along with the rest—a brass-nailed little old concern—and there was Willomene out of a job and afoot a long, long ways from her own range; and so she kept sitting, and onced in a while she'd cry some more. We got her a room in the cheap hotel where the Park drivers sleeps when they're in at the Springs, and she acted grateful like, thanking the boys in her tanglefoot English. Next mawnin' her folks druv off in a private team to Norris Basin, and she seemed dazed. For I talked with her then, and questioned her as to her wishes, but she could not say what she wished, nor if it was East or West she would go; and I reckon she was too stricken to have wishes.

"Our stuff for Galena Creek delayed on the railroad, and I got to know her, and then I quit givin' Hank cause for jealousy. I kept myself with the boys, and I played more cyards, while Hank he sca'cely played at all. One night I came on them—Hank and Willomene—walkin' among the pines where the road goes down the hill. Yu' should have saw that pair o' lovers. Her big shape was plain and kind o' steadfast in the moon, and alongside of her little black Hank! And there it was. Of course it ain't nothing to be surprised at that a mean and triflin' man tries to seem what he is not when he wants to please a good woman. But why does she get fooled, when it's so plain to other folks that are not givin' it any special thought? All the rest of the men and women at the Mammoth understood Hank. They knowed he was a worthless proposition. And I cert'nly relied on his gettin' back to his whiskey and openin' her eyes that way. But he did not. I met them next evening again by the Liberty Cap. Supposin' I'd been her brother or her mother, what use was it me warning her? Broth-ers and mothers don't get believed.

"The railroad brought the stuff for Galena Creek, and Hank would not look at it on account of his courtin'. I took it alone myself by Yancey's and the second bridge and Miller Creek to the camp, nor I didn't tell Willomene good-bye, for I had got disgusted at her blindness."

The Virginian shifted his position, and jerked his overalls to a more comfortable fit. Then he continued:

"They was married the Tuesday after at Livingston, and Hank must have been pow'ful pleased at himself. For he gave Willomene a wedding present, with the balance of his cash, spending his last nickel on buying her a red-tailed parrot they had for sale at the First National Bank. The son-of-a-gun hollad so freely at the bank, the president awde'd the cashier to get shed of the out-ragious bird, or he would wring its neck.

"So Hank and Willomene stayed a week up in Livingston on her money, and then he fetched her back to Gardner, and bought their grub, and bride and groom came up to the camp we had on Galena Creek.

"She had never slep' out before. She had never been on a hawss, neither. And she mighty near rolled off down into Pitchstone Cañon, comin' up by the cut-off trail. Why, seh, I would not willingly take you through that place, except yu' promised me yu' would lead your hawss when I said to. But Hank takes the woman he had married, and he takes heavy-loaded pack-hawsses. 'Tis the first time such a thing has been known of in the country. Yu' remember them big tall grass-topped mountains over in the Hoodoo country, and how they descends slam down through the cross-timber that yu' can't sca'cely work through afoot, till they pitches over into lots an' lots o' little cañons, with maybe two inches of water runnin' in the bottom? All that is East Fork water, and over the divide is Clark's Fork, or Stinkin' Water, if yu' take the country yondeh to the southeast. But any place yu' go is them undesirable steep slopes, and the cut-off trail takes along about the worst in the business.

"Well, Hank he got his outfit over it somehow, and, gentlemen, hush! but yu'd ought t've seen him and that poor girl pull into our camp. Yu'd cert'nly never have conjectured them two was a weddin' journey. He was leadin', but skewed around in his saddle to jaw back at Willomene for riding so ignorant. Suppose it was a thing she was responsible for, yu'd not have talked to her that-a-way even in private; and hyeh was the camp a-lookin', and a-listenin', and some of us ashamed. She was setting straddle-ways like a mountain, and between him and her went the three pack-animals, plumb shiverin' played out, and the flour—they had two hundred pounds—tilted over hellwards, with the red-tailed parrot shoutin' land-slides in his cage tied on top o' the leanin' sacks.

"It was that mean to see, that shameless and unkind, that even a thoughtless kid like the McLean boy felt offended, and favorable to some sort of remonstrance. 'The son-of-a—!' he said to me. 'The son of-a—! If he don't stop, let's stop him.' And I reckon we might have.

"But Hank he quit. 'Twas plain to see he'd got a genu-wine scare comin' through Pitchstone Cañon, and it turned him sour, so he'd hardly talk to us, but just mumbled 'How!' kind o' gruff, when the boys come up to congratulate him as to his marriage.

"But Willomene, she says when she saw me, 'Oh, I am so glad!' and we shook hands right friendly. And I wished I'd told her good-bye that day at the Mammoth. For she bore no spite, and maybe I had forgot her feelings in thinkin' of my own. I had talked to her down at the Mammoth at first, yu' know, and she said a word about old friends. Our friendship was three weeks old that day, but I expect her new experiences looked like years to her. And she told me how near she come to gettin' killed.

"Yu' ain't ever been over that trail, seh? Yu' cert'nly must see Pitchstone Cañon. But we'll not go there with packs. And we will get off our hawsses a good ways back. For many animals feels that there's something the matter with that place, and they act very strange about it.

"The Grand Cañon is grand, and makes yu' feel good to look at it, and a geyser is grand and all right, too. But this hyeh Pitchstone hole, if Willomene had went down into that—well, I'll tell yu', that you may judge.

"She seen the trail a-drawin' nearer and nearer the aidge, between the timber and the jumpin'-off place, and she seen how them little loose stones and the crumble stuff would slide and slide away under the hawss's feet. She could hear the stuff rattlin' continually from his steps, and when she turned her haid to look, she seen it goin' down close beside her, but into what it went she could not see. Only, there was a queer steam would come up now and agayn, and her hawss trembled. So she tried to get off and walk without sayin' nothin' to Hank. He kep' on ahaid, and her hawss she had pulled up started to follo' as she was half off him, and that gave her a tumble, but there was an old crooked dead tree. It growed right out o' the aidge. There she hung.

"Down below is a little green water tricklin', green as the stuff that gets on brass, and tricklin' along over soft cream-colored formation, like pie.

And it ain't so far to fall but what a man might not be too much hurt for crawlin' out. But there ain't no crawlin' out o' Pitchstone Cañon, they say. Down in there is caves that yu' cannot see. 'Tis them that coughs up the stream now and agayn. With the wind yu' can smell 'em a mile away, and in the night I have been layin' quiet and heard 'em. Not that it's a big noise, even when a man is close up. It's a fluffy kind of a sigh. But it sounds as if some awful thing was a-makin' it deep down in the guts of the world. They claim there's poison air comes out o' the caves and lays low along the water. They claim if a bear or an elk strays in from below, and the caves sets up their coughin', which they don't regular every day, the animals die. I have seen it come in two seconds. And when it comes that-a-way risin' upon yu' with that fluffy kind of a sigh, yu' feel mighty lonesome, seh.

"So Hank he happened to look back and see Willomene hangin' at the aidge o' them black rocks. And his scare made him mad. And his mad stayed with him till they come into camp. She looked around, and when she seen Hank's tent that him and her was to sleep in she showed surprise. And he showed surprise when he see the bread she cooked.

"'What kind of a Dutch woman are yu',' says he, strainin' for a joke, 'if yu' can't use a Dutch-oven?'

"'You say to me you have a house to live in,' says Willomene. 'Where is that house?'

"'I did not figure on gettin' a woman when I left camp,' says Hank, grinnin', but not pleasant, 'or I'd have hurried up with the shack I'm a buildin'.'

"He was buildin' one. When I left Galena Creek and come away from that country to meet you, the house was finished enough for the couple to move in. I hefted her brass-nailed trunk up the hill from their tent myself, and I watched her take out her crucifix. But she would not let me help her with that. She'd not let me touch it. She'd fixed it up agaynst the wall her own self her own way. But she accepted some flowers I picked, and set them in a can front of the crucifix. Then Hank he come in, and seein', says to me, 'Are you one of the kind that squats before them silly dolls?' 'I would tell yu'', I answered him; 'but it would not inter-est yu'.' And I cleared out, and left him and Willomene to begin their house-keepin'.

"Already they had quit havin' much to say to each other down in their tent. The only steady talkin' done in that house was done by the parrot.

I've never saw any go ahaid of that bird. I have told yu' about Hank, and how when he'd come home and see her prayin' to that crucifix he'd always get riled up. He would mention it freely to the boys. Not that she neglected him, yu' know. She done her part, workin' mighty hard, for she was a willin' woman. But he could not make her quit her religion; and Willomene she had got to bein' very silent before I come away. She used to talk to me some at first, but she dropped it. I don't know why. I expect maybe it was hard for her to have us that close in camp, witnessin' her troubles every day, and she a foreigner. I reckon if she got any comfort, it would be when we was off prospectin' or huntin', and she could shut the cabin door and be alone."

The Virginian stopped for a moment.

"It will soon be a month since I left Galena Creek," he resumed. "But I cannot get the business out o' my haid. I keep a studyin' over it."

His talk was done. He had unburdened his mind. Night lay deep and quiet around us, with no sound far or near, save Buffalo Fork splashing over its riffle.

II

We left Snake River. We went up Pacific Creek, and through Two Ocean Pass, and down among the watery willow-bottoms and beaver-dams of the Upper Yellowstone. We fished; we enjoyed existence along the lake. Then we went over Pelican Creek trail and came steeply down into the giant country of grass-topped mountains. At dawn and dusk the elk had begun to call across the stillness. And one morning in the Hoodoo country, where we were looking for sheep, we came round a jut of the strange, organ-pipe formation upon a long-legged boy of about nineteen, also hunting.

"Still hyeh?" said the Virginian, without emotion.

"I guess so," returned the boy, equally matter-of-fact. "Yu' seem to be around yourself," he added.

They might have been next-door neighbors, meeting in a town street for the second time in the same day.

The Virginian made me known to Mr. Lin McLean, who gave me a brief nod.

"Any luck?" he inquired, but not of me.

"Oh," drawled the Virginian, "luck enough."

Knowing the ways of the country, I said no word. It was bootless to interrupt their own methods of getting at what was really in both their minds.

The boy fixed his wide-open hazel eyes upon me. "Fine weather," he mentioned.

"Very fine," said I.

"I seen your horses a while ago," he said. "Camp far from here?" he asked the Virginian.

"Not specially. Stay and eat with us. We've got elk meat."

"That's what I'm after for camp," said McLean. "All of us is out on a hunt to-day—except him."

"How many are yu' now ?"

"The whole six."

"Makin' money?"

"Oh, some days the gold washes out good in the pan, and others it's that fine it'll float off without settlin'."

"So Hank ain't huntin' to-day?"

"Huntin'! We left him layin' out in that clump o' brush below their cabin. Been drinkin' all night."

The Virginian broke off a piece of the Hoodoo mud-rock from the weird eroded pillar that we stood beside. He threw it into a bank of last year's snow. We all watched it as if it were important. Up through the mountain silence pierced the long quivering whistle of a bull-elk. It was like an unearthly singer practising an unearthly scale.

"First time she heard that," said McLean, "she was scared."

"Nothin' maybe to resemble it in Austria," said the Virginian.

"That's so," said McLean. "That's so, you bet! Nothin' just like Hank over there, neither."

"Well, flesh is mostly flesh in all lands, I reckon," said the Virginian. "I expect yu' can be drunk and disorderly in every language. But an Austrian Hank would be liable to respect her crucifix."

"That's so!"

"He 'ain't made her quit it yet?"

"Not him. But he's got meaner."

"Drunk this mawnin', yu' say?"

"That's his most harmless condition now."

"Nobody's in camp but them two? Her and him alone?"

"Oh, he dassent touch her."

"Who did he tell that to?"

"Oh, the camp is backin' her. The camp has explained that to him several times, you bet! And what's more, she has got the upper hand of him herself. She has him beat."

"How beat?"

"She has downed him with her eye. Just by endurin' him peacefully; and with her eye. I've saw it. Things changed some after yu' pulled out. We had a good crowd still, and it was pleasant, and not too lively nor yet too slow. And Willomene, she come more among us. She'd not stay shut in-doors, like she done at first. I'd have like to've showed her how to punish Hank."

"Afteh she had downed yu' with her eye?" inquired the Virginian. Young McLean reddened, and threw a furtive look upon me, the stranger, the outsider. "Oh, well," he said, "I done nothing onusual. But that's all different now. All of us likes her and respects her, and makes allowances for her bein' Dutch. Yu' can't help but respect her. And she shows she knows."

"I reckon maybe she knows how to deal with Hank," said the Virginian.

"Shucks!" said McLean, scornfully. "And her so big and him so puny! She'd ought to lift him off the earth with one arm and lam him with a baste or two with the other, and he'd improve."

"Maybe that's why she don't," mused the Virginian, slowly; "because she is so big. Big in the spirit, I mean. She'd not stoop to his level. Don't yu' see she is kind o' way up above him and camp and everything—just her and her crucifix?"

"Her and her crucifix!" repeated young Lin McLean, staring at this interpretation, which was beyond his lively understanding. "Her and her crucifix. Turrible lonesome company! Well, them are things yu' don't know about. I kind o' laughed myself the first time I seen her at it. Hank, he says to me soft, 'Come here, Lin,' and I peeped in where she was a-prayin'. She seen us two, but she didn't quit. So I quit, and Hank came with me, sayin' tough words about it. Yes, them are things yu' sure don't know about. What's the matter with you camping with us boys tonight?"

We had been going to visit them the next day. We made it to-day, instead. And Mr. McLean helped us with our packs, and we carried our welcome in the shape of elk meat. So we turned our faces down the grass-topped mountains towards Galena Creek. Once, far through an open gap away below us, we sighted the cabin with the help of our field-glasses.

"Pity we can't make out Hank sleepin' in that brush," said McLean.

"He has probably gone into the cabin by now," said I.

"Not him! He prefers the brush all day when he's that drunk, you bet!"

"Afraid of her?"

"Well—oneasy in her presence. Not that she's liable to be in there now. She don't stay inside nowadays so much. She's been comin' round the ditch, silent-like but friendly. And she'll watch us workin' for a spell, and then she's apt to move off alone into the woods, singin' them Dutch songs of hern that ain't got no toon. I've met her walkin' that way, tall and earnest, lots of times. But she don't want your company, though she'll patch your overalls and give yu' lunch always. Nor she won't take pay."

Thus we proceeded down from the open summits into the close pines; and while we made our way among the cross-timber and over the little streams, McLean told us of various days and nights at the camp, and how Hank had come to venting his cowardice upon his wife's faith.

"Why, he informed her one day when he was goin' to take his dust to town, that if he come back and found that thing in the house, he'd do it up for her. 'So yu' better pack off your wooden dummy somewheres,' says he. And she just looked at him kind o' stone-like and solemn. For she don't care for his words no more.

"And while he was away she'd have us all in to supper up at the shack, and look at us eatin' while she'd walk around puttin' grub on your plate. Day time she'd come around the ditch, watchin' for a while, and move off slow, singin' her Dutch songs. And when Hank comes back from spendin' his dust, he sees the crucifix same as always, and he says, 'Didn't I tell yu' to take that down?' 'You did,' says Willomene, lookin' at him very quiet. And he quit. "And Honey Wiggin says to him, 'Hank, leave her alone.' And Hank, bein' all trembly from spreein' in town, he says, 'You're all agin me!' like as if he were a baby."

"I should think you would run him out of camp," said I.

"Well, we've studied over that some," McLean answered. "But what's to be done with Willomene?"

I did not know. None of us seemed to know.

"The boys got together night before last," continued McLean, "and after holdin' a unanimous meetin', we visited her and spoke to her about goin' back to her home. She was slow in corrallin' our idea on account of her bein' no English scholar. But when she did, after three of us takin' their turn at puttin' the proposition to her, she would not accept any of our dust. And though she started to thank us the handsomest she knowed how, it seemed to grieve her, for she cried. So we thought we'd better get out. She's tried to tell us the name of her home, but yu' can't pronounce such outlandishness."

As we went down the mountains, we talked of other things, but always came back to this; and we were turning it over still when the sun had departed from the narrow cleft that we were following, and shone only on the distant grassy tops which rose round us into an upper world of light.

"We'll all soon have to move out of this camp, anyway," said McLean, unstrapping his coat from his saddle and drawing it on. "It gets chill now in the afternoons. D'yu' see the quakin' -asps all turned yello', and the leaves keeps fallin' without no wind to blow 'em down? We're liable to get snowed in on short notice in this mountain country. If the water goes to freeze on us we'll have to quit workin'. There's camp."

We had rounded a corner, and once more sighted the cabin. I suppose it may have been still half a mile away, upon the further side of a ravine into which our little valley opened. But field-glasses were not needed now to make out the cabin clearly, windows and door. Smoke rose from it; for supper-time was nearing, and we stopped to survey the scene. As we were looking, another hunter joined us, coming from the deep woods to the edge of the pines where we were standing. This was Honey Wiggin. He had killed a deer, and he surmised that all the boys would be back soon. Others had met luck besides himself; he had left one dressing an elk over the next ridge. Nobody seemed to have got in yet, from appearances. Didn't the camp look lonesome?

"There's somebody, though," said McLean.

The Virginian took the glasses. "I reckon—yes, that's Hank. The cold has woke him up, and he's comin' in out o' the brush."

Each of us took the glasses in turn; and I watched the figure go up the hill to the door of the cabin. It seemed to pause and diverge to the window. At the window it stood still, head bent, looking in. Then it returned quickly to the door. It was too far to discern, even through the glasses, what the figure was doing. Whether the door was locked, whether he was knocking or fumbling with a key, or whether he spoke through the door to the person within—I cannot tell what it was that came through the glasses straight to my nerves, so that I jumped at a sudden sound; and it was only the distant shrill call of an elk. I was handing the glasses to the Virginian for him to see when the figure opened the door and disappeared in the dark interior. As I watched the square of darkness which the door's opening made, something seemed to happen there—or else it was a spark, a flash, in my own straining eyes.

But at that same instant the Virginian dashed forward upon his horse, leaving the glasses in my hand. And with the contagion of his act the rest of us followed him, leaving the pack animals to follow us as they should choose.

"Look!" cried McLean. "He's not shot her."

I saw the tall figure of a woman rush out of the door and pass quickly round the house.

"He's missed her!" cried McLean, again. "She's savin' herself."

But the man's figure did not appear in pursuit. Instead of this, the woman returned as quickly as she had gone, and entered the dark interior.

"She had something," said Wiggin. "What would that be?"

"Maybe it's all right, after all," said McLean. "She went out to get wood."

The rough steepness of our trail had brought us down to a walk, and as we continued to press forward at this pace as fast as we could, we compared a few notes. McLean did not think he saw any flash. Wiggin thought that he had heard a sound, but it was at the moment when the Virginian's horse had noisily started away.

Our trail had now taken us down where we could no longer look across and see the cabin. And the half-mile proved a long one over this ground. At length we reached and crossed the rocky ford, overtaking the Virginian there.

"These hawsses," said he, "are played out. We'll climb up to camp afoot. And just keep behind me for the present."

We obeyed our natural leader, and made ready for whatever we might be going into. We passed up the steep bank and came again in sight of the door. It was still wide open. We stood, and felt a sort of silence which the approach of two new-comers could not break. They joined us. They had been coming home from hunting, and had plainly heard a shot here. We stood for a moment more after learning this, and then one of the men called out the names of Hank and Willomene. Again we—or I at least—felt that same silence, which to my disturbed imagination seemed to be rising round us as mists rise from water.

"There's nobody in there," stated the Virginian. "Nobody that's alive," he added. And he crossed the cabin and walked into the door.

Though he made no gesture, I saw astonishment pass through his body, as he stopped still; and all of us came after him. There hung the crucifix, with a round hole through the middle of it. One of the men went to it and took it down; and behind it, sunk in the log, was the bullet. The cabin was but a single room, and every object that it contained could be seen at a glance; nor was there hiding-room for anything. On the floor lay the axe from the wood-pile; but I will not tell of its appearance. So he had shot her crucifix, her Rock of Ages, the thing which enabled her to bear her life, and that lifted her above life; and she—but there was the axe to show what she had done then. Was this cabin really empty? I looked more slowly about, half dreading to find that I had overlooked something. But it was as the Virginian had said; nobody was there.

As we were wondering, there was a noise above our heads, and I was not the only one who started and stared. It was the parrot; and we stood away in a circle, looking up at his cage. Crouching flat on the floor of the cage, his wings huddled tight to his body, he was swinging his head from side to side; and when he saw that we watched him, he began a low croaking and monotonous utterance, which never changed, but remained rapid and continuous. I heard McLean whisper to the Virginian, "You bet he knows."The Virginian stepped to the door, and then he bent to the gravel and beckoned us to come and see. Among the recent footprints at the threshold the man's boot-heel was plain, as well as the woman's broad tread. But while the man's steps led into the cabin, they did not lead away from it. We tracked his course just as we had seen it through the glasses: up the hill from the brush to the window, and then to the door. But he had never walked out again. Yet in the cabin he was not; we tore up the half-floor that it had. There was no use to dig in the earth. And all the while that we were at this search the parrot remained crouched in the bottom of his cage, his black eye fixed upon our movements.

"She has carried him," said the Virginian. "We must follow up Willomene."

The latest heavy set of footprints led us from the door along the ditch, where they sank deep in the softer soil; then they turned off sharply into the mountains.

"This is the cut-off trail," said McLean to me. "The same he brought her in by."

The tracks were very clear, and evidently had been made by a person moving slowly. Whatever theories our various minds were now shaping, no one spoke a word to his neighbor, but we went along with a hush over us. After some walking, Wiggin suddenly stopped and pointed.

We had come to the edge of the timber, where a narrow black cañon began, and ahead of us the trail drew near a slanting ledge, where the footing was of small loose stones. I recognized the odor, the volcanic whiff, that so often prowls and meets one in the lonely woods of that region, but at first I failed to make out what had set us all running.

"Is he looking down into the hole himself?" some one asked; and then I did see a figure, the figure I had looked at through the glasses, leaning strangely over the edge of Pitchstone Cañon, as if indeed he was peering to watch what might be in the bottom.

We came near. But those eyes were sightless, and in the skull the story of the axe was carved. By a piece of his clothing he was hooked in the twisted roots of a dead tree, and hung there at the extreme verge. I went to look over, and Lin McLean caught me as I staggered at the sight I saw. He would have lost his own foothold in saving me had not one of the others held him from above.

She was there below; Hank's woman, brought from Austria to the New World. The vision of that brown bundle lying in the water will never leave me, I think. She had carried the body to this point; but had she intended this end? Or was some part of it an accident? Had she meant to take him with her? Had she meant to stay behind herself? No word came from these dead to answer us. But as we stood speaking there, a giant puff of breath rose up to us between the black walls.

"There's that fluffy sigh I told yu' about," said the Virginian.

"He's talkin' to her! I tell yu' he's talkin' to her!" burst out McLean, suddenly, in such a voice that we stared as he pointed at the man in the tree. "See him lean over! He's sayin' 'I have yu' beat after all.'" And McLean fell to whimpering.

Wiggin took the boy's arm kindly and walked him along the trail. He did not seem twenty yet. Life had not shown this side of itself to him so plainly before.

"Let's get out of here," said the Virginian. It seemed one more pitiful straw that the lonely bundle should be left in such a vault of doom, with no last touches of care from its fellow-beings, and no heap of kind earth to hide it. But whether the place is deadly or not, man dares not venture into it. So they took Hank from the tree that night, and early next morning they buried him near camp on the top of a little mound.

But the thought of Willomene lying in Pitchstone Cañon had kept sleep from me through that whole night, nor did I wish to attend Hank's burial. I rose very early, while the sunshine had still a long way to come down to us from the mountain-tops, and I walked back along the cut-off trail. I was moved to look once more upon that frightful place. And as I came to the edge of the timber, there was the Virginian. He did not expect any one. He had set up the crucifix as near the dead tree as it could be firmly planted.

"It belongs to her, anyway," he explained.

Some lines of verse came into my memory, and with a change or two I wrote them as deep as I could with my pencil upon a small board that he smoothed for me.

"Call for the robin redbreast and the wren,
Since o'er shady groves they hover,
And with flowers and leaves do cover
The friendless bodies of unburied men.
Call to this funeral dole
The ant, the field-mouse, and the mole,
To rear her hillocks that shall keep her warm."

"That kind o' quaint language reminds me of a play I seen onced in Saynt Paul," said the Virginian. "About young Prince Henry."

I told him that another poet was the author.

"They are both good writers," said the Virginian. And as he was finishing the monument that we had made, young Lin McLean joined us. He was a little ashamed of the feelings that he had shown yesterday, a little anxious to cover those feelings with brass.

"Well," he said, taking an offish, man-of-the-world tone, "all this fuss just because a woman believed in God."

"You have put it down wrong," said the Virginian; "it's just because a man didn't."

TWELVE O'CLOCK

Stephen Crane

"Where were you at twelve o'clock, noon, on the 9th of June, 1875?"
– Question on intelligent cross-examination.

I

66 "EXCUSE *ME*," said Ben Roddle with graphic gestures to a group of citizens in Nantucket's store. "Excuse *me!* When them fellers in leather pants an' six-shooters ride in, I go home an' set in th' cellar. That's what I do. When you see me pirooting through the streets at th' same time an' occasion as them punchers, you kin put me down fer bein' crazy. Excuse *me!*"

"Why, Ben," drawled old Nantucket, "you ain't never really seen 'em turned loose. Why, I kin remember—in th' old days—when——"

"Oh, damn yer old days!" retorted Roddle. Fixing Nantucket with the eye of scorn and contempt, he said, "I suppose you'll be sayin' in a minute that in th' old days you used to kill Injuns, won't you?"

There was some laughter, and Roddle was left free to expand his ideas on the periodic visits of cowboys to the town. "Mason Rickets, he had ten big punkins a-sittin' in front of his store, an' them fellers from the Upside-down-P ranch shot 'em—shot 'em all—an' Rickets lyin' on his belly in th' store a-callin' fer 'em to quit it. An' what did they do? Why, they *laughed* at 'im—just *laughed* at 'im! That don't do a town no good. Now, how would an eastern capiterlist"—(it was the town's humor to be always gassing of phantom investors who were likely to come any moment and pay a thousand prices for everything)—"how would an eastern capiterlist like that? Why, you couldn't see 'im fer th' dust on his trail. Then he'd tell all his friends: 'That there town may be all right, but ther's too much loose-handed shootin' fer my money.' An' he'd be right, too. Them rich fellers, they don't make no bad breaks with their money. They watch it all th' time b'cause they know blame well there ain't hardly room fer their feet fer th' pikers an' tinhorns an' thimble-riggers what are layin' fer 'em. I tell you, one puncher racin' his cow-pony hell-bent-fer-election down Main Street an' yellin' an' shootin', an' nothin' at all done about it, would scare away a whole herd of capiterlists. An' it ain't right. It oughter be stopped."

A pessimistic voice asked: "How you goin' to stop it, Ben?"

"Organize," replied Roddle, pompously. "Organize. That's the only way to make these fellers lay down. I——"

From the street sounded a quick scudding of pony hoofs, and a party of cowboys swept past the door. One man, however, was seen to draw rein and dismount. He came clanking into the store. "Mornin', gentlemen," he said civilly.

"Mornin'," they answered in subdued voices.

He stepped to the counter and said, "Give me a paper of fine cut, please." The group of citizens contemplated him in silence. He certainly did not look threatening. He appeared to be a young man of twenty-five years, with a tan from wind and sun, with a remarkably clear eye from perhaps a period of enforced temperance, a quiet young man who wanted to buy some tobacco. A six-shooter swung low on his hip, but at the moment it looked more decorative than warlike; it seemed merely a part of his old gala dress—his sombrero with its band of rattlesnake-skin, his great flaming neckerchief, his belt of embroidered Mexican leather, his high-heeled boots, his huge spurs. And, above all, his hair had been watered and brushed until it lay as close to his head as the fur lies to a wet cat. Paying for his tobacco, he withdrew.

Ben Roddle resumed his harangue. "Well, there you are! Looks like a calm man now, but in less 'n half an hour he'll be as drunk as three bucks an' a squaw, an' then—excuse *me!*"

II

On this day the men of two outfits had come into town, but Ben Roddle's ominous words were not justified at once. The punchers spent most of the morning in an attack on whiskey which was too earnest to be noisy.

At five minutes of eleven, a tall, lank, brick-colored cowboy strode over to Placer's Hotel. Placer's Hotel was a notable place. It was the best hotel within two hundred miles. Its office was filled with armchairs and brown papier-maché spittoons. At one end of the room was a wooden counter painted a bright pink, and on this morning a man was behind the counter writing in a ledger. He was the proprietor of the hotel, but his customary humor was so sullen that all strangers immediately wondered why in life he had chosen to play the part of mine host. Near his left hand, double doors opened into the dining room, which in warm weather was always kept darkened in order to discourage the flies, which was not compassed at all.

Placer, writing in his ledger, did not look up when the tall cowboy entered.

"Mornin', mister," said the latter. "I've come to see if you kin grubstake th' hull crowd of us fer dinner t'day."

Placer did not then raise his eyes, but with a certain churlishness, as if it annoyed him that his hotel was patronized, he asked: "How many?"

"Oh, about thirty," replied the cowboy. "An' we want th' best dinner you kin raise an' scrape. Everything th' best. We don't care what it costs s' long as we git a good square meal. We'll pay a dollar a head: by God, we will! We won't kick on nothin' in th' bill if you do it up fine. If you ain't got it in the house, rustle th' hull town fer it. That's our gait. So you just tear loose, an' we'll——"

At this moment the machinery of a cuckoo clock on the wall began to whirr, little doors flew open, and a wooden bird appeared and cried "Cuckoo!" And this was repeated until eleven o'clock had been announced, while the cowboy, stupefied, glass-eyed, stood with his red throat gulping. At the end he wheeled upon Placer and demanded: *"What in hell is that?"*

Placer revealed by his manner that he had been asked this question too many times. "It's a clock," he answered shortly.

"I know it's a clock," gasped the cowboy; "but what *kind* of a clock?"

"A cuckoo clock. Can't you see?"

The cowboy, recovering his self-possession by a violent effort, suddenly went shouting into the street. "Boys! Say, boys! Come 'ere a minute!"

His comrades, comfortably inhabiting a nearby saloon, heard his stentorian calls, but they merely said one to another: "What's th' matter with Jake?—he's off his nut again."

But Jake burst in upon them with violence. "Boys," he yelled, "come over to th' hotel! They got a clock with a bird inside it, an' when it's eleven o'clock or anything like that, th' bird comes out and says '*Toot*-toot, *toot*-toot!' that way, as many times as whatever time of day it is. It's immense! Come on over!"

The roars of laughter which greeted his proclamation were of two qualities; some men laughing because they knew all about cuckoo clocks, and other men laughing because they had concluded that the eccentric Jake had been victimized by some wise child of civilization.

Old Man Crumford, a venerable ruffian who probably had been born in a corral, was particularly offensive with his loud guffaws of contempt. "Bird a-comin' out of a clock an' a-tellin' ye th' time! Haw-haw-haw!" He swallowed his whiskey. "A bird! a-tellin' ye th' time! Haw-haw! Jake, you ben up agin some new drink. You ben drinkin' lonely an' got up agin some snake-medicine licker. A bird a-tellin' ye th' time! Haw-haw!"

The shrill voice of one of the younger cowboys piped from the background. "Brace up, Jake. Don't let 'em laugh at ye. Bring 'em that salt codfish of yourn what kin pick out th' ace."

"Oh, he's only kiddin' us. Don't pay no 'tention to 'im. He thinks he's smart."

A cowboy whose mother had a cuckoo clock in her house in Philadelphia spoke with solemnity. "Jake's a liar. There's no such clock in the world. What? a bird inside a clock to tell the time? Change your drink, Jake."

Jake was furious, but his fury took a very icy form. He bent a withering glance upon the last speaker. "I don't mean a *live* bird," he said, with terrible dignity. "It's a wooden bird, an'——"

"A wooden bird!" shouted Old Man Crumford. "Wooden bird a-tellin' ye th' time! Haw-haw!"

But Jake still paid his frigid attention to the Philadelphian. "An' if yer sober enough to walk, it ain't such a blame long ways from here to th' hotel, an' I'll bet my pile agin yours if you only got two bits."

"I don't want your money, Jake," said the Philadelphian. "Somebody's been stringin' you—that's all. I wouldn't take your money." He cleverly appeared to pity the other's innocence.

"You couldn't *git* my money," cried Jake, in sudden hot anger. "You couldn't git it. Now—since yer so fresh—let's see how much you got." He clattered some large gold pieces noisily upon the bar.

The Philadelphian shrugged his shoulders and walked away. Jake was triumphant. "Any more bluffers round here?" he demanded. "Any more? Any more bluffers? Where's all these here hot sports? Let 'em step up. Here's my money—come an' git it."

But they had ended by being afraid. To some of them his tale was absurd, but still one must be circumspect when a man throws forty-five dollars in gold upon the bar and bids the world come and win it. The general feeling was expressed by Old Man Crumford, when with deference he asked: "Well, this here bird, Jake—what kinder lookin' bird is it?"

"It's a little brown thing," said Jake, briefly. Apparently he almost disdained to answer.

"Well—how does it work?" asked the old man, meekly.

"Why in blazes don't you go an' look at it?" yelled Jake. "Want me to paint it in iles fer you? Go an' look!"

III

Placer was writing in his ledger. He heard a great trample of feet and clink of spurs on the porch, and there entered quietly the band of cowboys, some of them swaying a trifle, and these last being the most painfully decorous of all. Jake was in advance. He waved his hand toward the clock. "There she is," he said laconically. The cowboys drew up and stared. There was some giggling, but a serious voice said half-audibly, "I don't see no bird."

Jake politely addressed the landlord. "Mister, I've fetched these here friends of mine in here to see yer clock——"

Placer looked up suddenly. "Well, they can see it, can't they?" he asked in sarcasm. Jake, abashed, retreated to his fellows.

There was a period of silence. From time to time the men shifted their feet. Finally, Old Man Crumford leaned toward Jake, and in a penetrating whisper demanded, "Where's th' bird?" Some frolicsome spirits on the outskirts began to call "Bird! Bird!" as men at a political meeting call for a particular speaker.

Jake removed his big hat and nervously mopped his brow.

The young cowboy with the shrill voice again spoke from the skirts of the crowd. "Jake, is ther' sure 'nough a bird in that thing?"

"Yes. Didn't I tell you once?"

"Then," said the shrill-voiced man, in a tone of conviction, "it ain't a clock at all. It's a bird cage."

"I tell you it's a clock," cried the maddened Jake, but his retort could hardly be heard above the howls of glee and derision which greeted the words of him of the shrill voice.

Old Man Crumford was again rampant. "Wooden bird a-tellin' ye th' time! Haw-haw!"

Amid the confusion Jake went again to Placer. He spoke almost in supplication. "Say, mister, what time does this here thing go off ag'in?"

Placer lifted his head, looked at the clock, and said, "Noon."

There was a stir near the door, and Big Watson of the Square-X outfit, at this time very drunk indeed, came shouldering his way through the crowd and cursing everybody. The men gave him much room, for he was notorious as a quarrelsome person when drunk. He paused in front of Jake, and spoke as through a wet blanket. "What's all this Goddamn monkeyin' about?"

Jake was already wild at being made a butt for everybody, and he did not give backward. "None a' your damn business, Watson."

"Huh?" growled Watson, with the surprise of a challenged bull.

"I said," repeated Jake, distinctly, "it's none a' your damn business."Watson whipped his revolver half out of its holster. "I'll make it m' business, then, you——"

But Jake had backed a step away, and was holding his left hand palm outward toward Watson, while in his right he held his six-shooter, its muzzle pointing at the floor. He was shouting in a frenzy, "No—don't you try it, Watson! Don't you dare try it, or, by Gawd, I'll kill you, sure—*sure!*"

He was aware of a torment of cries about him from fearful men; from men who protested, from men who cried out because they cried out. But he kept his eyes on Watson, and those two glared murder at each other, neither seeming to breathe, fixed like two statues.

A loud new voice suddenly rang out: "Hol' on a minute!" All spectators who had not stampeded turned quickly, and saw Placer standing behind his bright pink counter, with an aimed revolver in each hand.

"Cheese it!" he said. "I won't have no fightin' here. If you want to fight, git out in the street."

Big Watson laughed, and speeding up his six-shooter like a flash of blue light, he shot Placer through the throat—shot the man as he stood behind his absurd pink counter with his two aimed revolvers in his incompetent hands. With a yell of rage and despair, Jake smote Watson on the pate with his heavy weapon, and knocked him sprawling and bloody.

Somewhere a woman shrieked like windy, midnight death. Placer fell behind the counter, and down upon him came his ledger and his ink-stand, so that one could not have told blood from ink.

The cowboys did not seem to hear, see, nor feel, until they saw numbers of citizens with Winchesters running wildly upon them. Old Man Crumford threw high a passionate hand. "Don't shoot! We'll not fight ye fer 'im."

Nevertheless two or three shots rang, and a cowboy who had been about to gallop off suddenly slumped over on his pony's neck, where he held for a moment like an old sack, and then slid to the ground, while his pony, with flapping rein, fled to the prairie.

"In God's name, don't shoot!" trumpeted Old Man Crumford. "We'll not fight ye fer 'im!"

"It's murder," bawled Ben Roddle.

In the chaotic street it seemed for a moment as if everybody would kill everybody. "Where's the man what done it?" These hot cries seemed to declare a war which would result in an absolute annihilation of one side. But the cowboys were singing out against it. They would fight for nothing—yes—they often fought for nothing—but they would not fight for this dark something.

At last, when a flimsy truce had been made between the inflamed men, all parties went to the hotel. Placer, in some dying whim, had made his way out from behind the pink counter, and, leaving a horrible trail, had traveled to the center of the room, where he had pitched headlong over the body of Big Watson.

The men lifted the corpse and laid it at the side.

"Who done it?" asked a white, stern man.

A cowboy pointed at Big Watson. "That's him," he said huskily.

There was a curious grim silence, and then suddenly, in the death chamber, there sounded the loud whirring of the clock's works, little doors flew open, a tiny wooden bird appeared and cried "Cuckoo"—twelve times.

HYGEIA AT THE SOLITO

O. Henry

I F YOU ARE KNOWING in the chronicles of the ring you will recall to mind an event in the early 'nineties when, for a minute and sundry odd seconds, a champion and a "would-be" faced each other on the alien side of an international river. So brief a conflict had rarely imposed upon the fair promise of true sport. The reporters made what they could of it, but, divested of padding, the action was sadly fugacious. The champion merely smote his victim, turned his back upon him, remarking, "I know what I done to dat stiff," and extended an arm like a ship's mast for his glove to be removed.

Which accounts for a trainload of extremely disgusted gentlemen in an uproar of fancy vests and neckwear being spilled from their Pullmans in San Antonio in the early morning following the fight. Which also partly accounts for the unhappy predicament in which "Cricket" McGuire found himself as he tumbled from his car and sat upon the depot platform, torn by a spasm of that hollow, racking cough so familiar to San Antonian ears. At that time, in the uncertain light of dawn, that way passed Curtis Raidler, the Nueces County cattleman—may his shadow never measure under six feet two.

The cattleman, out this early to catch the southbound for his ranch station, stopped at the side of the distressed patron of sport, and spoke in the kindly drawl of his ilk and region, "Got it pretty bad, bud?"

"Cricket" McGuire, ex-feather-weight prizefighter, tout, jockey, follower of the "ponies," all-round sport, and manipulator of the gum balls and walnut shells, looked up pugnaciously at the imputation cast by "bud." "G'wan," he rasped, "telegraph pole. I didn't ring for yer."

Another paroxysm wrung him, and he leaned limply against a convenient baggage truck. Raidler waited patiently, glancing around at the white hats, short overcoats, and big cigars thronging the platform. "You're from the No'th, ain't you, bud?" he asked when the other was partially recovered. "Come down to see the fight?"

"Fight!" snapped McGuire. "Puss-in-the-corner! 'Twas a hypodermic injection. Handed him just one like a squirt of dope, and he's asleep, and no tanbark needed in front of his residence. Fight!" He rattled a bit, coughed, and went on, hardly addressing the cattleman, but rather for the relief of voicing his troubles. "No more dead sure t'ings for me. But Rus Sage himself would have snatched at it. Five to one dat de boy from Cork wouldn't stay t'ree rounds is what I invested in. Put my last cent on, and could already smell the sawdust in dat all-night joint of Jimmy Delaney's on T'irty-seventh Street I was goin' to buy. And den—say, telegraph pole, what a gazaboo a guy is to put his whole roll on one turn of the gaboozlum!"

"You're plenty right," said the big cattleman; "more 'specially when you lose. Son, you get up and light out for a hotel. You got a mighty bad cough. Had it long?"

"Lungs," said McGuire comprehensively. "I got it. The croaker says I'll come to time for six months longer—maybe a year if I hold my gait. I wanted to settle down and take care of myself. Dat's why I speculated on dat five to one perhaps. I had a t'ousand iron dollars saved up. If I winned I was goin' to buy Delaney's café. Who'd a t'ought dat stiff would take a nap in de foist round—say?"

"It's a hard deal," commented Raidler, looking down at the diminutive form of McGuire crumpled against the truck. "But you go to a hotel and rest. There's the Menger and the Maverick, and—"

"And the Fi'th Av'noo, and the Waldorf-Astoria," mimicked McGuire. "Told you I went broke. I'm on de bum proper. I've got one dime left. Maybe a trip to Europe or a sail in me private yacht would fix me up—pa'per!"

He flung his dime at a newsboy, got his *Express*, propped his back against the truck, and was at once rapt in the account of his Waterloo, as expanded by the ingenious press.

Curtis Raidler interrogated an enormous gold watch, and laid his hand on McGuire's shoulder.

"Come on, bud," he said. "We got three minutes to catch the train."

Sarcasm seemed to be McGuire's vein.

"You ain't seen me cash in any chips or call a turn since I told you I was broke, a minute ago, have you? Friend, chase yourself away."

"You're going down to my ranch," said the cattleman, "and stay till you get well. Six months 'll fix you good as new." He lifted McGuire with one hand, and half-dragged him in the direction of the train.

"What about the money?" said McGuire, struggling weakly to escape. "Money for what?" asked Raidler, puzzled. They eyed each other, not understanding, for they touched only as at the gear of bevelled cog-wheels—at right angles, and moving upon different axles.

Passengers on the south-bound saw them seated together, and wondered at the conflux of two such antipodes. McGuire was five feet one, with a countenance belonging to either Yokohama or Dublin. Bright-beady of eye, bony of cheek and jaw, scarred, toughened, broken and reknit, indestructible, grisly, gladiatorial as a hornet, he was a type neither new nor unfamiliar. Raidler was the product of a different soil. Six feet two in height, miles broad, and no deeper than a crystal brook, he represented the union of the West and South. Few accurate pictures of his kind have been made, for art galleries are so small and the mutoscope is as yet unknown in Texas. After all, the only possible medium of portrayal of Raidler's kind would be the fresco—something high and simple and cool and unframed.

They were rolling southward on the International. The timber was huddling into little, dense green motts at rare distances before the inundation of the downright, vert prairies. This was the land of the ranches; the domain of the kings of the kine.

McGuire sat, collapsed into his corner of the seat, receiving with acid suspicion the conversation of the cattleman. What was the "game" of this big "geezer" who was carrying him off? Altruism would have been McGuire's last guess. "He ain't no farmer," thought the captive, "and he ain't no con man, for sure. W'at's his lay? You trail in, Cricket, and see how many cards he draws. You're up against it, anyhow. You got a nickel and gallopin' consumption, and you better lay low. Lay low and see w'at's his game."

At Rincon, a hundred miles from San Antonio, they left the train for a buckboard which was waiting there for Raidler. In this they travelled the thirty miles between the station and their destination. If anything could, this drive should have stirred the acrimonious McGuire to a sense of his ransom. They sped upon velvety wheels across an exhilarant savanna. The pair of Spanish ponies struck a nimble, tireless trot, which gait they occasionally relieved by a wild, untrammelled gallop. The air was wine and seltzer, perfumed, as they absorbed it, with the delicate redolence of prairie flowers. The road perished, and the buckboard swam the uncharted billows of the grass itself, steered by the practised hand of Raidler, to whom each tiny distant mott of trees was a signboard, each convolution of the low hills a voucher of course and distance. But McGuire reclined upon his spine, seeing nothing but a desert, and receiving the cattleman's advances with sullen distrust. "W'at's he up to?" was the burden of his thoughts; "w'at kind of a gold brick has the big guy got to sell?" McGuire was only applying the measure of the streets he had walked to a range bounded by the horizon and the fourth dimension.

A week before, while riding the prairies, Raider had come upon a sick and weakling calf deserted and bawling. Without dismounting he had reached and slung the distressed bossy across his saddle, and dropped it at the ranch for the boys to attend to. It was impossible for McGuire to know or comprehend that, in the eyes of the cattleman, his case and that of the calf were identical in interest and demand upon his assistance. A creature was ill and helpless; he had the power to render aid—these were the only postulates required for the cattleman to act. They formed his system of logic and the most of his creed. McGuire was the seventh invalid whom Raidler had picked up thus casually in San Antonio, where so many thousand go for the ozone that is said to linger about its contracted streets. Five of them had been guests of Solito Ranch until they had been able to leave, cured or better, and exhausting the vocabulary of tearful gratitude. One came too late, but rested very comfortably, at last, under a ratama tree in the garden.

So, then, it was no surprise to the ranchhold when the buckboard spun to the door, and Raidler took up his debile *protégé* like a handful of rags and set him down upon the gallery.

McGuire looked upon things strange to him. The ranch-house was the best in the country. It was built of brick hauled one hundred miles by wagon, but it was of but one story, and its four rooms were completely encircled by a mud floor "gallery." The miscellaneous setting of horses, dogs, saddles, wagons, guns, and cow-punchers' paraphernalia oppressed the metropolitan eye of the wrecked sportsman.

"Well, here we are at home," said Raidler, cheeringly.

"It's a h—l of a looking place," said McGuire promptly, as he rolled upon the gallery floor, in a fit of coughing.

"We'll try to make it comfortable for you, buddy," said the cattleman gently. "It ain't fine inside; but it's the outdoors, anyway, that'll do you the most good. This'll be your room, in here. Anything we got, you ask for it."

He led McGuire into the east room. The floor was bare and clean. White curtains waved in the gulf breeze through the open windows. A big willow rocker, two straight chairs, a long table covered with newspapers, pipes, tobacco, spurs, and cartridges stood in the centre. Some well-mounted heads of deer and one of an enormous black javeli projected from the walls. A wide, cool cot-bed stood in a corner. Nueces County people regarded this guest chamber as fit for a prince. McGuire showed his eyeteeth at it. He took out his nickel and spun it up to the ceiling.

"T'ought I was lyin' about the money, did ye? Well, you can frisk me if you wanter. Dat's the last simoleon in the treasury. Who's goin' to pay?"

The cattleman's clear grey eyes looked steadily from under his grizzly brows into the huckleberry optics of his guest. After a little he said simply, and not ungraciously, "I'll be much obliged to you, son, if you won't mention money any more. Once was quite a plenty. Folks I ask to my ranch don't have to pay anything, and they very scarcely ever offers it. Supper'll be ready in half an hour. There's water in the pitcher, and some, cooler, to drink, in that red jar hanging on the gallery."

"Where's the bell?" asked McGuire, looking about.

"Bell for what?"

"Bell to ring for things. I can't—see here," he exploded in a sudden, weak fury, "I never asked you to bring me here. I never held you up for a cent. I never gave you a hard-luck story till you asked me. Here I am fifty miles from a bellboy or a cocktail. I'm sick. I can't hustle. Gee! but I'm up against it!" McGuire fell upon the cot and sobbed shiveringly.

Raidler went to the door and called. A slender, bright-complexioned Mexican youth about twenty came quickly. Raidler spoke to him in Spanish.

"Ylario, it is in my mind that I promised you the position of *vaquero* on the San Carlos range at the fall *rodea*."

"*Si, señor,* such was your goodness."

"Listen. This *señorito* is my friend. He is very sick. Place yourself at his side. Attend to his wants at all times. Have much patience and care with him. And when he is well, or—and when he is well, instead of *vaquero* I will make you *mayordomo* of the Rancho de las Piedras. *Esta bueno?*"

"*Si, si—mil gracias, señor.*" Ylario tried to kneel upon the floor in his gratitude, but the cattleman kicked at him benevolently, growling, "None of your opery-house antics, now."

Ten minutes later Ylario came from McGuire's room and stood before Raidler.

"The little *señor,*" he announced, "presents his compliments" (Raidler credited Ylario with the preliminary) "and desires some pounded ice, one hot bath, one gin feez-z, that the windows be all closed, toast, one shave, one Newyorkheral', cigarettes, and to send one telegram."

Raidler took a quart bottle of whisky from his medicine cabinet. "Here, take him this," he said.

Thus was instituted the reign of terror at the Solito Ranch. For a few weeks McGuire blustered and boasted and swaggered before the cow-punchers who rode in for miles around to see this latest importation of Raidler's. He was an absolutely new experience to them. He explained to them all the intricate points of sparring and the tricks of training and defence. He opened to their minds' view all the indecorous life of a tag-ger after professional sports. His jargon of slang was a continuous joy and surprise to them. His gestures, his strange poses, his frank ribaldry of tongue and principle fascinated them. He was like a being from a new world.

Strange to say, this new world he had entered did not exist to him. He was an utter egoist of bricks and mortar. He had dropped out, he felt, into open space for a time, and all it contained was an audience for his reminiscences. Neither the limitless freedom of the prairie days nor the grand hush of the close-drawn, spangled nights touched him. All the hues of Aurora could not win him from the pink pages of a sporting journal. "Get something for nothing," was his mission in life; "T'irty-seventh" Street was his goal.

Nearly two months after his arrival he began to complain that he felt worse. It was then that he became the ranch's incubus, its harpy, its Old Man of the Sea. He shut himself in his room like some venomous kobold or flibbertigibbet, whining, complaining, cursing, accusing. The keynote of his plaint was that he had been inveigled into a gehenna against his will; that he was dying of neglect and lack of comforts. With all his dire protestations of increasing illness, to the eye of others he remained unchanged. His currant-like eyes were as bright and diabolic as ever; his voice was as rasping; his callous face, with the skin drawn tense as a drum-head, had no flesh to lose. A flush on his prominent cheek bones each afternoon hinted that a clinical thermometer might have revealed a symptom, and percussion might have established the fact that McGuire was breathing with only one lung, but his appearance remained the same.

In constant attendance upon him was Ylario, whom the coming reward of the *mayordomo*ship must have greatly stimulated, for McGuire chained him to a bitter existence. The air—the man's only chance for life—he commanded to be kept out by closed windows and drawn curtains. The room was always blue and foul with cigarette smoke; whosoever entered it must sit, suffocating, and listen to the imp's interminable gasconade concerning his scandalous career.

The oddest thing of all was the relation existing between McGuire and his benefactor. The attitude of the invalid toward the cattleman was something like that of a peevish, perverse child toward an indulgent parent. When Raidler would leave the ranch McGuire would fall into a fit of malevolent, silent sullenness. When he returned, he would be met by a string of violent and stinging reproaches. Raidler's attitude toward his charge was quite inexplicable in its way. The cattleman seemed actually to assume and feel the character assigned him by McGuire's intemperate accusations—the character of tyrant and guilty oppressor. He seemed to have adopted the responsibility of the fellow's condition, and he always met his tirades with a pacific, patient, and even remorseful kindness that never altered.

One day Raidler said to him, "Try more air, son. You can have the buckboard and a driver every day if you'll go. Try a week or two in one of the cow camps. I'll fix you up plum comfortable. The ground, and the air next to it—them's the things to cure you. I knowed a man from Philadelphy, sicker than you are, got lost on the Guadalupe, and slept on the bare grass in sheep camps for two weeks. Well sir, it started him getting well, which he done. Close to the ground—that's where the medicine in the air stays. Try a little hossback riding now. There's a gentle pony—"

"What've I done to yer?" screamed McGuire. "Did I ever doublecross yer? Did I ask you to bring me here? Drive me out to your camps if you wanter; or stick a knife in me and save trouble. Ride! I can't lift my feet. I couldn't sidestep a jab from a five-year-old kid. That's what your d—d ranch has done for me. There's nothing to eat, nothing to see, and nobody to talk to but a lot of Reubens who don't know a punching bag from a lobster salad."

"It's a lonesome place, for certain," apologized Raidler abashedly. "We got plenty, but it's rough enough. Anything you think of you want, the boys'll ride up and fetch it down for you."

It was Chad Murchison, a cow-puncher from the Circle Bar outfit, who first suggested that McGuire's illness was fraudulent. Chad had brought a basket of grapes for him thirty miles, and four out of his way, tied to his saddle-horn. After remaining in the smoke-tainted room for a while, he emerged and bluntly confided his suspicions to Raidler.

"His arm," said Chad, "is harder'n a diamond. He interduced me to what he called a shore-perplexus punch, and 'twas like being kicked twice by a mustang. He's playin' it low down on you, Curt. He ain't no sicker'n I am. I hate to say it, but the runt's workin' you for range and shelter."

The cattleman's ingenuous mind refused to entertain Chad's view of the case, and when, later, he came to apply the test, doubt entered not into his motives.

One day, about noon, two men drove up to the ranch, alighted, hitched, and came in to dinner; standing and general invitations being the custom of the country. One of them was a great San Antonio doctor, whose costly services had been engaged by a wealthy cowman who had been laid low by an accidental bullet. He was now being driven to the station to take the train back to town. After dinner Raidler took him aside, pushed a twenty-dollar bill against his hand, and said:

"Doc, there's a young chap in that room I guess has got a bad case of consumption. I'd like for you to look him over and see just how bad he is, and if we can do anything for him."

"How much was that dinner I just ate, Mr. Raidler?" said the doctor bluffly, looking over his spectacles. Raidler returned the money to his pocket. The doctor immediately entered McGuire's room, and the cattle-man seated himself upon a heap of saddles on the gallery, ready to reproach himself in the event the verdict should be unfavourable.

In ten minutes the doctor came briskly out. "Your man," he said promptly, "is as sound as a new dollar. His lungs are better than mine. Respiration, temperature, and pulse normal. Chest expansion four inches. Not a sign of weakness anywhere. Of course I didn't examine for the bacillus, but it isn't there. You can put my name to the diagnosis. Even cigarettes and a vilely close room haven't hurt him. Coughs, does he? Well, you tell him it isn't necessary. You asked if there is anything we could do for him. Well, I advise you to set him digging post-holes or breaking mustangs. There's our team ready. Good-day, sir." And like a puff of wholesome, blustery wind the doctor was off.

Raidler reached out and plucked a leaf from a mesquite bush by the railing, and began chewing it thoughtfully.

The branding season was at hand, and the next morning Ross Hargis, foreman of the outfit, was mustering his force of some twenty-five men at the ranch, ready to start for the San Carlos range, where the work was to begin. By six o'clock the horses were all saddled, the grub wagon ready, and the cow-punchers were swinging themselves upon their mounts, when Raidler bade them wait. A boy was bringing up an extra pony, bridled and saddled, to the gate. Raidler walked to McGuire's room and threw open the door. McGuire was lying on his cot, not yet dressed, smoking.

"Get up," said the cattleman, and his voice was clear and brassy, like a bugle.

"How's that?" asked McGuire, a little startled.

"Get up and dress. I can stand a rattlesnake, but I hate a liar. Do I have to tell you again?" He caught McGuire by the neck and stood him on the floor.

"Say, friend," cried McGuire wildly, "are you bug-house? I'm sick—see? I'll croak if I got to hustle. What've I done to yer?"—he began his chronic whine—"I never asked yer to—"

"Put on your clothes," called Raidler in a rising tone.

Swearing, stumbling, shivering, keeping his amazed, shiny eyes upon the now menacing form of the aroused cattleman, McGuire managed to tumble into his clothes. Then Raidler took him by the collar and shoved him out and across the yard to the extra pony hitched at the gate. The cow-punchers lolled in their saddles, open-mouthed.

"Take this man," said Raidler to Ross Hargis, "and put him to work. Make him work hard, sleep hard, and eat hard. You boys know I done what I could for him, and he was welcome. Yesterday the best doctor in San Antone examined him, and says he's got the lungs of a burro and the constitution of a steer. You know what to do with him, Ross."

Ross Hargis only smiled grimly.

"Aw," said McGuire, looking intently at Raidler, with a peculiar expression upon his face, "the croaker said I was all right, did he? Said I was fakin', did he? You put him onto me. You t'ought I wasn't sick. You said I was a liar. Say, friend, I talked rough, I know, but I didn't mean most of it.

If you felt like I did—aw! I forgot—I ain't sick, the croaker says. Well, friend, now I'll go work for yer. Here's where you play even."

He sprang into the saddle easily as a bird, got the quirt from the horn, and gave his pony a slash with it. "Cricket," who once brought in Good Boy by a neck at Hawthorne—and a 10 to 1 shot—had his foot in the stirrups again.

McGuire led the cavalcade as they dashed away for San Carlos, and the cow-punchers gave a yell of applause as they closed in behind his dust.

But in less than a mile he had lagged to the rear, and was last man when they struck the patch of high chaparral below the horse pens. Behind a clump of this he drew rein, and held a handkerchief to his mouth. He took it away drenched with bright, arterial blood, and threw it carefully into a clump of prickly pear. Then he slashed with his quirt again, gasped "G'wan" to his astonished pony, and galloped after the gang.

That night Raidler received a message from his old home in Alabama. There had been a death in the family; an estate was to divide and they called for him to come. Daylight found him in the buckboard, skimming the prairies for the station. It was two months before he returned. When he arrived at the ranch house he found it well-nigh deserted save for Ylario, who acted as a kind of steward during his absence. Little by little the youth made him acquainted with the work done while he was away. The branding camp, he was informed, was still doing business. On account of many severe storms the cattle had been badly scattered, and the branding had been accomplished but slowly. The camp was now in the valley of the Guadalupe, twenty miles away.

"By the way," said Raidler, suddenly remembering, "that fellow I sent along with them—McGuire—is he working yet?"

"I do not know," said Ylario. "Mans from the camp come verre few times to the ranch. So plentee work with the leetle calves. They no say. Oh, I think that fellow McGuire he dead much time ago."

"Dead!" said Raidler. "What you talking about?"

"Verree sick fellow, McGuire," replied Ylario, with a shrug of his shoulder. "I theenk he no live one, two month when he go away."

"Shucks!" said Raidler. "He humbugged you, too, did he? The doctor examined him and said he was sound as a mesquite knot."

"That doctor," said Ylario, smiling, "he tell you so? That doctor no see McGuire."

"Talk up," ordered Raidler. "What the devil do you mean?"

"McGuire," continued the boy tranquilly, "he getting drink water out-side when that doctor come in room. That doctor take me and pound me all over here with his fingers"—putting his hand to his chest—"I not know for what. He put his ear here and here and here, and listen—I not know for what. He put little glass stick in my mouth. He feel my arm here. He make me count like whisper—so—twenty, *treinta, cuarenta*. Who knows," concluded Ylario, with a deprecating spread of his hands, "for what that doctor do those verree droll and such-like things?"

"What horses are up?" asked Raidler shortly.

"Paisano is grazing but behind the little corral, *señor.*"

"Saddle him for me at once."

Within a very few minutes the cattleman was mounted and away. Paisano, well named after that ungainly but swift-running bird, struck into his long lope that ate up the road like a strip of macaroni. In two hours and a quarter Raidler, from a gentle swell, saw the branding camp by a water hole in the Guadalupe. Sick with expectancy of the news he feared, he rode up, dismounted, and dropped Paisano's reins. So gentle was his heart that at that moment he would have pleaded guilty to the murder of McGuire.

The only being in the camp was the cook, who was just arranging the hunks of barbecued beef, and distributing the tin coffee cups for supper. Raidler evaded a direct question concerning the one subject in his mind.

"Everything all right in camp, Pete?" he managed to inquire.

"So, so," said Pete conservatively. "Grub give out twice. Wind scattered the cattle, and we've had to rake the brush for forty mile. I need a new coffee-pot. And the mosquitos is some more hellish than common."

"The boys—all well?"

Pete was no optimist. Besides, inquiries concerning the health of cow-punchers were not only superfluous, but bordered on flaccidity. It was not like the boss to make them.

"What's left of 'em don't miss no calls to grub," the cook conceded.

"What's left of 'em?" repeated Raidler in a husky voice. Mechanically he began to look around for McGuire's grave. He had in his mind a white slab such as he had seen in the Alabama church-yard. But immediately he knew that was foolish.

"Sure," said Pete; "what's left. Cow camps change in two months. Some's gone."

Raidler nerved himself.

"That—chap—I sent along—McGuire—did—he—"

"Say," interrupted Pete, rising with a chunk of corn bread in each hand, "that was a dirty shame, sending that poor, sick kid to a cow camp. A doctor that couldn't tell he was graveyard meat ought to be skinned with a cinch buckle. Game as he was, too—it's a scandal among snakes—lemme tell you what he done. First night in camp the boys started to initiate him in the leather breeches degree. Ross Hargis busted him one swipe with his chaparreras, and what do you reckon the poor child did? Got up, the little skeeter, and licked Ross. Licked Ross Hargis. Licked him good. Hit him plenty and everywhere and hard. Ross'd just get up and pick out a fresh place to lay down on agin.

"Then that McGuire goes off there and lays down with his head in the grass and bleeds. A hem'ridge they calls it. He lays there eighteen hours by the watch, and they can't budge him. Then Ross Hargis, who loves any man who can lick him, goes to work and damns the doctors from Greenland to Poland Chiny; and him and Green Branch Johnson they gets McGuire in a tent, and spells each other feedin' him chopped raw meat and whisky.

"But it looks like the kid ain't got no appetite to git well, for they misses him from the tent in the night and finds him rootin' in the grass, and likewise a drizzle fallin'. 'Gwan,' he says, 'lemme go and die like I wanter. He said I was a liar and a fake and I was playin' sick. Lemme alone.'

"Two weeks," went on the cook, "he laid around, not noticin' nobody, and then—"

A sudden thunder filled the air, and a score of galloping centaurs crashed through the brush into camp.

"Illustrious rattlesnakes!" exclaimed Pete, springing all ways at once; "here's the boys come, and I'm an assassinated man if supper ain't ready in three minutes."

But Raidler saw only one thing. A little, brown-faced, grinning chap, springing from his saddle in the full light of the fire. McGuire was not like that, and yet—

In another instant the cattleman was holding him by the hand and shoulder.

"Son, son, how goes it?" was all he found to say.

"Close to the ground, says you," shouted McGuire, crunching Raidler's fingers in a grip of steel; "and dat's where I found it—healt' and strengt', and tumbled to what a cheap skate I been actin'. T'anks fer kickin' me out, old man. And—say! de joke's on dat croaker, ain't it? I looked t'rough the window and see him playin' tag on dat Dago kid's solar plexus."

"You son of a tinker," growled the cattleman, 'whyn't you talk up and say the doctor never examined you?"

"Aw—g'wan!" said McGuire, with a flash of his old asperity, "nobody can't bluff me. You never ast me. You made your spiel, and you t'rowed me out, and I let it go at dat. And, say, friend, dis chasin' cows is outer sight. Dis is de whitest bunch of sports I ever travelled with. You'll let me stay, won't yer, old man?"

Raidler looked wonderingly toward Ross Hargis.

"That cussed little runt," remarked Ross tenderly, "is the Jo-dartin'est hustler—and the hardest hitter in anybody's cow camp."

THE CATTLE RUSTLERS

Stewart Edward White

AWN BROKE, so we descended through wet grasses to the cañon. There, after some difficulty, we managed to start a fire, and so ate breakfast, the rain still pouring down on us. About nine o'clock, with miraculous suddenness, the torrent stopped. It began to turn cold. The Cattleman and I decided to climb to the top of the butte after meat, which we entirely lacked.

It was rather a stiff ascent, but once above the sheer cliffs we found ourselves on a rolling meadow tableland, a half-mile broad by, perhaps, a mile and a half in length. Grass grew high; here and there were small live oaks planted park-like; slight and rounded ravines accommodated brooklets. As we walked back, the edges blended in the edges of the mesa across the cañon. The deep gorges, which had heretofore seemed the most prominent elements of the scenery, were lost. We stood, apparently, in the middle of a wide and undulating plain, diversified by little ridges, and running with a free sweep to the very foot of the snowy Galiuros. It seemed as though we should be able to ride horseback in almost any given direction. Yet we knew that ten minutes' walk would take us to the brink of most stupendous chasms—so deep that the water flowing in them hardly seemed to move; so rugged that only with the greatest difficulty could a horseman make his way through the country at all; and yet so ancient that the bottoms supported forests, rich grasses, and rounded, gentle knolls. It was a most astonishing set of double impressions.

We succeeded in killing a nice, fat white-tail buck, and so returned to camp happy. The rain held off. We dug ditches, organized shelters, cooked a warm meal. For the next day we planned a bear hunt afoot, far up a manzañita cañon where Uncle Jim knew of some "holing up" caves.

But when we awoke in the morning we threw aside our coverings with some difficulty to look on a ground covered with snow; trees laden almost to the breaking point with snow, and the air filled with it.

"No bear to-day," said the Cattleman.

"No," agreed Uncle Jim drily. "No b'ar. And what's more, unless yo're aimin' to shop here somewhat of a spell, we'll have to make out to-day."

We cooked with freezing fingers, ate while dodging avalanches from the trees, and packed reluctantly. The ropes were frozen, the hobbles stiff, everything either crackling or wet. Finally the task was finished. We took a last warming of the fingers and climbed on.

The country was wonderfully beautiful with the white not yet shaken from the trees and rock ledges. Also it was wonderfully slippery. The snow was soft enough to ball under the horses' hoofs, so that most of the time the poor animals skated and stumbled along on stilts. Thus we made our way back over ground which, naked of these difficulties, we had considered bad enough. Imagine riding along a slant of rock shelving off to a bad tumble, so steep that your pony has to do more or less expert ankle work to keep from slipping off sideways. During the passage of that rock you are apt to sit very light. Now cover it with several inches of snow, stick a snowball on each hoof of your mount, and try again. When you have ridden it—or its duplicate—a few score of times, select a steep mountain side, cover it with round rocks the size of your head, and over that spread a concealing blanket of the same sticky snow. You are privileged to vary these to the limits of your imagination.

Once across the divide, we ran into a new sort of trouble. You may remember that on our journey over we had been forced to travel for some distance in a narrow stream-bed. During our passage we had scrambled up some rather steep and rough slopes, and hopped up some fairly high ledges. Now we found the heretofore dry bed flowing a good eight inches deep. The steep slopes had become cascades; the ledges, waterfalls. When we came to them we had to "shoot the rapids" as best we could, only to land with a *plunk* in an indeterminately deep pool at the bottom. Some of the pack horses went down, sousing again our unfortunate bedding, but by the grace of fortune not a saddle pony lost his feet.

After a time the gorge widened. We came out into the box cañon with its trees. Here the water spread and shoaled to a depth of only two or three inches. We splashed along gaily enough, for, with the exception of an occasional quicksand or boggy spot, our troubles were over.

Jed Parker and I happened to ride side by side, bringing up the rear and seeing to it that the pack animals did not stray or linger. As we passed the first of the rustlers' corrals, he called my attention to them.

"Go take a look," said he. "We only got those fellows out of here two years ago."

I rode over. At this point the rim-rock broke to admit the ingress of a ravine into the main cañon. Riding a short distance up the ravine, I could see that it ended abruptly in a perpendicular cliff. As the sides also were precipitous, it became necessary only to build a fence across the entrance into the main cañon to become possessed of a corral completely closed in. Remembering the absolute invisibility of these sunken cañons until the rider is almost directly over them, and also the extreme roughness and remoteness of the district, I could see that the spot was admirably adapted to concealment.

"There's quite a yarn about the gang that held this hole," said Jed Parker to me, when I had ridden back to him. "I'll tell you about it sometime."

We climbed the hill, descended on the Double R, built a fire in the stove, dried out, and were happy. After a square meal—and a dry one—I reminded Jed Parker of his promise, and so, sitting cross-legged on his "so-gun" in the middle of the floor, he told us the following yarn:

There's a good deal of romance been written about the "bad man," and there's about the same amount of nonsense. The bad man is just a plain murderer, neither more nor less. He never does get into a real, good, plain, stand-up gun fight if he can possibly help it. His killin's are done from behind a door, or when he's got his man dead to rights. There's Sam Cook. You've all heard of him. He had nerve, of course, and when he was backed into a corner he made good; and he was sure sudden death with a gun. But when he went out for a man deliberate, he didn't take no special chances. For a while he was marshal at Willets. Pretty soon it was noted that there was a heap of cases of resisting arrest, where Sam as marshal had to shoot, and that those cases almost always happened to be his personal enemies. Of course, that might be all right, but it looked suspicious. Then one day he killed poor old Max Schmidt out behind his own saloon. Called him out and shot him in the stomach. Said Max resisted arrest on a warrant for keepin' open out of hours! That was a sweet warrant to take out in Willets, anyway! Mrs. Schmidt always claimed that she saw that deal played, and that, while they were talkin' perfectly peaceable, Cook let drive from the hip at about two yards' range. Anyway, we decided we needed another marshal. Nothin' else was ever done, for the Vigilantes hadn't been formed, and your individual and decent citizen doesn't care to be marked by a bad man of that stripe. Leastways, unless he wants to go in for bad-man methods and do a little ambusheein' on his own account.

The point is, that these yere bad men are a low-down, miserable proposition, and plain, cold-blood murderers, willin' to wait for a sure thing, and without no compunctions whatever. The bad man takes you unawares, when you're sleepin', or talkin', or drinkin', or lookin' to see what for a day it's goin' to be, anyway. He don't give you no show, and sooner or later he's goin' to get you in the safest and easiest way for himself. There ain't no romance about that.

And, until you've seen a few men called out of their shacks for a friendly conversation, and shot when they happen to look away; or asked for a drink of water, and killed when they stoop to the spring; or potted from behind as they go into a room, it's pretty hard to believe that any man can be so plumb lackin' in fair play or pity or just natural humanity.

As you boys know, I come in from Texas to Buck Johnson's about ten year back. I had a pretty good mount of ponies that I knew, and I hated to let them go at prices they were offerin' then, so I made up my mind to ride across and bring them in with me. It wasn't so awful far, and I figured that I'd like to take in what New Mexico looked like anyway.

About down by Albuquerque I tracked up with another outfit headed my way. There was five of them, three men, and a woman, and a yearlin' baby. They had a dozen hosses, and that was about all I could see. There was only two packed, and no wagon. I suppose the whole outfit—pots, pans, and kettles—was worth five dollars. It was just supper when I run across them, and it didn't take more'n one look to discover that flour, coffee, sugar, and salt was all they carried. A yearlin' carcass, half-skinned, lay near, and the fry-pan was full of meat.

"Howdy, strangers," says I, ridin' up.

They nodded a little, but didn't say nothin'. My hosses fell to grazin', and I eased myself around in my saddle, and made a cigareet. The men was tall, lank fellows, with kind of sullen faces, and sly, shifty eyes; the woman was dirty and generally mussed up. I knowed that sort all right. Texas was gettin' too many fences for them.

"Havin' supper?" says I, cheerful.

One of 'em grunted "Yes" at me; and, after a while, the biggest asked me very grudgin' if I wouldn't light and eat, I told them "No," that I was travellin' in the cool of the evenin'.

"You seem to have more meat than you need, though," says I. "I could use a little of that."

"Help yourself," says they. "It's a maverick we come across."

I took a steak, and noted that the hide had been mighty well cut to ribbons around the flanks, and that the head was gone.

"Well," says I to the carcass, "no one's goin' to be able to swear whether you're a maverick or not, but I bet you knew the feel of a brandin' iron all right."

I gave them a thank-you, and climbed on again. My hosses acted some surprised at bein' gathered up again, but I couldn't help that.

"It looks like a plumb imposition, cavallos," says I to them, "after an all-day, but you sure don't want to join that outfit any more than I do the angels, and if we camp here we're likely to do both."

I didn't see them any more after that until I'd hit the Lazy Y, and had started in runnin' cattle in the Soda Springs Valley. Larry Eagen and me rode together those days, and that's how I got to know him pretty well. One day, over in the Elm Flat, we ran smack on this Texas outfit again, headed north. This time I was on my own range, and I knew where I stood, so I could show a little more curiosity in the case.

"Well, you got this far," says I.

"Yes," says they.

"Where you headed?"

"Over towards the hills."

"What to do?"

"Make a ranch, raise some truck; perhaps buy a few cows."

They went on.

"Truck farmin'," says I to Larry, "is fine prospects in this country."

He sat on his horse lookin' after them.

"I'm sorry for them," says he. "It must be almighty hard scratchin'."

Well, we rode the range for upwards of two year. In that time we saw our Texas friends—name of Hahn—two or three times in Willets, and heard of them off and on. They bought an old brand of Steve McWilliams for seventy-five dollars, carryin' six or eight head of cows. After that, from time to time, we heard of them buyin' more—two or three head from one man, and two or three from another. They branded them all with that

McWilliams iron —T O—so, pretty soon, we began to see the cattle on the range.

Now, a good cattleman knows cattle just as well as you know people, and he can tell them about as far off. Horned critters look alike to you, but even in a country supportin' a good many thousand head, a man used to the business can recognise most every individual as far as he can see him. Some is better than others at it. I suppose you really have to be brought up to it. So we boys at the Lazy Y noted all the cattle with the new T O, and could estimate pretty close that the Hahn outfit might own, maybe, thirty-five head all told.

That was all very well, and nobody had any kick comin'. Then, one day in the spring, we came across our first "sleeper."

What's a sleeper? A sleeper is a calf that has been ear-marked, but not branded. Every owner has a certain brand, as you know, and then he crops and slits the ears in a certain way, too. In that manner he don't have to look at the brand, except to corroborate the ears; and, as the critter generally sticks his ears up inquirin'-like to anyone ridin' up, it's easy to know the brand without lookin' at it, merely from the ear-marks. Once in a great while, when a man comes across an unbranded calf, and it ain't handy to build a fire, he just ear-marks it and let's the brandin' go till later. But it isn't done often, and our outfit had strict orders never to make sleepers.

Well, one day in the spring, as I say, Larry and me was ridin', when we came across a Lazy Y cow and calf. The little fellow was ear-marked all right, so we rode on, and never would have discovered nothin' if a bush rabbit hadn't jumped and scared the calf right across in front of our hosses. Then we couldn't help but see that there wasn't no brand.

Of course we roped him and put the iron on him. I took the chance to look at his ears, and saw that the marking had been done quite recent, so when we got in that night I reported to Buck Johnson that one of the punchers was gettin' lazy and sleeperin'. Naturally he went after the man who had done it; but every puncher swore up and down, and back and across, that he'd branded every calf he'd had a rope on that spring. We put it down that someone was lyin', and let it go at that.

And then, about a week later, one of the other boys reported a Triangle-H sleeper. The Triangle-H was the Goodrich brand, so we didn't have nothin' to do with that. Some of them might be sleeperin' for all we knew. Three other cases of the same kind we happened across that same spring.

So far, so good. Sleepers runnin' in such numbers was a little astonish-in', but nothin' suspicious. Cattle did well that summer, and when we come to round up in the fall, we cut out maybe a dozen of those T O cat-tle that had strayed out of that Hahn country. Of the dozen there was five grown cows, and seven yearlin's.

"My Lord, Jed," says Buck to me, "they's a heap of these youngsters comin' over our way."

But still, as a young critter is more apt to stray than an old one that's got his range established, we didn't lay no great store by that neither. The Hahns took their bunch, and that's all there was to it.

Next spring, though, we found a few more sleepers, and one day we came on a cow that had gone dead lame. That was usual, too, but Buck, who was with me, had somethin' on his mind. Finally he turned back and roped her, and threw her.

"Look here, Jed," says he, "what do you make of this?"

I could see where the hind legs below the hocks had been burned.

"Looks like somebody had roped her by the hind feet," says I.

"Might be," says he, "but her bein' lame that way makes it look more like hobbles."

So we didn't say nothin' more about that neither, until just by luck we came on another lame cow. We threw her, too.

"Well, what do you think of this one?" Buck Johnson asks me.

"The feet is pretty well tore up," says I, "and down to the quick, but I've seen them tore up just as bad on the rocks when they come down out of the mountains."

You sabe what that meant, don't you? You see, a rustler will take a cow and hobble her, or lame her so she can't follow, and then he'll take her calf a long ways off and brand it with his iron. Of course, if we was to see a calf of one brand followin' of a cow with another, it would be just too easy to guess what had happened.

We rode on mighty thoughtful. There couldn't be much doubt that cat-tle rustlers was at work. The sleepers they had ear-marked, hopin' that no one would discover the lack of a brand. Then, after the calf was weaned, and quit followin' of his mother, the rustler would brand it with his own iron, and change its ear-mark to match. It made a nice, easy way of gettin' together a bunch of cattle cheap.

But it was pretty hard to guess off-hand who the rustlers might be. There were a lot of renegades down towards the Mexican line who made a raid once in a while, and a few oilers livin' near had water holes in the foothills, and any amount of little cattle holders, like this T O outfit, and any of them wouldn't shy very hard at a little sleeperin' on the side. Buck Johnson told us all to watch out, and passed the word quiet among the big owners to try and see whose cattle seemed to have too many calves for the number of cows.

The Texas outfit I'm tellin' you about had settled up above in this Double R cañon where I showed you those natural corrals this morning. They'd built them a 'dobe, and cleared some land, and planted a few trees, and made an irrigated patch for alfalfa. Nobody never rode over his way very much, 'cause the country was most too rough for cattle, and our ranges lay farther to the southward. Now, however, we began to extend our ridin' a little. I was down towards Dos Cabesas to look over the cattle there, and they used to send Larry up into the Double R country. One evenin' he took me to one side.

"Look here, Jed," says he, "I know you pretty well, and I'm not ashamed to say that I'm all new at this cattle business—in fact, I haven't been at it more'n a year. What should be the proportion of cows to calves anyhow?"

"There ought to be about twice as many cows as there're calves," I tells him.

"Then, with only about fifty head of grown cows, there ought not to be an equal number of yearlin's?"

"I should say not," says I. "What are you drivin' at?"

"Nothin' yet," says he.

A few days later he tackled me again.

"Jed," says he, "I'm not good, like you fellows are, at knowin' one cow from another, but there's a calf down there branded T O that I'd pretty near swear I saw with an X Y cow last month. I wish you could come down with me."

We got that fixed easy enough, and for the next month rammed around through this broken country, lookin' for evidence. I saw enough to satisfy me to a moral certainty, but nothin' for a sheriff; and, of course, we couldn't go shoot up a peaceful rancher on mere suspicion. Finally, one day, we run on a four-months' calf all by himself, with the T O iron onto him—a mighty healthy lookin' calf, too.

"Wonder where *his* mother is!" says I.

"Maybe it's a 'dogie,'" says Larry Eagen—we calls calves whose mothers have died "dogies."

"No," says I, "I don't hardly think so. A dogie is always under size and poor, and he's layin' around water holes, and he always has a big, sway belly onto him. No, this is no dogie; and, if it's an honest calf, there sure ought to be a T O cow around somewhere."

So we separated to have a good look. Larry rode up on the edge of a little rim-rock. In a minute I saw his hoss jump back, dodgin' a rattlesnake or somethin', and then fall back out of sight. I jumped my hoss up there tur'ble quick, and looked over, expectin' to see nothin' but mangled remains. It was only about fifteen foot down, but I couldn't see bottom 'count of some brush.

"Are you all right?" I yells.

"Yes, yes!" cries Larry, "but for the love of God get down here as quick as you can."

I hopped off my hoss and scrambled down somehow.

"Hurt?" says I, as soon as I lit.

"Not a bit—look here."

There was a dead cow with the Lazy Y on her flank.

"And a bullet-hole in her forehead," adds Larry. "And, look here, that T O calf was bald-faced, and so was this cow."

"Reckon we found our sleepers," says I.

So, there we was. Larry had to lead his cavallo down the barranca to the main cañon. I followed along on the rim, waitin' until a place gave me a chance to get down, too, or Larry a chance to get up. We were talkin' back and forth when, all at once, Larry shouted again.

"Big game this time," he yells. "Here's a cave and a mountain lion squallin' in it."

I slid down to him at once, and we drew our six shooters and went up to the cave openin', right under the rim-rock. There, sure enough, were fresh lion tracks, and we could hear a little faint cryin' like a woman.

"First chance," claims Larry, and dropped to his hands and knees at the entrance.

"Well, damn me!" he cries, and crawls in at once, payin' no attention to me tellin' him to be more cautious. In a minute he backs out, carryin' a three-year-old girl.

"We seem to be in for adventures to-day," says he. "Now, where do you suppose that came from, and how did it get here?"

"Well," says I, "I've followed lion tracks where they've carried yearlin's across their backs like a fox does a goose. They're tur'ble strong."

"But where did she come from?" he wonders.

"As for that," says I, "don't you remember now that T O outfit had a yearlin' kid when it came into the country?"

"That's right," says he. "It's only a mile down the cañon. I'll take it home. They must be most distracted about it."

So I scratched up to the top where my pony was waitin'. It was a tur'ble hard climb, and I 'most had to have hooks on my eyebrows to get up at all. It's easier to slide down than to climb back. I dropped my gun out of my holster, and she went way to the bottom, but I wouldn't have gone back for six guns. Larry picked it up for me.

So we went along, me on the rim-rock and around the barrancas, and Larry in the bottom carryin' of the kid.

By and by we came to the ranch house, and stopped to wait. The minute Larry hove in sight everybody was out to once, and in two winks the woman had that baby. They didn't see me at all, but I could hear, plain enough, what they said. Larry told how he had found her in the cave, and all about the lion tracks, and the woman cried and held the kid close to her, and thanked him about forty times. Then when she'd wore the edge off a little, she took the kid inside to feed it or somethin'.

"Well," says Larry, still laughin', "I must hit the trail."

"You say you found her up the Double R?" asks Hahn. "Was it that cave near the three cottonwoods?"

"Yes," says Larry.

"Where'd you get into the cañon?"

"Oh, my hoss slipped off into the barranca just above.

"The barranca just above," repeats Hahn, lookin' straight at him.

Larry took one step back.

"You ought to be almighty glad I got into the cañon at all," says he.

Hahn stepped up, holdin' out his hand.

"That's right," says he. "You done us a good turn there."

Larry took his hand. At the same time Hahn pulled his gun and shot him through the middle.

It was all so sudden and unexpected that I stood there paralysed. Larry fell forward the way a man mostly will when he's hit in the stomach, but somehow he jerked loose a gun and got it off twice. He didn't hit nothin', and I reckon he was dead before he hit the ground. And there he had my gun, and I was about as useless as a pocket in a shirt!

No, sir, you can talk as much as you please, but the killer is a low-down ornery scub, and he don't hesitate at no treachery or ingratitude to keep his carcass safe.

Jed Parker ceased talking. The dusk had fallen in the little room, and dimly could be seen the recumbent figures lying at ease on their blankets. The ranch foreman was sitting bolt upright, cross-legged. A faint glow from his pipe barely distinguished his features.

"What became of the rustlers?" I asked him.

"Well, sir, that is the queer part. Hahn himself, who had done the killin', skipped out. We got out warrants, of course, but they never got served. He was a sort of half outlaw from that time, and was killed finally in the train hold-up of '97. But the others we tried for rustling. We didn't have much of a case, as the law went then, and they'd have gone free if the woman hadn't turned evidence against them. The killin' was too much for her. And, as the precedent held good in a lot of other rustlin' cases, Larry's death was really the beginnin' of law and order in the cattle business."

We smoked. The last light suddenly showed red against the grimy window. Windy Bill arose and looked out the door.

"Boys," said he, returning, "she's cleared off. We can get back to the ranch to-morrow."

ON THE BRAZOS AND WICHITA

Andy Adams

A S WE NEARED BUFFALO GAP a few days later, a deputy sheriff of Taylor County, who resided at the Gap, rode out and met us. He brought an urgent request from Hames to Flood to appear as a witness against the rustlers, who were to be given a preliminary trial at Abilene the following day. Much as he regretted to leave the herd for even a single night, our foreman finally consented to go. To further his convenience we made a long evening drive, camping for the night well above Buffalo Gap, which at that time was little more than a landmark on the trail. The next day we made an easy drive and passed Abilene early in the afternoon, where Flood rejoined us, but refused any one permission to go into town, with the exception of McCann with the wagon, which was a matter of necessity. It was probably for the best, for this cow town had the reputation of setting a pace that left the wayfarer purseless and breathless, to say nothing about headaches. Though our foreman had not reached those mature years in life when the pleasures and frivolities of dissipation no longer allure, yet it was but natural that he should wish to keep his men from the temptation of the cup that cheers and the wiles of the siren. But when the wagon returned that evening, it was evident that our foreman was human, for with a box of cigars which were promised us were several bottles of Old Crow.

After crossing the Clear Fork of the Brazos a few days later, we entered a well-watered, open country, through which the herd made splendid progress. At Abilene, we were surprised to learn that our herd was the twentieth that had passed that point. The weather so far on our trip had been exceptionally good; only a few showers had fallen, and those during the daytime. But we were now nearing a country in which rain was more frequent, and the swollen condition of several small streams which have their headwaters in the Staked Plains was an intimation to us of recent rains to the westward of our route. Before reaching the main Brazos, we passed two other herds of yearling cattle, and were warned of the impassable condition of that river for the past week. Nothing daunted, we made our usual drive; and when the herd camped that night, Flood, after scouting ahead to the river, returned with the word that the Brazos had been unfordable for over a week, five herds being waterbound.

As we were then nearly twenty miles south of the river, the next morning we threw off the trail and turned the herd to the northeast, hoping to strike the Brazos a few miles above Round Timber ferry. Once the herd was started and their course for the day outlined to our point men by definite landmarks, Flood and Quince Forrest set out to locate the ferry and look up a crossing. Had it not been for our wagon, we would have kept the trail, but as there was no ferry on the Brazos at the crossing of the western trail, it was a question either of waiting or of making this detour. Then all the grazing for several miles about the crossing was already taken by the waterbound herds, and to crowd up and trespass on range already occupied would have been a violation of an unwritten law. Again, no herd took kindly to another attempting to pass them when in traveling condition the herds were on an equality. Our foreman had conceived the scheme of getting past these waterbound herds, if possible, which would give us a clear field until the next large watercourse was reached.

Flood and Forrest returned during the noon hour, the former having found, by swimming, a passable ford near the mouth of Monday Creek, while the latter reported the ferry in "apple-pie order." No sooner, then, was dinner over than the wagon set out for the ferry under Forrest as pilot, though we were to return to the herd once the ferry was sighted. The mouth of Monday Creek was not over ten miles below the regular trail crossing on the Brazos, and much nearer our noon camp than the regular one; but the wagon was compelled to make a direct elbow, first turning to the eastward, then doubling back after the river was crossed. We held the cattle off water during the day, so as to have them thirsty when they reached the river. Flood had swum it during the morning, and warned us to be prepared for fifty or sixty yards of swimming water in crossing. When within a mile, we held up the herd and changed horses, every man picking out one with a tested ability to swim. Those of us who were expected to take the water as the herd entered the river divested ourselves of boots and clothing, which we intrusted to riders in the rear. The approach to crossing was gradual, but the opposite bank was abrupt, with only a narrow passageway leading out from the channel. As the current was certain to carry the swimming cattle downstream, we must, to make due allowance, take the water nearly a hundred yards above the outlet on the other shore. All this was planned out in advance by our foreman, who now took the position of point man on the right hand or down the riverside; and with our saddle horses in the immediate lead, we breasted the angry Brazos.

The water was shallow as we entered, and we reached nearly the middle of the river before the loose saddle horses struck swimming water. Honeyman was on their lee, and with the cattle crowding in their rear, there was no alternative but to swim. A loose horse swims easily, however, and our *remuda* readily faced the current, though it was swift enough to carry them below the passageway on the opposite side. By this time the lead cattle were adrift, and half a dozen of us were on their lower side, for the footing under the cutbank was narrow, and should the cattle become congested on landing, some were likely to drown. For a quarter of an hour it required cool heads to keep the trail of cattle moving into the water and the passageway clear on the opposite landing. While they were crossing, the herd represented a large letter "U," caused by the force of the current drifting the cattle downstream, or until a foothold was secured on the farther side. Those of us fortunate enough to have good swimming horses swam the river a dozen times, and then after the herd was safely over, swam back to get our clothing. It was a thrilling experience to us younger lads of the outfit, and rather attractive; but the elder and more experienced men always dreaded swimming rivers. Their reasons were made clear enough when, a fortnight later, we crossed Red River, where a newly made grave was pointed out to us, amongst others of men who had lost their lives while swimming cattle.

Once the bulk of the cattle were safely over, with no danger of congestion on the farther bank, they were allowed to loiter along under the cutbank and drink to their hearts' content. Quite a number strayed above the passageway, and in order to rout them out, Bob Blades, Moss Strayhorn, and I rode out through the outlet and up the river, where we found some of them in a passageway down a dry arroyo. The steers had found a soft, damp place in the bank, and were so busy horning the waxy, red mud, that they hardly noticed our approach until we were within a rod of them. We halted our horses and watched their antics. The kneeling cattle were cutting the bank viciously with their horns and matting their heads with the red mud, but on discovering our presence, they curved their tails and stampeded out as playfully as young lambs on a hillside.

"Can you sabe where the fun comes in to a steer, to get down on his knees in the mud and dirt, and horn the bank and muss up his curls and enjoy it like that?" inquired Strayhorn of Blades and me. "Because it's healthy and funny besides," replied Bob, giving me a cautious wink. "Did you never hear of people taking mud baths? You've seen dogs eat grass, haven't you? Well, it's something on the same order. Now, if I was a student of the nature of animals, like you are, I'd get off my horse and imagine I had horns, and scar and otherwise mangle that mud bank shamefully. I'll hold your horse if you want to try it—some of the secrets of the humor of cattle might be revealed to you."

The banter, though given in jest, was too much for this member of a craft that can always be depended on to do foolish things; and when we rejoined the outfit, Strayhorn presented a sight no sane man save a member of our tribe ever would have conceived of.

The herd had scattered over several thousand acres after leaving the river, grazing freely, and so remained during the rest of the evening. Forrest changed horses and set out down the river to find the wagon and pilot it in, for with the long distance that McCann had to cover, it was a question if he would reach us before dark. Flood selected a bed ground and camp about a mile out from the river, and those of the outfit not on herd dragged up an abundance of wood for the night, and built a roaring fire as a beacon to our absent commissar. Darkness soon settled over camp, and the prospect of a supperless night was confronting us; the first guard had taken the herd, and yet there was no sign of the wagon. Several of us youngsters then mounted our night horses and rode down the river a mile or over in the hope of meeting McCann. We came to a steep bank, caused by the shifting of the first bottom of the river across to the north bank, rode up this bluff some little distance, dismounted, and fired several shots; then with our ears to the earth patiently awaited a response. It did not come, and we rode back again. "Hell's fire and little fishes!" said Joe Stallings, as we clambered into our saddles to return, "it's not supper or breakfast that's troubling me, but will we get any dinner tomorrow? That's a more pregnant question."

It must have been after midnight when I was awakened by the braying of mules and the rattle of the wagon, to hear the voices of Forrest and Mc-Cann, mingled with the rattle of chains as they unharnessed, condemning to eternal perdition the broken country on the north side of the Brazos, between Round Timber ferry and the mouth of Monday Creek.

"I think that when the Almighty made this country on the north side of the Brazos," said McCann the next morning at breakfast, "the Creator must have grown careless or else made it out of odds and ends. There's just a hundred and one of these dry arroyos that you can't see until you are right onto them. They wouldn't bother a man on horseback, but with a loaded wagon it's different. And I'll promise you all right now that if Forrest hadn't come out and piloted me in, you might have tightened up your belts for breakfast and drank out of cow tracks and smoked cigarettes for nourishment. Well, it'll do you good; this high living was liable to spoil some of you, but I notice that you are all on your feet this morning. The black strap? Honeyman, get that molasses jug out of the wagon—it sits right in front of the chuck box. It does me good to see this outfit's tastes once more going back to the good old staples of life."

We made our usual early start, keeping well out from the river on a course almost due northward. The next river on our way was the Wichita, still several days' drive from the mouth of Monday Creek. Flood's intention was to parallel the old trail until near the river, when, if its stage of water was not fordable, we would again seek a lower crossing in the hope of avoiding any waterbound herds on that watercourse. The second day out from the Brazos it rained heavily during the day and drizzled during the entire night. Not a hoof would bed down, requiring the guards to be doubled into two watches for the night. The next morning, as was usual when of the trail, Flood scouted in advance, and near the middle of the afternoon's drive we came into the old trail. The weather in the mean time had faired off, which revived life and spirit in the outfit, for in trail work there is nothing that depresses the spirits of men like falling weather. On coming into the trail, we noticed that no herds had passed since the rain began. Shortly afterward our rear guard was overtaken by a horseman who belonged to a mixed herd which was encamped some four or five miles below the point where we came into the old trail. He reported the Wichita as having been unfordable for the past week, but at that time falling; and said that if the rain of the past few days had not extended as far west as the Staked Plains, the river would be fordable in a day or two.

Before the stranger left us, Flood returned and confirmed this information, and reported further that there were two herds lying over at the Wichita ford expecting to cross the following day. With this outlook, we grazed our herd up to within five miles of the river and camped for the night, and our visitor returned to his outfit with Flood's report of our expectation of crossing on the morrow. But with the fair weather and the prospects of an easy night, we encamped entirely too close to the trail, as we experienced to our sorrow. The grazing was good everywhere, the recent rains having washed away the dust, and we should have camped farther away. We were all sleepy that night, and no sooner was supper over than every mother's son of us was in his blankets. We slept so soundly that the guards were compelled to dismount when calling the relief, and shake the next guards on duty out of their slumber and see that they got up, or men would unconsciously answer in their sleep. The cattle were likewise tired, and slept as willingly as the men.

About midnight, however, Fox Quarternight dashed into camp, firing his six-shooter and yelling like a demon. We tumbled out of our blankets in a dazed condition to hear that one of the herds camped near the river had stampeded, the heavy rumbling of the running herd and the shooting of their outfit now being distinctly audible. We lost no time getting our horses, and in less than a minute were riding for our cattle, which had already got up and were timidly listening to the approaching noise. Although we were a good quarter mile from the trail, before we could drift our herd to a point of safety, the stampeding cattle swept down the trail like a cyclone and our herd was absorbed into the maelstrom of the onrush like leaves in a whirlwind. It was then that our long-legged Mexican steers set us a pace that required a good horse to equal, for they easily took the lead, the other herd having run between three and four miles before striking us, and being already well winded. The other herd were Central Texas cattle, and numbered over thirty-five hundred, but in running capacity were never any match for ours.

Before they had run a mile past our camp, our outfit, bunched well together on the left point, made the first effort to throw them out and off the trail and try to turn them. But the waves of an angry ocean could as easily have been brought under subjection as our terrorized herd during this first mad dash. Once we turned a few hundred of the leaders, and about the time we thought success was in reach, another contingent of double the number had taken the lead; then we had to abandon what few we had, and again ride to the front. When we reached the lead, there, within half a mile ahead, burned the campfire of the herd of mixed cattle which had moved up the trail that evening. They had had ample warning of impending trouble, just as we had; and before the running cattle reached them about half a dozen of their outfit rode to our assistance, when we made another effort to turn or hold the herds from mixing. None of the outfit of the first herd had kept in the lead with us, their horses fagging, and when the foreman of this mixed herd met us, not knowing that we were as innocent of the trouble as himself, he made some slighting remarks about our outfit and cattle. But it was no time to be sensitive, and with his outfit to help we threw our whole weight against the left point a second time, but only turned a few hundred; and before we could get into the lead again their campfire had been passed and their herd of over three thousand cattle more were in the run. As cows and calves predominated in this mixed herd, our own southerners were still leaders in the stampede.

It is questionable if we would have turned this stampede before daybreak, had not the nature of the country come to our assistance. Something over two miles below the camp of the last herd was a deep creek, the banks of which were steep and the passages few and narrow. Here we succeeded in turning the leaders, and about half the outfit of the mixed herd remained, guarding the crossing and turning the lagging cattle in the run as they came up. With the leaders once turned and no chance for the others to take a new lead, we had the entire run of cattle turned back within an hour and safely under control. The first outfit joined us during the interim, and when day broke we had over forty men drifting about ten thousand cattle back up the trail. The different outfits were unfortunately at loggerheads, no one being willing to assume any blame. Flood hunted up the foreman of the mixed herd and demanded an apology for his remarks on our abrupt meeting with him the night before; and while it was granted, it was plain that it was begrudged. The first herd disclaimed any responsibility, holding that the stampede was due to an unavoidable accident, their cattle having grown restless during their enforced lay-over. The indifferent attitude of their foreman, whose name was Wilson, won the friendly regard of our outfit, and before the wagon of the mixed cattle was reached, there was a compact, at least tacit, between their outfit and ours. Our foreman was not blameless, for had we taken the usual precaution and camped at least a mile off the trail, which was our custom when in close proximity to other herds, we might and probably would have missed this mix-up, for our herd was inclined to be very tractable. Flood, with all his experience, well knew that if stampeded cattle ever got into a known trail, they were certain to turn backward over their course; and we were now paying the fiddler for lack of proper precaution.

Within an hour after daybreak, and before the cattle had reached the camp of the mixed herd, our saddle horses were sighted coming over a slight divide about two miles up the trail, and a minute later McCann's mules hove in sight, bringing up the rear. They had made a start with the first dawn, rightly reasoning, as there was no time to leave orders on our departure, that it was advisable for Mahomet to go to the mountain. Flood complimented our cook and horse wrangler on their foresight, for the wagon was our base of sustenance; and there was little loss of time before Barney McCann was calling us to a hastily prepared breakfast. Flood asked Wilson to bring his outfit to our wagon for breakfast, and as fast as they were relieved from herd, they also did ample justice to McCann's cooking. During breakfast, I remember Wilson explaining to Flood what he believed was the cause of the stampede. It seems that there were a few remaining buffalo ranging north of the Wichita, and at night when they came into the river to drink they had scented the cattle on the south side. The bellowing of buffalo bulls had been distinctly heard by his men on night herd for several nights past. The foreman stated it as his belief that a number of bulls had swum the river and had by stealth approached near the sleeping cattle,—then, on discovering the presence of the herders, had themselves stampeded, throwing his herd into a panic.

We had got a change of mounts during the breakfast hour, and when all was ready Flood and Wilson rode over to the wagon of the mixed herd, the two outfits following, when Flood inquired of their foreman,—

"Have you any suggestions to make in the cutting of these herds?"

"No suggestions," was the reply, "but I intend to cut mine first and cut them northward on the trail."

"You intend to cut them northward, you mean, provided there are no objections, which I'm positive there will be," said Flood. "It takes me some little time to size a man up, and the more I see of you during our brief acquaintance, the more I think there's two or three things that you might learn to your advantage. I'll not enumerate them now, but when these herds are separated, if you insist, it will cost you nothing but the asking for my opinion of you. This much you can depend on: when the cutting's over, you'll occupy the same position on the trail that you did before this accident happened. Wilson, here, has nothing but jaded horses, and his outfit will hold the herd while yours and mine cut their cattle. And instead of you cutting north, you can either cut south where you belong on the trail or sulk in your camp, your own will and pleasure to govern. But if you are a cowman, willing to do your part, you'll have your outfit ready to work by the time we throw the cattle together."

Not waiting for any reply, Flood turned away, and the double outfit circled around the grazing herd and began throwing the sea of cattle into a compact body ready to work. Rod Wheat and Ash Borrowstone were detailed to hold our cut, and the remainder of us, including Honeyman, entered the herd and began cutting. Shortly after we had commenced the work, the mixed outfit, finding themselves in a lonesome minority, joined us and began cutting out their cattle to the westward. When we had worked about half an hour, Flood called us out, and with the larger portion of Wilson's men, we rode over and drifted the mixed cut around to the southward, where they belonged. The mixed outfit pretended they meant no harm, and were politely informed that if they were sincere, they could show it more plainly. For nearly three hours we sent a steady stream of cattle out of the main herd into our cut, while our horses dripped with sweat. With our advantage in the start, as well as that of having the smallest herd, we finished our work first. While the mixed outfit were finishing their cutting, we changed mounts, and then were ready to work the separated herds. Wilson took about half his outfit, and after giving our herd a trimming, during which he recut about twenty, the mixed outfit were given a similar chance, and found about half a dozen of their brand. These cattle of Wilson's and the other herd amongst ours were not to be wondered at, for we cut by a liberal rule. Often we would find a number of ours on the outside of the main herd, when two men would cut the squad in a bunch, and if there was a wrong brand amongst them, it was no matter,—we knew our herd would have to be retrimmed anyhow, and the other outfits might be disappointed if they found none of their cattle amongst ours.

The mixed outfit were yet working our herd when Wilson's wagon and saddle horses arrived, and while they were changing mounts, we cut the mixed herd of our brand and picked up a number of strays which we had been nursing along, though when we first entered the main herd, strays had received our attention, being well known to us by ranch brands as well as flesh marks. In gathering up this very natural flotsam of the trail, we cut nothing but what our herd had absorbed in its travels, showing due regard to a similar right of the other herds. Our work was finished first, and after Wilson had recut the mixed herd, we gave his herd one more looking over in a farewell parting. Flood asked him if he wanted the lead, but Wilson waived his right in his open, frank manner, saying, "If I had as long-legged cattle as you have, I wouldn't ask no man for the privilege of passing. Why, you ought to out-travel horses. I'm glad to have met you and your outfit, personally, but regret the incident which has given you so much trouble. As I don't expect to go farther than Dodge or Ogalalla at the most, you are more than welcome to the lead. And if you or any of these rascals in your outfit are ever in Coryell County, hunt up Frank Wilson of the Block Bar Ranch, and I'll promise you a drink of milk or something stronger if possible."

We crossed the Wichita late that afternoon, there being not over fifty feet of swimming water for the cattle. Our wagon gave us the only trouble, for the load could not well be lightened, and it was an imperative necessity to cross it the same day. Once the cattle were safely over and a few men left to graze them forward, the remainder of the outfit collected all the ropes and went back after the wagon. As mules are always unreliable in the water, Flood concluded to swim them loose. We lashed the wagon box secured to the gearing with ropes, arranged our bedding in the wagon where it would be on top, and ran the wagon by hand into the water as far as we dared without flooding the wagon box. Two men, with guy ropes fore and aft, were then left to swim with the wagon in order to keep it from toppling over, while the remainder of us recrossed to the farther side of the swimming channel, and fastened our lariats to two long ropes from the end of the tongue. We took a wrap on the pommels of our saddles with the loose end, and when the word was given our eight horses furnished abundant motive power, and the wagon floated across, landing high and dry amid the shoutings of the outfit.

BEYOND THE DESERT

Eugene Manlove Rhodes

MACGREGOR WAS IN HASTE. He pressed forward in a close, fine rain. A huge and graceless bulk of a man, he rode craftily, a brisk jog, a brisk walk; where the trail was steep, he slipped from the saddle and led the way to the next smooth bit.

Hard by the head of the pass, where the peaks of San Ouentin—monstrous, exaggerated, fantastic—frowned through fog and mist, he paused on a jutting shoulder in a brief lull between showers. The night drew near. The fog lifted for a space as a gust of wind whipped between the hills: far behind and below there was a glimpse of toiling horsemen, a black wavering line where the trail clung to the hillside.

MacGregor lifted the heavy brows that pent his piggy little red eyes. His face was a large red face, heavy, square, coarse-featured, stubbly. It now expressed no emotion. Unhurriedly, he took up a long thirty-forty from the sling below the stirrup leather, raised the sights high, and dropped two bullets in the trail before the advancing party. They shrank back to a huddling clump. The mist shut down.

Under shelter of his long slicker, he wiped the rifle carefully and returned it to the scabbard. "Persons of no experience," he grumbled. "They ride with small caution for a country of boulders and such-like cover. If the half o' them had stayed behind at yonder well and the best few followed, each with a led horse, they might well ha' caught me oop ere I could win across yonder weary plain. No judgment at all!"

The critic clicked his teeth disparagingly as he remounted.

"'Tis plain I have naught to fear from these gentry for all the heavy weight this red horse of mine must carry. For they will think twice and again at each bend and rockfall. Aweell—I hae seen worse days. Thanks to this good rain, I needna fear the desert either for mysel' or the beastie. Hunger and great weariness, pain and jostling death, these I can make shift to bear—but against naked thirst no man can strive for long—But beyont the desert? Ay, there's the kittle bit. There's a telephone line awa' to the north, and if the good folk of Datil be at all of enterprising mind, 'tis like I shall hear tidings."

Dawn found him beyond the desert, breasting the long slow ridges beneath the wooded mountain of the Datils. The storm was passed away. Behind, the far peaks of San Quentin fluttered on the horizon, dreampale; and then, in one swift moment, flamed at a touch of sudden sun, radiant and rejoicing, sharp against a clean-washed sky. The desert brimmed with a golden flood of light, a flood which rolled eastward across the level, to check and break and foam against the dense, cool shadow of the Datil Range. So dense and so black was the shadow that the rambling building of the CLA ranch scarce bulked blacker; hardly to be seen, save for a thin wisp of wood smoke that feathered in the windless air.

"Ay," said the horseman. "Now the pot boils. And indeed I am wondering if my name is in that pot. For here comes one at a hard gallop—wrangling horses, belike. And now he sees me and swerves this way. Truly, I am very desirous that this man may be Mundy himself. I would ever like best to deal with principals—and Mundy is reputed a man of parts. Be it Clay Mundy or another, yon bit wire has gien him word and warning to mark who comes this way. I must e'en call science to my own employ. Hullo, Central! . . . Hullo! Give me Spunk, please . . . Hullo, Spunk. MacGregor speaking. Spunk, I am now come to a verra strait place, and I would be extremely blithe to hae your company. For to deal plainly wi' you, my neck is set on the venture, no less . . . I am obligit to you. Ye hae aye been dependable. See if you canna bring Common-sense wi' you. Hullo, Central! Gimme Brains . . . What's that? No answer? Try again, Central! Central, gin ye please. The affair is verra urgent."

The oncoming rider slowed down: MacGregor turned to meet him, his two hands resting on the saddle horn.

"'Tis Mundy's self, thanks be," he muttered. "Now, do you twa walk cannily, Spunk and Common-sense. Here is the narrow bit. Aha, Brains! Are ye there at the last of it? That's weel! I shall need you!"

He rode on at a walk. The riders drew abreast.

"Hands up, you!" Mundy's gun was drawn and leveled with incredible swiftness.

MacGregor's hands did not move from the saddle horn: he leaned on them easily. "And that is no just what ye might call a ceevil greeting, Mr. Mundy. Ye give me but a queer idea of your hospitality. Man, ye think puirly! Do ye see this rifle under my knee? Thirty-forty, smokeless—and had I meant ye ill, it was but stepping behind a bit bush to tumble you from the saddle or e'er ye clapped eyes on me."

"You have my name, I see," said Mundy. "And there is certainly some truth in your last saying. You might have taken a pot shot at me from ambush, easy enough. Guess you didn't know we were expecting you. Unless all signs fail, you are fresh from the loot of Luna. Now I've had about enough nonsense from you. Stick up those hands or I'll blow you into eternity."

"And that is a foolish obsairve," said MacGregor, composedly. "'Into eternity!' says he! Man, I wonder at ye! We're in eternity just noo—every minute of it—as much as we e'er shall be. For the ambush, you do me great wrong. I was well knowing to yon mischief-making telephone—but I took my chance of finding you a man of sense. For my hands, they are very well where they are. You have me covered—what more would you wish? I have conscientious scruples aboot this hands-up business. It is undeegnified in the highest degree. Man, theenk ye I have nae self-luve at all! Hands up might be all verra weel for a slim young spark like you, wi' looks and grace to bear it off with. But me, wi' my years and the hulking carcass of me, in such a bairnly play—man, I should look just reedeeculous! The thing cannae be done."

"Very well. I am coming to get your gun. Keep your hands on the saddle horn. I have you covered, and if you crook a finger, I'll crook mine."

"'Tis early yet in the day, Mr. Mundy." MacGregor held the same attitude and the same unmoved composure. "Dinna be hasty in closing in upon me. I was thinking to propose a compromise."

"A compromise? And me with finger on trigger—me that could hit you blindfolded?"

"Nae doot of it at all. I am well acquaint wi' you by repute. Ye have the name of a man of speerit and of one skilly wi' his gun and unco' swift to the back o' that. Myself, I am slow on the draw. 'Tis lamentable, but I must needs admit it. I am no what ye might ca' preceesely neemble of body or of mind—but, man! if I'm slow, I'm extraordinary eefeecient! If you crook that finger you are speaking of, I am thinking that the two of us may miss the breakfast cooking yonder. For myself, I am free to say I had liefer crook elbows wi' you over a thick beefsteak."

"Fool! I can shoot you three times before you get to your gun."

"Nae doot, nae doot," said MacGregor pacifically. "It has been done—yet here am I, little the waur o't. Mr. Mundy, I must deal plainly wi' you. Long ago, that place where your ranch is was pointit oot to me by yon square-capped peak behind for landmark—and I came here the noo rather than to any ither spot round about this wide circle of the plains of San Quentin, preceesly because ye are bespoken a man of parts and experience—and thereby the better able to judge weel and deal wisely with another man as good as yoursel'."

"Sure of that?"

"Positeeve. Now, understand me weel. I am laying no traps to tempt your eye to rove—so dinna look, but e'en take my word for it. But gin ye were free to look ye wad see, as I did just ere you came, some ten-twelve black specks coming this way ahindt me on the plain, a long hour back, or near two—and ye may draw your ain conclusions thereby. To speak the plain truth, I doot they mean me nae guid at a'."

"I should conclude that this was your unlucky day. Mr. Whatever-your-name-is. Quite aside from these gentlemen behind, or from myself—and you may possibly be underrating me—the whole country east of here is warned by telephone. Heavy, heavy hangs over your head!"

"I am a little struck wi' that circumstance myself," said MacGregor simply. "Ye see the seetuation wi' great clearness, Mr. Mundy. But I have seen worse days and have good hopes to come fairly off from this one yet. For if you can eenstruct me in what way I should be any worse off to be shot by you just now, than to be hanged in a tow from a pleasant juniper a little later, after tedious delays and parley-wows, I shall be the more obleegit. For then I can plainly see my way to give myself up to you. If you cannae do this, then I shall expect ye, as a reasoning man yourself, to note that ye can have naught to gain by changing shots wi' one who has naught to lose, and to conseeder the proposeetion I mak to you—as I should surely do and the cases were changed."

"You put it very attractively and I see your point," said Mundy. A slow smile lit up his face. He put his gun back in the scabbard. "Well, let's have it."

"And a verra guid choice, too. If it be not askin' too much, let us e'en be riding toward your ranch gate while ye hear my offer, for when the sun reaches here we should be seen—and yonder weary bodies gain on us while we stand here daffing."

They made a strange contrast: Mundy, smooth, slender and graceful, black of hair and eye, poised, lithe and tense, a man to turn and look after: MacGregor, stiff, unwieldy, awkward, gross, unkempt, battered, year-bitten.

"For the first of it, ye should know that not one of these gentry behind have seen my face, the which I kep' streectly covered durin' my brief stay in Luna. Second, though no great matter, ye may care to know that the bit stroke I pulled off in Luna was even less than justice. For within a year and a day a good friend of mine was there begowked and cozened by that same partnership—yes and that wi' treachery and broken trust to the back of it—of mair then I regained for him by plain and open force at noonday. So much for that—though I do not hold you squeamish. Third, for your own self, it is far known that you and the Wyandotte Company and Steel-foot Morgan are not agreeing verra weel—"

"You never heard that I've taken any the worst of it, did you?"

"No, but that they keep you well occupied. Also, that hired warriors from the Tonto are to join wi' Webb of the Wyandotte. So hear me now. I need nae ask of ye if ye have ony but discreet persons aboot ye?"

Mundy laughed. "Boys are floating in the Malibu hills with a pack outfit. No one at the ranch today but Hurley, the watermason. He's all right."

"Verra weel. Do you send him away betimes on that beastie atween your knees, and I will be water-mason to you—the mair that I can run your steam-pump as well as the best, though there will be small need of pumps till these rains be over. The story will be that the outlaw-body passed by night, unseen, liftin' your night-horse as he flitted, and leavin' this sorrel of mine. Your man Hurley can join your outfit and lose himself. That will be my gain, for I shall be blameless Maxwell, your water-mason—and who so eager to run down the rungate robber as he? And when they see how it is, that their man has got clean away, these men from Luna will know that the jig is definitely up and they will be all for the eating and sleeping."

"Very pretty, and it can be done—since they do not know you," agreed Mundy. "They will not be expecting their outlaw to call them in to breakfast, certainly. But I do not see where I am to gain anything."

"You are to hear, then," said the outlaw. "I will praise the bridge that carries me over, but I will do more too: I will mend that bridge. I will fight your battles with you against all comers. Not murder, mind you, but plain warfare against men fit for war."

"A fighting man, and slow on the draw?"

"I am that same, both the one and the other. Slow, I cannot deny it— slow, in compare with the best. But man, I'm experienced. I'm judgmatical, and I'm fine on the latter end. I'm a good person to have at your right hand or your left. Some way, I dinna prosper verra weel as chief man— but as the next best, there is none better rides leather."

"You come well recommended."

"By myself, you are meaning? And just that you may know the worth of that recommend, I am telling ye that my name is no exactly Maxwell. You have had word of me, your ownself, in El Paso, where indeed I saw your face, though you saw not mine. And I would have ye to observe, Mr. Mundy, that I keepit my name streectly to myself for such time as ye might have taken the sound of it as a threat, and give it to you now only when it comes mair as a promise. So now I offer to you the naked choice, peace or war—and the last word is with you. A hundred miles and twenty, at the least of it, I have now made in sax-and thirty hours—and blow high, blow low, I ride no step beyond yonder gate."

"I am decidedly inclined toward peace," said Clay Mundy, smiling again, "if only to hear you talk. For you talk convincingly. My own risk in the matter—which you have been kind enough not to mention—also moves me that way. And, after all, your late exploit at Luna is nothing to me. But as to your value in my little range war—you forgot to mention the name, you know."

"The name is MacGregor."

"Not Sandy MacGregor? Of Black Mountain?"

"That same. Plain shooting done neatly."

"You're on," said Clay Mundy.

So MacGregor became Maxwell, and Mundy's. The search party came, and swore, and slept; for they were weary. None mistrusted Maxwell, that kindly and capable cook, who sympathized so feelingly with them concerning the upness of the jig. In the seven-up tournament organized after that big sleep, Maxwell won the admiration of all and the money of most: and they went home mingling praises of their new friend with execrations of the escaped outlaw.

II

"And the herdsmen of Gerar did strive with Isaac's herdsmen, saying, The water is ours."

That was at the well Esek. The patriarchs were always quarreling with their neighbors or with each other over wells, pasturage and other things—mavericks, maybe. Abraham, Laban, Lot, Isaac, Jacob—they led a stirring life, following the best grass. You ought to read about them, sometime.

It is entirely probable that Terah went forth from Ur of the Chaldees either because the grass was short or because he had no friends on the grand jury.

Cattlemen have not changed much since then. They still swing a big loop: it is as risky as ever to let the stock out on shares: and we still have cattle wars wherever there is free range, because of the spirit so justly expressed by Farmer Jones: "He said he wasn't no land-hog—all he wants is just what joins his'n."

Human nature is the same on the plains of Mamre or of San Quentin: so there is no new thing to tell about the Mundy Morgan war. Wrong and folly and stubbornness; small matter now whose first the blame; this might have been a page of history.

Strong warriors, able leaders, Ben "Steel-foot" Morgan, Webb of the Wyandotte outfit, and Clay Mundy; sharp and bitter hate was in their hearts, and the feud was more savage than the usual run of cattle wars: carried on (of course) upon a higher plane than any "civilized" warfare. For there were restrictions, there were limits. To rise up from a man's table and war upon that man while the taste of his bread was still sweet in your mouth—such dealing would have been unspeakable infamy in the San Quentin country.

Again, you might be unfriendly with a man and yet meet on neutral ground or when each was on his lawful occasions, without trouble. It was not the custom to war without fresh offense, openly given. You must not smile and shoot. You must not shoot an unarmed man, and you must not shoot an unwarned man. Here is a nice distinction, but a clear one: you might not ambush your enemy; but when you fled and your enemy followed, you might then waylay and surprise without question to your honor, for they were presumed to be on their guard and sufficiently warned. The rattlesnake's code, to warn before he strikes, no better: a queer, lop-sided, topsy-turvy, jumbled and senseless code—but a code for all that. And it is worthy of note that no better standard has ever been kept with such faith as this barbarous code of the fighting man.

Roundup season passed with no fresh outbreak of hostilities. After the steer-shipping, Mr. Maxwell had been given a mount, a rope and a branding iron, and so turned loose to learn the range. This was equivalent to letters of Marque and Reprisal.

Mr. Maxwell was camped at Whitewater, alone. So far, he had passed a pleasant day. He had killed a fat buck at daybreak, when he wrangled horses. Later, he had ridden leisurely in nooks and corners, branding two of his employer's calves, overlooked by the roundup, two of the Y calves, and one long-eared yearling—a pleasant total of five for the CLA tally-book. So far his services had been confined to such peaceful activities as these: the war had languished since the rains set in. It was late October now, and the rains were still falling. The desert was glorified with the magic of belated spring.

All day it had been cloudy. While Mr. Maxwell was branding his maverick it began to sprinkle; when he turned it loose the sprinkle had become rain, the clouds were banked dark and sullen against the mountains. He wriggled into his slicker and started for camp, but the rain turned to a blinding storm and he was glad to turn his back to its fury and ride his straightest for the next shelter.

Pictured Rock is an overhanging cliff of limestone, sheltered from three winds. Gray walls and creamy roof are close covered with the weird picture writing of Apache and Navajo, a record of the wars and journeys of generations.

As he turned the bend in the canon, Maxwell saw a great light glowing under Pictured Rock, now veiled by the driving sheets of rain, now beating out in gusts across the murky dark, reflected and magnified by the cliff behind. Another, storm driven like himself, was before him. He paused at the hill-foot and shouted:

"Hullo, the house! Will your dog bite?"

"Hi!" It was a startled voice: a slender figure in a yellow slicker appeared beside the fire. "Dog's dead, poor fellow—starved to death! Come on up!"

The CLA man rode up the short zigzag of the trail to the firelit level. He took but one glance and swept off his hat, for the face he saw beneath the turned-up sombrero was the bright and sparkling face of a girl.

"You will be Miss Bennie May Morgan? I saw you in Magdalena at the steer-shipping."

"Quite right. And you are Mr. Sandy Maxwell, the new warrior for Clay Mundy."

"Faces like ours are not easily forgot," said Maxwell.

Miss Bennie laughed. Her eyes crinkled when she laughed. "I will give you a safe-conduct. Get down—unless you are afraid of hurting your reputation, that is." She sat upon her saddle blankets where they were spread before the fire, and leaned back against the saddle.

The CLA man climbed heavily down and strode to the fire, where he stood dripping and silent. The grinding of boulders in the flooded canon rose louder and louder, swelled to a steady ominous roar by the multitudinous echoes of the hills.

"Well! How about that lunch?" demanded Miss Bennie sharply. "It's past noon."

"Sorry, Miss Morgan, but I have not so much as a crumb. And that is a bad thing, for you are far from home, and who knows when this weary storm will be by? But doubtless they will be abroad to seek for you."

Miss Bennie laid aside her hat and shook her curly head decidedly. "Not for me. Dad thinks I'm visiting Effie at the XL and Effie thinks I'm home by this time. But this storm won't last. The sun will be out by three. You'll see! And now, if you please, since you can't feed me, hadn't you better entertain me? Sit down, do!"

"It is like that I should prove entertaining for a young maid, too!" said Maxwell, carrying a flat stone to the fire to serve for a seat.

"Oh, you never can tell! Suppose, for a starter, you tell me what you are thinking so busily."

"I am thinking," said Maxwell, slowly, "that you are a bonnie lass and a merry one. And I was thinking one more thing, too. The XL is awa' to the southeast and the Morgan home ranch as far to the southwest. Now what may Miss Bennie Morgan need of so much northing, ten long miles aside from the straight way, and her friend Effie thinking she was safe home and all? And then I thought to myself, the folk at San Quentin are very quiet now. It is to be thought that the season of great plenty has put them in better spunk with the world. And it is an ill thing that a way cannae be found to make an end of this brawling for good and all. And, thinks I, the bonny Earl of Murray himself was not more goodly to the eye than Clay Mundy—and it is a great peety for all concerned that Clay Mundy is not storm-bound this day at Picture Rock, rather than I!"

"Well!" Miss Bennie gasped and laughed frankly, blushed red, neck and cheek. "Oh, you men! And while you were making this up—"

"It is what I thought," said Maxwell stoutly. "Only I was nae thinking words, d'ye see? I was just thinking thoughts. And it is no verra easy to put thoughts into words."

"Well, then—while you were thinking all those preposterous thoughts, I was seeing a wonderful picture, very much like this storm, and this cave, and this fire, and us. If I were a painter, this is what I would try to paint: a hill-side like this—so you might feel what you could not see, the black night and the wild storm. The black night, and a red fire glowing in a cave-mouth, and a wind-bent tree close beside: and by the fire a man straining into the night at some unseen danger; a cave man, clad in skins, with long matted hair, broad-shouldered, long-armed, ferocious, brutal—but unafraid. He is half-crouching, his knees bent to spring: he is peering under his hand: the other hand clutches a knotted club: a dog strains beside his foot, snarling against the night, teeth bared, glaring, stiff legs braced back, neck bristling: behind them, half-hidden, shrinking in the shadow—a woman and a child. And the name of that picture would be 'Home!'

Maxwell's heavy face lit up, his dull and little eyes gleamed with an answering spark, his sluggish blood thrilled at the spirit and beauty of her: his voice rang with a heat of frank admiration. "And that is a brave thought you have conjured up, too, and I will be warrant you would be unco' fine woman to a cave-man—though I'm judgin' you would be having a bit club of your own." He paused, fixed her with a meditative eye, and spoke again in a lighter tone. "I recognize myself, and the dog is dead, puir fellow—starved to death, you said. But I would have you observe that the thoughts of the two of us differed but verra little when all is said—forbye it ran in my mind that a much younger person was to be cave-man to you. And you gave me safe-conduct, too! Are you to be man-sworn, then, and me trusting to you?"

"Now you are trying to torment me," said Miss Bennie briskly. "I can't have that, you know. Better give it up. Roll a smoke. I know you want to. The storm is slackening already—we will be going soon."

"A pipe, since you are so kind," said Maxwell, fumbling for it.

"Do you admire your friend Clay Mundy so much?" said Miss Bennie next, elbows on knees, chin in hands.

Maxwell rolled a slow eye on her, and blew out a cloud of smoke. "My employer. I did not say friend, though if I like him no worse it may come to that yet. He has the devil's own beauty—which thing calls the louder to me, misshapen as you see me. He is a gallant horseman, fame cries him brave and proven. But I am not calling him friend yet till I know the heart of him. Fifty-and-five I am, and I can count on the fingers of my twa hands, the names of those I have been willing to call wholly friends—for-bye one of those few was my enemy to my overthrow. So you will not be taking Clay Mundy to your cave upon my say-so till I am better acquaint wi' him. But dootless you know him verra well yourself."

Miss Bennie evaded this issue. She became suddenly gloomy. "It is plain that you are a stranger here, since you talk so glibly of any lasting peace in the San Quentin. A wicked, stiff-necked unreasoning pack, they are—dad and all! There has never been anything but wrong and hate here, outrage and revenge, and there never will be. It is enough to make one believe in the truth of original sin and total depravity!"

"No truth at all!" cried Maxwell warmly. "Oreeginal sin is just merely a fact—no truth at a'! Folks are aye graspin' at some puir halflin fact and settin' it up to be the truth. It takes at least three trees to make a row, and it needs at least three facts to make a truth. Mankind is blind, foolish and desperately wicked—yes, take it from me that am an old ruffian. But mankind is also eencurably good—wise and strong and splendid and kindly and brave—in your time of sorrow and danger you will find it so—and there's another glaring fact for you! Wi' endless rain earth would drown, wi' endless sun it would be a cinder: look about you now, see what sun and rain and evil and good have wrought together, grass and flower and bud and fruit, the bonny world and the bonny race o' men! World and man, the machine Works! And there's the third fact for you, lassie, and the weightiest fact. We are a Going Concern: we pay a profit to our Owner! And for the truth behind these three facts, may not this be it: That if we are at once evil and good, it is the good God who made us that way, not in sloth, but because He wanted us to be that way? It is so I think. But it is a strange thing to me that I am most roundly abused for disrespect to the Maker whene'er I dare venture the mild guess that perhaps He knew what He was about!"

"A very fine sermon, reverend sir, though I did not get the text," said Miss Bennie, twinking. "And now if you will give me your benediction, I will be on my way soon. The storm is breaking. It will clear as suddenly as it came on."

Maxwell shook out the saddle blankets and saddled her horse. "For the text it is this: 'And God saw everything that He had made and behold it was very good.'—And I am an old fool as well as an old ruffian," he grumbled, "for I have wearied you."

"Oh, no, you haven't. Your theology took my breath away, rather—that's all. It was so very unexpected."

"Of course, I will be seeing that you get safe home—"

"You mustn't. It would only make you a hard ride for nothing. No need of it at all. There is time for me to get home while the sun is still an hour high."

"It doesn't seem right," protested Maxwell.

"Really, I'd rather you wouldn't," said Miss Bennie earnestly. "I don't want to be rude, but I am still—" She gave him her eyes and blushed to her hair—"am still . . . north of where I should be, as you so shrewdly observed. And your camp lies farther yet to the north."

"Good-bye, then, Miss Morgan."

"Good-bye, Mr. MacGregor."

He stared after her as she rode clattering down the steep. "MacGregor!" he repeated. "MacGregor, says she! And never a soul of the San Quentin kens aught of the late MacGregor save Clay Mundy's own self! Here is news! Is she so unco' chief wi' him as that, then? And who told her whaur my camp was; she was glib to say that she had time enow to go home or sundown—but she was careful she didna say she was gaun there! Little lady, it is in my mind that you are owre far north!"

She waved her hand gaily; her fresh young voice floated back to him, lingering, soft and slow:

He was a braw gallant,
And he rid at the ring;
And the bonny Earl of Murray
Oh! He might have been a king.

He was a braw gallant
And he played at the glove;
And the bonny Earl of Murray
Oh! He was the Queen's love!

Oh! Lang may his lady
Luke owre the castle down,
Ere she see the Earl of Murray
Come sounding thro' the town.

The girl passed from sight down the narrow canon. MacGregor-Maxwell gave his head a shaking then, to clear his thoughts, and put foot to stirrup. When he came to the beaten trail again, where the horse's feet pattered rhythmically on the firm ground, MacGregor half sang, half crooned, a plaintive and wandering air:

Then I pray you do not trust the hawk again,
The cruel hawk that mocks thy love, like me.
Oh, alone, betrayed and sad although I leave thee,
Yet the wandering traitor weeps, poor love, for thee—
Ay! Paloma azul!

"The de'il and his horns! Now why do I sing such an ill-omened and unchancy song as that?" He shook his great shoulders, as if to shake off a weight: he held his cupped hand to his mouth. "Hullo, Central! Can you get Brains for me? . . . Try again, please . . . Now, Brains, you are partly acquaint wi' this day's doings. But did you mark the bonny blush of her at the name of Clay Mundy—and her so far from the plain way, wi' no cause given? . . . Ye didna? . . . Brains, you're but a cauld, feckless, dusty-dry thing, when all's said. Well then, I am telling you of it. And what am I to do in such case as that? . . . A little louder, please! . . . Oh! I am to see where Clay Mundy rides this day, if it is any affair of mine—is that it? . . . Surely it is my business. Any man is natural protector to any woman against any man except himself . . . And if he means her naething but good? . . . It is what I will know. And then I will be best man—and to be best man at this employ should be no empty form. For indeed I think the Morgans are like to be little pleased.

"Aweel, Brains, I will e'en do your bidding, and I will seek proof where Clay Mundy fares this day—though I tell you plainly that I know very well now. And I scorn for a slow-speeritless, doddering sluggard—you and your proofs! You can but look through a hole in a stone wall, at the most of it. What are walls for but to leap over—can you tell me that? Show me once a braw lass and a high hard wall and a lad beyond, and I will show you a place where there shall be a fine climbing done—the more when the young folk are so bold and bonny as the twa of them yonder towards the sunset . . . What's that? How do I know? . . . Brains, I wonder at ye, I fairly peety you—and that's the truth of it: Where else should he be?"

III

I thought it was you," said Miss Bennie May Morgan. "So I waited for you. Aren't you rather out of your own range, Mr. Maxwell? The Morgans'll get you if you don't watch out!"

With elaborate surprise, MacGregor took his bearings from the distant circling hills. "Why so I am! I was on my way to Datil," he explained. "I see now"—he jerked a thumb back over his shoulder—"that I should have ridden east-like this morning instead of west."

"It is shorter that way—and dryer," she agreed. "This road to Datil is very damp after you pass California."

"Shall I ride with you a bit on your way?" said MacGregor. "I can still get back to my camp before sundown. Mind you, I am not saying at all that I shall go to my camp by that hour, but only that there is time enough."

Then Miss Bennie Morgan knew where she stood. She flicked at her stirrup with a meditative quirt. "Why, I said something about like that to you last week at Pictured Rock, didn't I?"

"Very much like that."

"When you got lost today," said Miss Bennie thoughtfully, "I suppose you were composing a sermon?"

"Why, no, I wasnae. It was like this. Clay Mundy set off for Datil early this morning, you see, whilst I staid in camp, shoeing horses. He was riding his Jugador horse—fine I ken the crooked foot of him. And when later in the day I came upon the track of that twisted hoof, I found suddenly a great desire to go after him to Datil, where I have never yet been. And I said to myself, 'Plainly if you follow this track you will come to that place.' And so you see me here."

"And now that you're here, Mr.—?"

"Maxwell—not MacGregor," said MacGregor.

"Thank you; Maxwell. Not MacGregor. I must remember that." She turned clear, unflinching eyes upon him. "Well, let's have it!"

"Er—why—eh!" said MacGregor, and swallowed hard. "I don't quite understand you."

"Oh, yes you do!" said Miss Bennie cheerfully. "Don't squirm. What's on your mind?"

"It is now on my mind that it would be none such a bad scheme for me to turn tail bravely and run awa' from this place," said MacGregor, truthfully; quite taken aback at this brisk and matter of-fact directness.

In her innermost heart Miss Bennie knew certainly—without reason, as women know these things—that this grim old man-at-arms liked her very well, and came as a friend.

"Blackmail? Oh no—that is not your line. And I do not take you for a tell-tale, either." She looked him over slowly and attentively; a cruel, contemplative glance. It brought a dull glow to MacGregor's leathern face, even before she spoke. "I see!" She dropped the reins and clapped her hands together. "You were planning to take Clay Mundy's place with me—is that it?"

MacGregor plucked up spirit at the taunt. "And that was an unkind speech of you, Miss Morgan."

Her eyes danced at him. "There is but one thing left, then. You have come to plead with me for your friend—your employer—to ask me to spare his youth and innocence—to demand of me, as the phrase goes, if my intentions are honorable. Is that it?"

"It is something verra like that, then, if I must brave your displeasure so far as to say it. And it is my poor opinion that so much was verra needful—though it was in my mind to give you but the bare hint that your secret was stumbled upon. For what one has chanced upon this day another may chance tomorrow. And there was something else besides, which I find ill to put to words to."

The girl dropped all pretense. "I think you meant kindly to me, Mr. MacGregor, and I thank you for it. And you must consider that our case is hard indeed. For where can we meet, if not secretly? Fifty miles each way, every ranch is lined up on one side or the other of this feud. One word to my father's ear will mean bloodshed and death—and then, whoever wins, Bennie Morgan must lose."

"Yet you must meet?" said MacGregor.

She met his eyes bravely. "Yet we must meet!" She said it proudly. "You two should wed out of hand then, and put the round world between you and this place," said MacGregor.

Miss Bennie sighed. "That is what I tell Clay. It is the only way. Soon or late, if we live here, those two would clash, my father and my husband. If we go away, father may get over it in time. Clay does not want to go. He cannot bear to have it said that he had to run away from San Quentin. But I will never marry him till he is ready to go."

"He is a fool for his pains, and I will be the one who will tell him that same!" declared MacGregor, stoutly. "Him and his pride! He should be proud to run further and faster than ever man rode before on such an argument."

"No—you mustn't say one word to him about me—please! He would be furious—and he is a dangerous man!"

"I thank ye kindly for this unexpected care of my safety," said MacGregor humbly.

"Oh these men! Must you hear that you are so dangerous, too? There would be trouble, and you know it. Clay's as cross as a bear with a sore head, now—so I think he is coming to my way of thinking, and doesn't like to own up. Don't you say anything to him. I'll tell him—not that you have seen me, but that we might easily be seen—and that our meetings must be few and far between. That will help to make up his mind, too, if he feels—" She checked herself, with a startled shyness in her sudden drooping lids: she was only a young girl, for all her frank and boyish courage. "I will warn him, then. And yet I think there is no man who would not think twice before he whispered evil of Ben Morgan's daughter and"—she held her head proud, she lifted her brave eyes—"and Clay Mundy's sweetheart!"

MacGregor checked his horse, his poor, dull face for once lit up and uplifted: whatever had been best of him in all his wasted and misspent life stirred at the call of her gallant girlhood.

"I think there will be no man so vile as to think an evil thing of you," he said. "Miss Morgan, I was a puir meddlin' fool to come here on such an errand—and yet I am glad that I came, too. And now I shall go back and trouble you nae mair. Yet there is one thing, too, before I turn back—and I think you will not laugh."

She faced him where he stood: so that he carried with him a memory of her dazzling youth against a dazzle of sun. "I shall not laugh."

"It is better than fifty years, they tell me, since last the San Quentin knew any such rains as these," said MacGregor slowly. "This place has the ill name of a desert. Yet all this day the air has been heavy with sweetness; all day long I have ridden stirrup-deep in strange bright flowers—and no man knows the name of them! Fifty years they have slept in the blistered brown earth, the seeds of these nameless flowers, waiting for this year of many rains. Lassie, there are only too many men, like me, of deserved and earned ill name, as of waste places where no good thing can flourish. And when you think of us, I would have you remember how this bright, belated spring-tide came to San Quentin. I would have you think there may be hidden seeds of good in us yet—if only the rains might come! And if ever you have any need of me—as is most unlike—I shall be real friend to you, I shall stick at nothing in your service. It is so that I would have you think of old MacGregor. Good-bye!"

"I shall not forget," said Bennie. "But you said there was something else—something hard to put into words?"

MacGregor took off his hat. "I think there will be no need to say that—to you," he said.

Once more her eyes searched him and this time he did not flinch—so high he held her now in his thought. She read his answering look. "Yes—since this is the day for plain-speaking, let me say it for you. You mean . . . that it is not only whispering tongues I have to fear, or my father's anger—no, nor black death itself—but that I must fear myself most of all? But, Mr. MacGregor—there was need to say that indeed! And now you are my friend, for I have trusted you very greatly."

"Good-bye, then!" said MacGregor again. He bent over her hand. "Good-bye!"

IV

MacGregor worked out the Whitewater country and moved his camp to Bear Springs, on the southern frontier of the Mundy range. From here he rode the cedar brakes on the high flanks of the mountain, branding late calves. This work was most effectively done at early daybreak and at sundown, when the wild cattle ventured from the thickets into the open glades and valleys.

For a week, Milt Craig had ridden with him. But Milt had made his pack yesterday and moved on to the Cienaga, where MacGregor was to join him later, once he had picked up the few calves that still went unbranded in the Bear Spring country. So today MacGregor rode alone.

Ever drifting from one bunch of cattle to another and then on to an-other clump of red and white on the next hill-side, as the day wore on he found himself well across in the Wyandotte-Morgan country; prowling in the tangle of hills, south of the Magdalena road, which was the accepted dividing line.

As the sun rode on to afternoon, the prowler turned back, and made his way to Skullspring, with a thought of the trickle of water that dripped from the high cliffs there; and as he came down a ridge of backbone from the upper bench, he saw a little curl of smoke rising above the Skull-spring bluff.

MacGregor remarked upon this fact to Neighbor his horse. "We are in a hostile country, Neighbor," said he. "For all we are so quiet and peace-ful these days, it will be the part of prudence to have a look into this mat-ter, least we go blundering in where we arenae much wanted." He tied Neighbor in a little hollow of the hill, and went down with infinite pre-caution to the edge of the cliff above Skullspring.

Three men were by the fire below—all strangers to MacGregor. That gentleman lay flat on the rock, peering through a bush, and looked them over. Clearly, they had only stopped at Skullspring for nooning. Two were cowboys: their saddled horses stood by. The younger of these two stowed a little grub-sack under the seat of a light buggy that stood by the fire. The third person, a tall man of about thirty, had the look of a town-man. He wore a black suit and a "hard-boiled" hat.

"I tell you," said the older cowboy, a sullen-faced young man. "I'll be good and glad a-plenty when this thing is over with. It's a shaky busi-ness."

"Don't get cold feet, Joe," advised the tall man. You're getting big money, mighty big money, for a small risk."

"I notice there's none of these San Quentin *hombres* caring for any of it," grumbled Joe, sulkily.

"Aw, now, be reasonable," said the tall man. "He wouldn't risk letting any of the home people know. Too shakey. You get the chance just because you're a stranger. And because you're a stranger, you can get away without being noticed."

Plainly, here was mischief afoot. It seemed likely to MacGregor that Clay Mundy was to be the object of it. .

The younger man of the party spoke up. "I'm not only goin' to get away, but I'm goin' to keep on gettin' away. I'm after that dough all right, all right—but lemme tell you, Mr. Hamerick, this country'll be too hot for me when it's over."

MacGregor barely breathed. It appeared that the tall man was Hamerick, for he answered. "I'm going away myself. But this is too good a chance for easy money, and we don't want to make a hash of it. Keep your nerve. Your part is easy. You take the first right-hand trail and drift south across that saddle-back pass yonder, so you'll get there before I do. You'll find the Bent ranch right under the pass. Nobody there. The Bents have all gone to Magdalena for supplies. Mrs. Bent is going to Socorro and Brent'll wait for her. You're to make yourselves at home, so there won't be anything suspicious—new men working there; sorry the Bents are gone, and all that." He kicked out the dying fire.

"And if anyone comes, then what?" Joe glowered at him with the question.

"Then you're strangers, passing by. It isn't at all likely that anyone'll come. The nearest ranch is twenty-five miles. But if anyone should come, it's all off, for today. We want to have the longest start we can get. And for Mundy, he has his own reasons. You'll ride out to good grass and make camp. If we see your fire, Mundy and me'll turn back. We'll pull it off tomorrow."

Mundy! MacGregor's heart leaped. Were the men to entice Mundy to the Bent ranch and murder him there, while he was off his guard, thinking himself among friends? MacGregor drew his gun, minded to fall upon the plotters without more ado: the vantage of ground more than made up for the odds of numbers. But he put back his gun. They were to separate. He would follow the man Hamerick and deal with him alone.

"I am to meet Mundy at that little sugar-loaf hill yonder, four or five miles out on the plain," said Hamerick. "I'll be late, too—jawing with you fellows this way. Then I'll go on down the wagon road to Bent's with him. The play is that I'm supposed to think the Bent folks are at home. You boys'll have plenty of time to get settled down."

"If we don't run into a wasp's nest," said Joe sulkily.

Hamerick scowled. "I'm the one that's taking the biggest risk, with this damned buggy—but I've got to have it, to play the part. I'll leave it, once I get safe back to my saddle."

"We three want to ride in three different directions," said Joe. "I wish it was over."

Hamerick gave him a sinister look. "You get no money till I get a-straddle of a horse again—I'll tell you that right now, my laddie-buck! This buggy's too easy to track up, if anything goes wrong. You'd like it first-rate to ride off scot-free and leave me to hold the sack."

"I won't, eh!" Joe took a step forward, his ugly face blotched with crimson. "Damn you, I've took just about enough from you!"

Here the younger man interposed. "Oh, you both make me sick!" His voice was cutting and cold, venomous in its unforced evenness. "I guess I'll do a little telling now, myself. If you fellows get to fighting, I'll do my best to kill both of you. Got that?"

MacGregor almost hugged himself with delight. Oh, if they once get to shooting—if they only would! he thought. It would be a strange thing if between the four of us we should not do a good day's work of it!

"Now, now, Tait—"

"Don't Tait me!" said Tait, in the same deadly level. "This is a wise bunch for a ticklish job, ain't it? I know that no one but a dirty skunk would be found in such dirty work—but is that any reason why we should be fools, too? Hamerick's right, Joe. We'll string along with him till he gets to a saddle—and then may the devil take the hindmost! Maybe we'll find a saddle at the Bent ranch. If we do, all the better. The sooner I see the last of you two, the better pleased I'll be. For you, Hamerick—you're engineerin' this thing, but when it comes down to brass tacks, I'm the best man, and don't you forget it. So if you've been plannin' any nice little plans to hold out part of the price on me and Joe, you can throw 'em over for excess baggage, right here. For I'm to put it up to the paymaster, right to your face—you won't have no chance to fool us. Now don't up any more head to me! You'll stick to me against Joe till you're horseback again, with a fair chance for a getaway; Joe'll stick to me till we get a fair divvy on the money—and if either of you don't like it, you can double up on me whenever you feel lucky. I'm ready for you both any turn in the road."

The challenge went unmet. It was plain that Tait was to be master. MacGregor waited for no more. He rolled back from the bare rim with scarce more noise than a shadow would have made. He crawled to the nearest huddle of rocks and hid away. For a little, the muffled murmur of angry voices floated to him; then came the sound of wheels and a ringing of shod feet on rock; Tait and Joe toiled up the trail beyond the cliff-end, paced slowly by, black against the sky line, and dipped down into a dark hollow that twisted away towards Bent's Pass.

The tingling echoes died; and then MacGregor climbed back to Neighbor. The game was in his hands. Keeping to the ridge, he would gain a long mile on the wagon road, deep in the winding pass. He was in high feather as he followed the plunging slope; he laughed as he rode; his eyes drank in the brightness of the day. This would be a rare jest to tell at campfires!

"Now I wonder who can be at the bottom of this bonny scheme?" he chuckled. "It doesnae sound much like the San Quentin folk, who, if reports be true, are accustomed to do their own murders. And, if the man Hamerick tells the whole story, what then? That will be for Mundy to say. Any rate, 'tis a fine thing for Clay Mundy that my dry throttle drove me to Skullspring just at that time."

When he came into the wagon road the buggy was just before him, close to the mouth of the pass. MacGregor struck into a gallop.

The stranger had been going at a brisk gait, but at sight of the horseman he slowed to a prim and mincing little trot.

"A fine day, sir," said MacGregor civilly, as he rode alongside.

"It certainly is," said the stranger. He was plainly ill at ease at this ill-timed meeting, but tried to carry it off. "How far is it to Old Fort Tularosa, can you tell me?"

MacGregor squinted across the plain. "A matter of forty miles, I should say. Goin' across?"

The stranger shook his head. "Not today. I think I will camp here for the night and have a look in the hills for a deer. You're not going to the Fort yourself, are you?"

MacGregor grinned cheerfully. Knowing what he did, he knew that this was Hamerick's device to try to shake off his unwelcome company. "Well, no; not today. The fact is, sir"—he bent over close and sunk his voice to a confidential whisper—"the fact is, if you're for camping here the night, I must even camp here, too."

"What!"

"Just that. And first of all, do you remark this little gun which I hold here in my hand? Then I will ask you to stop and to get out upon this side, holding to your lines verra carefully lest the beastie should run away, while I search you for any bit weapons of your ain. For you spoke very glibly of hunting a deer—and yet I do not see any rifle."

Hamerick groaned as he climbed out; he had not thought of that. "I haven't any rifle. My revolver is under the cushion—but of course you can search me, if you think I've got another. What the devil do you want anyway? If it's money you're after, you'll get most mighty little."

"All in good time, all in good time," said MacGregor cheerfully. He went through Hamerick for arms; finding none, he went through the buggy, finding the gun under the cushion. He inspected this carefully, tried it, and stuck it in his waistband.

"Will you kindly go aside some few steps, sir?" said MacGregor politely. "I am dry, and I would have a good swig of water from your canteen, but I didnae wish to set myself in that defenseless posture of holding a canteen to my throat whilst ye were still armed."

"You see I have no money, you have my gun, you have your drink—what more do you want of me?" spluttered Hamerick. "Let me go! I have an appointment—I'll be late now."

"With that deer, ye are meaning?" MacGregor sat cross-legged on the ground and whittled off a pipeful of tobacco with loving care. He puffed a while in great satisfaction, watching his fuming captive with twinkling eyes. "Do you know, sir," he said at last, between whiffs, "that in my puir opeenion, if you knew how you are like to keep that appointment of yours, you would be little made up with it?"

Hamerick stammered. He had no idea of what his captor was driving at, but he had his own reasons for great uneasiness. He pulled himself together with an effort. "I—I don't know what you mean. I see now that you are not a robber, as I first thought. You are mistaking me for some other man. You can't be doing yourself any possible good by keeping me here. I tell you I am waited for."

"Take my word for it, sir—if you knew my way of it, you would be less impatient for that tryst of yours."

"What—what the devil do you mean?"

"I will tell you then, Mr. Hamerick." At this unexpected sound of his own name, Hamerick started visibly. "If Clay Mundy is at all of my mind, this is what we shall do: We will set you on Clay Mundy's horse and put Clay Mundy's hat upon your head; and we two will get in your bit wagon and drive you before our guns—just at dusk, d'ye mind?—to the Bent ranch; and there, if I do not miss my guess, you will be shot to death by hands of your own hiring!"

Here MacGregor, gloating on that pleasant inward vision, was extremely disconcerted by the behavior of his prospective victim. So far from being appalled, Hamerick was black with rage; he stamped, he shook his fist, he struggled for speech in a choking fury.

"You fool! You poor spy! Idiot! Bungler! Why couldn't you tell me you were Mundy's man?"

"Steady, there! Are you meaning to face it out that you did not plan to murder Clay Mundy! Because we are going on now to see him."

Hamerick gathered up the reins eagerly. "Come on, then, damn you— before it's too late!" There was relief and triumph in his voice—and at the sound of it MacGregor sickened with a guess at the whole dreadful business; the bright day faded. "Me, kill Clay Mundy? Why, you poor, pitiful bungler, Clay Mundy brought me here to play preacher for him!"

MacGregor drew back. His face flamed; his eyes were terrible. He jerked out Hamerick's gun and threw it at Hamerick's feet. There was a dreadful break in his voice. "Protect yourself!" he said.

But Hamerick shrank back, white-lipped, cringing. "I won't! I won't touch it!"

"Cur!"

"Oh, don't kill me, don't murder me!" Hamerick was winging his hands; he was almost screaming.

MacGregor turned shamed eyes away. He took up Hamerick's gun. "Strip the harness from that horse then, take the bridle and ride! And be quick, lest I think better of it. Go back the way you came, and keep on going! For I shall tell your name and errand, and there is no man of Morgan's men but will kill you at kirk or gallows-foot."

He watched in silence as Hamerick fled. Then he rode down the pass, sick-hearted, brooding, grieving. He came to the mouth of the pass: at the plain's edge he saw a horseman, near by, coming swiftly. It was Clay Mundy.

V

MacGregor slowed up. The flush of burning wrath had died away; his face was set to a heavy, impassive mask. He thrust Hamerick's gun between his left knee and the stirrup-leather and gripped it there. He rode on to meet Clay Mundy—and the nameless flowers of San Quentin were stirrup-high about him as he rode.

He drew rein so Mundy should come to his right side; and again, as at their first meeting, he laid both hands on the saddle horn as he halted.

Clay Mundy's face was dark with suspicion.

"Have you seen a fool in a buggy?" he demanded.

"I see a fool on a horse!" responded MacGregor calmly. "For the person you seek, I have put such a word in his ear that he will never stop this side of tidewater. What devil's work is this, Clay Mundy?"

"You damned meddler! Are you coward as well as meddler, that you dare not move your hands?"

"Put up your foolish gun, man—you cannae fricht me with it. The thing is done and shooting will never undo it. There will be no mock-marriage this day, nor any day—and now shoot, if you will, and damned to you! Man! Have ye gone clean daft? Or did ye wish to proclaim it that ye were no match for the Morgans in war? And did ye think to live the week out That had been a chance had you married her indeed, with bell and book—as whaur could ye find better mate? But after such black treachery as ye meant—Man, ye are not in your right mind, the devil is at your ear!"

"It is hard to kill a man who will not defend himself," said Mundy thickly. "I spared your life once because you amused me—"

"And because it was a verra judeecious thing, too—and you are well knowing to that same. Think ye I value my life owre high, or that I fear ye at all, that I come seeking you? Take shame to yourself, man! Have a better thought of it yet! Say you will marry the lass before my eyes, and I will go with you on that errand; or turn you back and I will go with her back to the house of the Morgans—and for her sake, I will keep your shame to mysel'. Or, if it likes you better, you may even fall to the shooting."

"Fool!" said Mundy. "I can kill you before you can touch your gun."

"It is what I doubt," said MacGregor. "Please yourself. For me there is but the clean stab of death—but you must leave behind the name of a false traitor to be a hissing and a byword in the mouths of men."

"I will say this much, that I was wrong to call you coward," said Mundy, in a changed voice. "You are a bold and stubborn man, and I think there is a chance that you might get your gun—yes, and shoot straight, too. I will not marry the girl—but neither will I harm her. But I will not be driven further. I am not willing to skulk away while you tell her your way of the story. That would be too sorry a part. I will go on alone, and tell her, and send her home."

"You will say your man fled before the Morgans, or was taken by them, or some such lies, and lure her on to her ruin," said MacGregor. "I will not turn back."

"I will give you the minute to turn back," said Mundy.

"It is what I will never do!"

"Then you will die here," said Mundy.

"Think of me as one dead an hour gone," said MacGregor steadily. "My life is long since forfeit to every law of God or man. I am beyond the question. Think rather of yourself. You have the plain choice before you—a bonny wife to cherish, and bairns to your knee—life and love, peace and just dealing and quiet days—or at the other hand but dusty death and black shame to the back of that!"

As a snake strikes, Mundy's hand shot out: he jerked MacGregor's gun from the scabbard and threw it behind him. His face lit up with ferocious joy.

"You prating old windbag! How about it now? I'll be driven by no man on earth, much less by a wordy old bluffer like you."

"You used other speech but now. Ye are false in war as in love. But I carenae for hard words, so you deal justly with the lassie. Wed her with me to witness, or let her go free."

"Talk to the wind!" said Mundy.

"For the last time, Mundy, give it up! In the name of God!"

"Get off that horse and drag it! I give you your life—you're not worth my killing. Never be seen on the San Quentin again!"

"Mundy—"

"Get off, I say!" Mundy spurred close, his cocked gun swung shoulder high.

"Aweel," said MacGregor. He began to slide off slowly, his right hand on the saddle horn; his left hand went to the gun at his left knee; he thrust it up under Neighbor's neck and fired once, twice—again! Crash of flames, roaring of gun shots: he was on his back, Neighbor's feet were in his ribs, he fired once more, blindly, from under the trampling feet.

Breathless, crushed, he struggled to his knees, the blood pumping from two bullet-holes in his great body. A yard away, Clay Mundy lay on his face, crumpled and still, clutching a smoking gun.

"I didnae touch his face," said MacGregor. He threw both guns behind him; he turned Mundy over and opened his shirt. One wound was in his breast, close beside his heart; another was through the heart. MacGregor looked down upon him.

"The puir, mad, misguided lad!" he said between pain-wrung lips. "Surely he was gone horn-mad with hate and wrong and revenge."

He covered the dead man's face, and straightened the stiffening arms, and sat beside him: he looked at the low sun, the splendor of the western range; he held his hand to his own breast to stay the pulsing blood.

"And the puir lassie—she will hear this shameful tale of him! Had I looked forward and killed yonder knave Hamerick, she had blamed none but me. 'Twas ill done . . . Ay, but she's young still. She will have a cave and a fire of her own yet."

There was a silence and a little space, and his hand slipped. Then he opened his dulling eyes:

"Hullo, Central! . . . Give me Body, please . . . Hullo, Body! Hullo! That you, Body? . . . MacGregor's Soul, speaking. I am going away. Good luck to you—good-bye! . . . I don't know where.

LONGROPE'S LAST GUARD

Charles M. Russell

66 W HOEVER TOLD YOU that cattle stampede without cause was talkin' like a shorthorn," says Rawhide Rawlins. "You can bet all you got that whenever cattle run, there's a reason for it. A whole lot of times cattle run, an' nobody knows why but the cows an' they won't tell.

"There's plenty of humans call it instinct when an animal does something they don't savvy. I don't know what it is myself, but I've seen the time when I'd like to a-had some. I've knowed of hosses bein' trailed a thousand miles an' turned loose, that pulled back for their home range, not goin' the trail they come, but takin' cut-offs across mountain ranges that would puzzle a bighorn. An' if you'd ask one of these wise boys how they done it, he'd back out of it easy by sayin' it's instinct. You'll find cow ponies that knows more about the business than the men that rides 'em.

"There's plenty of causes for a stampede; sometimes it's a green hand or a careless cowpuncher scratchin' a match to light a cigarette. Maybe it's something on the wind, or a tired nighthoss spraddles and shakes himself, an' the poppin' of the saddle leather causes them to jump the bedground. Scare a herd on the start, and you're liable to have hell with them all the way. I've seen bunches well trail-broke that you couldn't fog off the bed-ground with a slicker an' six-shooter; others, again, that had had a scare, you'd have to ride a hundred yards away from to spit. Some men's too careful with their herd an' go tiptoein' around like a mother with a sick kid. I've had some experience, an' claim this won't do. Break 'em so they'll stand noise; get 'em used to seein' a man afoot, an' you'll have less trouble.

"There's some herds that you dassen't quit your hoss short of five hundred yards of. Of course it's natural enough for cow-brutes that never see hoss an' man apart to scare some when they see 'em separate. They think the top of this animal's busted off, an' when they see the piece go movin' around they're plenty surprised; but as I said before, there's many reasons for stampedes unknown to man. I've seen herds start in broad daylight with no cause that anybody knows of. The smell of blood will start 'em goin'; this generally comes off in the mornin' when they're quittin' the bed-ground. Now, in every herd you'll find steers that's regular old rounders. They won't go to bed like decent folks, but put in the night perusin' around, disturbin' the peace. If there's any bulls in the bunch, there's liable to be fightin'. I've often watched an old bull walkin' around through the herd an' talkin' fight, hangin' up his bluff, with a bunch of these rounders at his heels. They're sure backin' him up—boostin' an' ribbin' up trouble, an' if there's a fight pulled off you should hear these trouble-builders takin' sides; every one of 'em with his tongue out an' his tail kinked, buckin' an' bellerin, like his money's all up. These night ramblers that won't go to bed at decent hours, after raisin' hell all night, are ready to bed down an' are sleepin' like drunks when decent cattle are walkin' off the bed-ground.

"Now, you know, when a cow-brute quits his bed he bows his neck, gaps an' stretches all the same as a human after a night's rest. Maybe he accidentally tromps on one of these rounders' tails that's layin' along the ground. This hurts plenty, and Mr. Night Rambler ain't slow about wakin' up; he raises like he's overslept an' 's afeared he'll miss the coach, leavin' the tossel of his tail under the other fellow's hoof. He goes off wringin' his stub an' scatterin' blood on his rump an' quarters. Now the minute them other cattle winds the blood, the ball opens. Every hoof's at his heels barkin' and bellerin'. Them that's close enough are hornin' him in the flank like they'd stuck to finish him off. They're all plumb hog-wild, an' if you want any beef left in your herd you'd better cut out the one that's causin' the excitement, 'cause an hour of this will take off more taller than they'll put on in a month.

"Cattle like open country to sleep in. I sure hate to hold a herd near any brakes or deep 'royos, cause no matter how gentle a herd is, let a coyote or any other animal loom up of a sudden close to 'em an' they don't stop to take a second look, but are gone like a flash in the pan. Old bulls comin' up without talkin' sometimes jump a herd this way, an' it pays a cowpuncher to sing when he's comin' up out of a 'royo close to the bed-ground.

"Some folks'll tell you that cowboys sing their cows to sleep, but that's a mistake, judgin' from my experience, an' I've had some. The songs an' voices I've heard around cattle ain't soothin'. A cowpuncher sings to keep himself company; it ain't that he's got any motherly love for these long-horns he's put to bed an' 's ridin' herd on; he's amusin' himself an' nobody else. These ditties are generally shy on melody an' strong on noise. Put a man alone in the dark, an' if his conscious is clear an' he ain't hidin' he'll sing an' don't need to be a born vocalist. Of course singin's a good thing around a herd, an' all punchers know it. In the darkness it lets the cows know where you're at. If you ever woke up in the darkness an' found somebody—you didn't know who or what—loomin' up over you, it would startle you, but if this somebody is singin' or whistlin', it wouldn't scare you none. It's the same with Mr. Steer; that snaky, noiseless glidin' up on him's what scares the animal.

"All herds has some of these lonesomes that won't lie down with the other cattle, but beds down alone maybe twenty-five to thirty yards from the edge of the herd. He's got his own reason for this; might be he's short an eye. This bein' the case you can lay all you got he's layin' with the good blinker next to the herd. He don't figure on lettin' none of his playful brothers beef his ribs from a sneak. One-eyed hoss is the same. Day or night you'll find him on the outside with his good eye watchin' the bunch. Like Mister Steer, the confidence he's got in his brother's mighty frail.

"But these lonesome cattle I started to tell you about, is the ones that a puncher's most liable to run onto in the dark, layin' out that way from the herd. If you ride onto him singin', it don't startle Mr. Steer; he raises easy, holdin' his ground till you pass; then he lays down in the same place. He's got the ground warm an' hates to quit her. Cows, the same as humans, like warm beds. Many's the time in cool weather I've seen some evil-minded, lowdown steer stand around like he ain't goin' to bed, but all the time he's got his eye on some poor, undersized brother layin' near by, all innocent. As soon as he thinks the ground's warm he walks over, horns him out an' jumps his claim. This low-down trick is sometimes practiced by punchers when they got a gentle herd. It don't hurt a cow-puncher's conscience none to sleep in a bed he stole from a steer.

"If you ride sneakin' an' noiseless onto one of these lonesome fellers, he gets right to his feet with dew-claws an' hoofs rattlin', an' 's runnin' before he's half up, hittin' the herd like a canned dog, an' quicker than you can bat an eye the whole herd's gone. Cows are slow animals, but scare 'em an' they're fast enough; a thousand will get to their feet as quick as one. It's sure a puzzler to cowmen to know how a herd will all scare at once, an' every animal will get on his feet at the same time. I've seen herds do what a cowpuncher would call 'jump'—that is, to raise an' not run. I've been lookin' across a herd in bright moonlight—a thousand head or more, all down; with no known cause there's a short, quick rumble, an' every hoof's standin'.

"I've read of stampedes that were sure dangerous an' scary, where a herd would run through a camp, upsettin' wagons an' trompin' sleepin' cowpunchers to death. When day broke they'd be fifty or a hundred miles from where they started, leavin' a trail strewn with blood, dead cowpunchers, an' hosses, that looked like the work of a Kansas cyclone. This is all right in books, but the feller that writes 'em is romancin' an' don't savvy the cow. Most stampedes is noisy, but harmless to anybody but the cattle. A herd in a bad storm might drift thirty miles in a night, but the worst run I ever see, we ain't four miles from the bed-ground when the day broke.

"This was down in Kansas; we're trailin' beef an' have got about seventeen hundred head. Barrin' a few dry ones the herd's straight steers, mostly Spanish longhorns from down on the Cimarron. We're about fifty miles south of Dodge. Our herd's well broke an' lookin' fine, an' the cowpunchers all good-natured, thinkin' of the good time comin' in Dodge.

"That evenin' when we're ropin' our hosses for night guard, the trail boss, 'Old Spanish' we call him—he ain't no real Spaniard, but he's rode some in Old Mexico an' can talk some Spanish— says to me: 'Them cattle ought to hold well; they ain't been off water four hours, an' we grazed 'em plumb onto the bed-ground. Every hoof of 'em's got a paunch full of grass an' water, an' that's what makes cattle lay good.'

"Me an' a feller called Longrope's on first guard. He's a centerfire or single-cinch man from California; packs a sixty-foot rawhide riata, an' when he takes her down an' runs about half of her into a loop she looks big, but when it reaches the animal, comes pretty near fittin' hoof or horn. I never went much on these longrope boys, but this man comes as near puttin' his loop where he wants as any I ever see. You know Texas men ain't got much love for a single rig, an' many's the argument me an' Longrope has on this subject. He claims a center-fire is the only saddle, but I 'low that they'll do all right on a shad-bellied western hoss, but for

Spanish pot-gutted ponies they're no good. You're ridin' up on his withers all the time.

"When we reach the bed-ground most of the cattle's already down, lookin' comfortable. They're bedded in open country, an' things look good for an easy night. It's been mighty hot all day, but there's a little breeze now makin' it right pleasant; but down the west I notice some nasty-lookin' clouds hangin' 'round the new moon that's got one horn hooked over the skyline. The storm's so far off that you can just hear her rumble, but she's walkin' up on us slow, an' I'm hopin' she'll go 'round. The cattle's all layin' quiet an' nice, so me an' Longrope stop to talk awhile.

"'They're layin' quiet,' says I.

"'Too damn quiet,' says he. 'I like cows to lay still all right, but I want some of the natural noises that goes with a herd this size. I want to hear 'em blowin' off, an' the creakin' of their joints, showin' they're easin' themselves in their beds. Listen, an' if you hear anything I'll eat that rimfire saddle of yours—grass rope an' all.'

"I didn't notice till then, but when I straighten my ears it's quiet as a grave. An' if it ain't for the lightnin' showin' the herd once in a while, I couldn't a-believed that seventeen hundred head of longhorns lay within forty feet of where I'm sittin' on my hoss. It's gettin' darker every minute, an' if it wasn't for Longrope's slicker I couldn't a-made him out, though he's so close I could have touched him with my hand. Finally it darkens up so I can't see him at all. It's black as the inside of a pocket; you couldn't find your nose with both hands.

"I remember askin' Longrope the time.

"'I guess I'll have to get help to find the timepiece,' says he, but gets her after feelin' over himself, an' holdin' her under his cigarette takes a long draw, lightin' up her face.

"'Half-past nine,' says he.

"'Half an hour more,' I says. 'Are you goin' to wake up the next guard, or did you leave it to the hoss-wrangler?'

"'There won't be but one guard to-night,' he answers, 'an' we'll ride it. You might as well hunt for a hoss thief in heaven as look for that camp. Well, I guess I'll mosey 'round.' An' with that he quits me.

"The lightnin's playin' every little while. It ain't making much noise, but lights up enough to show where you're at. There ain't no use ridin'; by the flashes I can see that every head's down. For a second it'll be like broad day, then darker than the dungeons of hell, an' I notice the little fire-balls on my hoss's ears; when I spit there's a streak in the air like strikin' a wet match. These little fire-balls is all I can see of my hoss, an' they tell me he's listenin' all ways; his ears are never still.

"I tell you, there's something mighty ghostly about sittin' up on a hoss you can't see, with them two little blue sparks out in front of you wigglin' an' movin' like a pair of spook eyes, an' it shows me the old night hoss is usin' his listeners pretty plenty. I got my ears cocked, too, hearing nothin' but Longrope's singin'; he's easy three hundred yards across the herd from me, but I can hear every word:

"Sam Bass was born in Injiana,
It was his native home,
'Twas at the age of seventeen
Young Sam began to roam.
He first went out to Texas,
A cowboy for to be;
A better hearted feller
You'd seldom ever see.

"It's so plain it sounds like he's singin' in my ear; I can even hear the click-clack of his spur chains against his stirrups when he moves 'round. An' the cricket in his bit—he's usin' one of them hollow conched half-breeds—she comes plain to me in the stillness. Once there's a steer layin' on the edge of the herd starts sniffin'. He's takin' long draws of the air, he's nosin' for something. I don't like this, it's a bad sign; it shows he's layin' for trouble, an' all he needs is some little excuse.

"Now every steer, when he beds down, holds his breath for a few seconds, then blows off; that noise is all right an' shows he's settlin' himself for comfort. But when he curls his nose an' makes them long draws it's a sign he's sniffin' for something, an' if anything crosses his wind that he don't like there's liable to be trouble. I've seen dry trail herds mighty thirsty, layin' good till a breeze springs off the water, maybe ten miles away; they start sniffin', an' the minute they get the wind you could comb Texas an' wouldn't have enough punchers to turn 'em till they wet their feet an' fill their paunches.

"I get tired sittin' there starin' at nothin', so start ridin' 'round. Now it's sure dark when animals can't see, but I tell you by the way my hoss moves he's feelin' his way. I don't blame him none; it's like lookin' in a black pot. Sky an' ground all the same, an' I ain't gone twenty-five yards till I hear cattle gettin' up around me; I'm in the herd an' it's luck I'm singing an' they don't get scared. Pullin' to the left I work cautious an' easy till I'm clear of the bunch. Ridin's useless, so I flop my weight over on one stirrup an' go on singin'.

"The lightin' 's quit now, an' she's darker than ever; the breeze has died down an' it's hotter than the hubs of hell. Above my voice I can hear Longrope. He's singin' the 'Texas Ranger' now; the Ranger's a long song an' there's few punchers that knows it all, but Longrope's sprung a lot of new verses on me an' I'm interested. Seems like he's on about the twenty-fifth verse, an' there's danger of his chokin' down, when there's a whisperin' in the grass behind me; it's a breeze sneakin' up. It flaps the tail of my slicker an' goes by; in another second she hits the herd. The ground shakes, an' they're all runnin'. My hoss takes the scare with 'em an' 's bustin' a hole in the darkness when he throws both front feet in a badger hole, goin' to his knees an' plowin' his nose in the dirt. But he's a good night hoss an' 's hard to keep down. The minute he gets his feet under him he raises, runnin' like a scared wolf. Hearin' the roar behind him he don't care to mix with them locoed longhorns. I got my head turned over my shoulder listenin', tryin' to make out which way they're goin', when there's a flash of lightnin' busts a hole in the sky—it's one of these kind that puts the fear of God in a man, thunder an' all together. My hoss whirls an' stops in his tracks, spraddlin' out an' squattin' like he's hit, an' I can feel his heart beatin' agin my leg, while mine's poundin' my ribs like it'll bust through. We're both plenty scared.

"This flash lights up the whole country, givin' me a glimpse of the herd runnin' a little to my left. Big drops of rain are pounding on my hat. The storm has broke now for sure, with the lightnin' bombardin' us at every jump. Once a flash shows me Longrope, ghostly in his wet slicker. He's so close to me that I could hit him with my quirt an' I hollers to him, 'This is hell.'

"'Yes,' he yells back above the roar; 'I wonder what damned fool kicked the lid off.'

'I can tell by the noise that they're runnin' straight; there ain't no clickin' of horns. It's a kind of hummin' noise like a buzzsaw, only a thousand times louder. There's no use in tryin' to turn 'em in this darkness, so I'm ridin' wide just herdin' by ear an' follerin' the noise. Pretty soon my ears tell me they're crowdin' an' comin' together; the next flash shows 'em all millin', with heads jammed together an' horns locked; some's rared up ridin' others, an' these is squirmin' like bristled snakes. In the same light I see Longrope, an' from the blink I get of him he's among 'em or too close for safety, an' in the dark I thought I saw a gun flash three times with no report. But with the noise these longhorns are makin' now, I doubt if I could a-heard a six-gun bark if I pulled the trigger myself, an' the next thing I know me an' my hoss goes over a bank, lightin' safe. I guess it ain't over four feet, but it seems like fifty in the darkness, an' if it hadn't been for my chin-string I'd a-went from under my hat. Again the light shows me we're in a 'royo with the cattle comin' over the edge, wigglin' an' squirmin' like army worms.

"It's a case of all night riding. Sometimes they'll mill an' quiet down, then start trottin' an' break into a run. Not till daybreak do they stop, an' maybe you think old day ain't welcome. My hoss is sure leg-weary, an' I ain't so rollicky myself. When she gets light enough I begin lookin' for Longrope, with nary a sign of him; an' the herd, you wouldn't know they were the same cattle—smeared with mud an' ga'nt as greyhounds; some of 'em with their tongues still lollin' out from their night's run. But sizin' up the bunch, I guess I got 'em all. I'm kind of worried about Longrope. It's a cinch that wherever he is he's afoot, an' chances is he's layin' on the prairie with a broken leg.

"The cattle's spread out, an' they begin feedin'. There ain't much chance of losin' 'em, now it's broad daylight, so I ride up on a raise to take a look at the back trail. While I'm up there viewin' the country, my eyes run onto somethin' a mile back in a draw. I can't make it out, but get curious, so spurrin' my tired hoss into a lope I take the back trail. 'Tain't no trouble to foller in the mud; it's plain as plowed ground. I ain't rode three hundred yard till the country raises a little an' shows me this thing's a hoss, an' by the white streak on his flank I heap savvy it's Peon—that's the hoss Longrope's ridin'. When I get close he whinners pitiful like; he's lookin' for sympathy, an' I notice, when he turns to face me, his right foreleg's broke. He's sure a sorry sight with that fancy, full-stamped cen-ter-fire saddle hangin' under his belly in the mud. While I'm lookin' him over, my hoss cocks his ears to the right, snortin' low. This scares me—I'm afeared to look. Somethin' tells me I won't see Longrope, only part of him—that part that stays here on earth when the man's gone. Bracin' up, I foller my hoss's ears, an' there in the holler of the 'royo is a patch of yeller; it's part of a slicker. I spur up to get a better look over the bank, an' there tromped in the mud is all there is left of Longrope. Pullin' my gun I empty her in the air. This brings the boys that are follerin' on the trail from the bed-ground. Nobody'd had to tell 'em we'd had hell, so they come in full force, every man but the cook an' hoss-wrangler.

"Nobody feels like talkin'. It don't matter how rough men are—I've known 'em that never spoke without cussin', that claimed to fear neither God, man, nor devil—but let death visit camp an' it puts 'em thinkin'. They generally take their hats off to this old boy that comes everywhere an' any time. He's always ready to pilot you—willin' or not—over the long dark trail that folks don't care to travel. He's never welcome, but you've got to respect him.

"'It's tough—damned tough,' says Spanish, raisin' poor Longrope's head an' wipin the mud from his face with his neck-handkerchief, tender, like he's feared he'll hurt him. We find his hat tromped in the mud not fur from where he's layin'. His scabbard's empty, an' we never do locate his gun.

"That afternoon when we're countin' out the herd to see if we're short any, we find a steer with a broken shoulder an' another with a hole plumb through his nose. Both these is gun wounds; this accounts for them flashes I see in the night. It looks like, when Longrope gets mixed in the mill, he tries to gun his way out, but the cattle crowd him to the bank an' he goes over. The chances are he was dragged from his hoss in a tangle of horns.

"Some's for takin' him to Dodge an' gettin' a box made for him, but Old Spanish says: 'Boys, Longrope is a prairie man, an' if she was a little rough at times, she's been a good foster mother. She cared for him while he's awake, let her nurse him in his sleep.' So we wrapped him in his blankets, an' put him to bed.

"It's been twenty years or more since we tucked him in with the end-gate of the bed-wagon for a headstone, which the cattle have long since rubbed down, leavin' the spot unmarked. It sounds lonesome, but he ain't alone, 'cause these old prairies has cradled many of his kind in their long sleep."

TRAIL
FEVER

S. Omar Barker

SUPPER AT THE U BAR WAGON that midsummer evening was by no means a-hurt with happiness, nor with cleanliness either. The only wahoo not mud-caked from boot heel to brisket was old Tuck Fargus, the cross-eyed cook.

"Dry me out an' you could lay me for a 'dobe," complained Midge Calley, heel-squatting where the glow of embers soon had his south end steaming.

"If dirt was a penny a pound," grunted Rusty Strayhorn, "I'd be worth a month's wages just for my scrapin's!"

"Which is more'n you'll ever add up to, clean!" Brazos Bill Endicott was eating left-handed tonight, thanks to an elbow painfully twisted in futile struggle with a bogged steer, but his arid drawl sounded as breezy as usual. "Which-away's Montana now, Cuff?"

Cuff Howell didn't answer. He and his nine-man crew of trail-toughened Texas cow hands had that day tried to push two thousand rebellious longhorns across a water called Pudgamalodgy Creek—and failed, at a cost of seventeen bog-buried steers.

There had been some cost in cowboy temper too. In six hundred hoof-beaten miles of dust and drought, good grass and bad, storms, stampedes and rivers to cross, these seventeen were the first U Bar cattle the prideful young trail boss had lost, and he was feeling a little stiff-necked about it. That could have been partly because he had tried the crossing despite the profane protests of red-haired Rusty Strayhorn that there wasn't a crossing within forty miles that would be safe for a mud turtle on stilts, much less a herd of steers. It was not the first time a little hair had been rubbed the wrong way between him and Rusty.

"Montana lays thataway!" Howell had gestured northward with a leather-cuffed arm. "We'll cross 'em!"

So they had tried. Almost all day they had tried, and no trail crew had ever tried harder. But tonight the U Bar herd, minus seventeen dead, was still south of the Pudgamalodgy, and Cuff Howell was in no pleasant temper.

They had hit the Cimarron and the Red in full flood and swum them both in true trail-driver style, but here was a different story. Mildly in flood from upcreek rains, still not more than a dozen feet of this sluggish little stream's sixty-foot width ran swimming water. The rest of its deceptive span was barely moving water no more than three to a dozen inches deep. But under that water lurked mud. Not quicksand. Mud. Mud without apparent bottom, tar-black when wet, turning a dull ash color as it caked dry on the legs of men, horses and the long-shanked Texas steers that balked and backed out of it in panic, in spite of all hell crowding hard behind them in the guise of whooping, rope-whapping cowboys.

Around midafternoon Cuff Howell's stubborn will had finally recognized reality and called it quits.

"I'll be a hog-tied horny toad!" he had sworn bitterly. "Six hundred miles behind us, and balked by a little crick that I could purt' near spit across! All right, boys, ream out your ears and let's see how many of these bogged beeves we can drag out before they drown!"

Around sundown, as they were dragging out the last still-living bog victims, an old speckled cow had come meandering through the cottonwoods on the opposite bank, paused to bawl a few times, then deliberately lunged into the muddy creek. She had floundered and struggled like a bug in a bowl of Pudgamalodgy pudding, but still somehow made it across, thus adding insult to the indignity of the trail crew's failure. Clambering out on the south bank, the cow had trotted off to join the herd of steers now grazing a quarter of a mile away out on the flat, as if wallowing across mud-bound creeks were an everyday pastime.

"By the holy horny toads!" said Cuff Howell. "If that crazy critter can cross it, why can't my idiot steers?"

"The female of the species," said Brazos Bill, hunching his bull-like, slightly humped-over shoulders in a sort of half-clowning way he had, "gits more lonesome than the he! She heard the bawlin' an' come lookin' for company!"

Cuff Howell had then ridden along the bank, a slim ramrod in his muddy saddle, scowling at the route by which the cow had crossed.

"Tomorrow we'll cross this herd," he said, "or know the reason why!"

"One cow on her own ain't like two thousand steers pushed, Cuff," observed Brazos Bill. "If I was bossin' this beef, I'd hold up an' graze till she dries."

Ordinarily such comment should have raised no hackles, but the young trail boss's judgment had that day been proved wrong, and Cuff Howell was a man who liked to be right. There was a raw edge of touchy temper in his answer.

"It so happens you ain't bossin' this herd, cowboy!"

"Might not be a bad idea if he was," put in Rusty Strayhorn dryly. "Sometimes you git awful high an' mighty for the size of your diapers, Mister Howell!"

There were times in those rough days of rawhide riding men when a certain way of saying "Mister" could touch off a ruckus. This might easily have been one of them if Brazos Bill hadn't picked that moment to pop Rusty Strayhorn behind the ear with a gob of mud. He followed it up by riding casually between the outspoken Rusty and their sore-minded trail boss.

"Cuff," he said, "let's go see if ol' Tuck's got the Java pot hot!"

So supper at the U Bar wagon that evening was something less than a joyous feast of fellowship; not the most propitious moment, perhaps, for a nester kid to come looking for his cow. Nobody noticed his approach. He simply materialized out of the shadows, a scrawny youngster, maybe around twelve years old, his old straw hat pushed back from a humorously pug-nosed face, his frazzled bib overalls rolled to the knees above mud-smeared bare feet and legs. He carried a cow halter and a short frazzled rope over one arm, an ax on the other shoulder.

"Howdy," he said without noticeable timidity. "Who's the top tuckahoo of this sorry Texican outfit?"

"Now that," observed Brazos Bill, "could be a matter of opinion."

Cuff Howell ignored the dig. "Where the devil," he said, "did you come from?"

"Pap's homestead's over acrost the crick," the boy informed him. "I come after my cow that your ol' Texican cattle tolled off with their bawlin'. We had her about done weanin' her calf, so I reckon she got lonesome. Her name's Josephine."

"Yeah? What's yours?"

"*G-l-a-d*, Glad; *d-i-s*, dis. Gladdis! An' the first feller that laughs, I'll stomp him!"

YOU DON'T H
HOME TO EX

Discove

THE LATEST BREAKTHROUGH
AND TECHNOLOGY DELIVERE
DOOR EVERY MONT

NAME_____

ADDRESS_____

CITY_____ PROVINCE_____

❏ Payment Enclosed   ❏ Bill Me

Please add 7% GST. Please allow 6 to 8 weeks for delivery.

For a couple of brief chuckles nobody got "stomped."

"Call me Gwendoline," said Brazos Bill. "How'd you manage to cross that crick without boggin'?"

"Rode over on a dang catfish!" The boy batted big blue eyes solemnly. "I'm fixin' to go ketch Josephine outa your herd, mister. You got any objections?"

He addressed himself to Brazos Bill, but it was Cuff Howell who answered. "You keep away from that herd, you savvy!" he warned sharply. "We got trouble enough without a stampede!"

"Then you better git Josephine outa there for me—or was you aimin' to steal her? Pap says a heap of Texicans ain't nothin' but cow thieves anyway!"

"You better mind your manners, Catfish," Brazos Bill warned him solemnly. "That's the ring-tailed ramrod himself you're talking to. He crumbles kids your size into his coffee! . . . Ain't that right, Cuff?"

Cuff Howell seemed to be in no mood for cowboy joshing. "You go back and tell your pa I said we'll cut out his cow in due time, after we get the herd across," he told the kid shortly. "I got no time now to fool with strays."

"You try drivin' Josephine acrost along with all them steers the way I seen you doin' today, an' you'll git her bogged down, sure as shootin'!" The Catfish Kid stood right up in the front row and laid it on the taw line. "I come after my cow, Mister Texican, an' I ain't goin' back till I git her!"

"And just how," inquired Cuff Howell sarcastically, "do you figger you'd get her back across, even if you had her cut out of the herd?"

"Let her ride a catfish, same as I did. Me an' Josephine ain't from Texas. We're smart enough to cross a little ol' muddy crick!"

Without comment, Cuff Howell got up and went to refill his tin coffee cup.

"Catfish," said Brazos Bill, "don't you realize you're liable to get yourself tromped on, insultin' the great Lone Star State with that kind of talk?"

"If I was scared of Texicans," stated the Catfish Kid scornfully, "I'd quit chawin' an' learn to suck eggs!"

It was a ludicrous thing, even a comical thing, this business of a scrawny, ragged, barefooted nester's young'un putting on such a show of bravado and bold talk before a bunch of tough Texas trail men. Yet mere smart-aleck show-off it surely was not. "Biggity behavior"—yes, but with something about it too frank and open-faced to be seriously offensive; something even a little pitiful, as if here was a boy trying, however mistakenly, to act like a man because for some reason or other he felt he had to be one.

Even as the kid's untimid tongue boasted how unafraid of "Texicans" he was, Brazos Bill saw his glance rest hungrily on the Dutch oven still half full of old Tuck's brown-crusted biscuits close beside the cook fire. Apparently the cross-eyed cooky saw it, too, but before either of them had time to act on a hospitable impulse, Cuff Howell spoke again.

"You got no business here, kid," he said brusquely, "but as long as you are, you just as well get you a plate and sample our beans."

"I'll bet they rattle in the plate," said the boy, but he got a tin plate, filled it and went to work on Texican chuck with considerable gusto.

"If you was that light in the gut," observed Brazos Bill, "no wonder you didn't bog down crossin' the crick!"

The Catfish Kid took time to relish a generous bite of sourdough biscuit, then grinned amiably.

"All I done," he announced, "was coon-trot an ol' cottonwood log across the deep part with a few armloads of brush I'd chopped, then kept throwin' it out ahead of me to step on till I got acrost the bog. The brush don't sink enough but what it holds you up till you hop onto the next one. That catfish ridin' was jest a joke."

"There you are, Mister Howell!" Rusty Strayhorn spread his red-knuckled hands. "Learn your longhorns to hop from brush to brush an' you've just as good as got 'em across!"

"You pick a poor time for smart-aleck talk, Rusty." The young trail boss spoke quietly, but by no means sweetly. "And while I think of it, I reckon you ain't forgot my callin' name."

Rusty set down his eating weapons and stood up. "I ain't forgot the tongue-whippin' you give me back at Doan's Crossing! Nor how long you've kept me eatin' dust on the drag. I've rode the trail with you as a plain cow hand, Mister Howell, an' by glory, if you don't start sweetenin' up purty soon, I'm liable to—"

"You're liable to swaller your cud, Rusty," broke in Brazos Bill, breezy as ever. "If anybody's goin' to whip a trail boss around here, it's gonna be me! . . . Ain't that right, Cuff?"

Cuff Howell gave him a queer look. "Let me know when," he shrugged.

"Sick 'em!" said the Catfish Kid, and everybody but Cuff and Rusty laughed.

"You 'tend to your biscuit-bitin', Catfish," warned Brazos Bill, "or you're liable to git your little tail stepped on!"

Still scowling, Rusty Strayhorn sat down again on his bedroll and began to make a smoke. The Catfish Kid sopped up the last of his gravy with a hunk of biscuit and began gathering up the U Bar crew's empty eating gear.

"You want these weapons washed," he asked the cook "or shall I wipe 'em out on my shirt tail?"

"You just leave 'em be," growled Tuck Fargus. "I don't want no mudcat messin' around my kitchen!"

"You go set on a stump an' scratch your itch, gran'pa," the boy advised him. "My ma learned me never to eat free without he'pin' the cook!"

It was some cause for surprise to the U Bar crew that the cranky old cook let him go ahead. Whether purposely or not, the song the kid picked to sing while he worked seemed singularly appropriate to the occasion:

> *"Oh, I come to a river an' I couldn't git across,*
> *Singin' polly-wolly-doodle all the day."*

"Boys," said Cuff Howell, abruptly breaking a considerable spell of silence, "tomorrow we're goin' to build us a bridge across this creek!"

"In a pig's eye!" said Rusty Strayhorn.

Cuff ignored him. "If a little brush throwed in the mud held up this kid, a lot of brush will hold up logs. There's plenty of cottonwoods within draggin' distance and we've got three axes, countin' this youngster's. How many of you boys ever done any ax work?"

"I chopped off an ol' rooster's head once for a preacher's daughter down in Deaf Smith County," said Brazos Bill. "She was a yaller-haired filly, sorter Percheron built an'—"

"I hired out to drive cattle," broke in Rusty, "not to swing an ax!"

"You'll get used to it," said the trail boss dryly. "I want to get this crossin' made. The Three Bar herd ain't over two days behind us."

"So what?"

"I still aim to get to Montana ahead of them. You know the U Bars ain't contracted. It'll be first come, best sold. Tomorrow we'll build a bridge."

Bridging Pudgamalodgy Creek turned out to be no simple task. Well before sunup, cowboy arms far more accustomed to swinging a rope were swinging axes, felling cottonwoods, lopping off the branches and chopping the trunks into logs about fifteen feet long. Other cowboys dragged the lopped brush to the bridge site by rope and saddle horn. Even old Tuck Fargus was pressed into service to snake logs with the chuck-wagon team.

Cuff Howell bossed the job of piling brush in the muck to serve as a foundation for the logs to rest on, but he didn't spare his own sweat either.

Neither did the Catfish Kid, though a good deal of his energy seemed to be used up in trotting back and forth from one part of the job to another, alternately giving unsought advice, getting in the way, and demanding the immediate return of his cow.

"You ox-wallopers chop like a one-eyed ol' woman whippin' a carpet," he commented. "Them stumps look like they'd been gnawed off by a sore-toothed beaver!"

"You go learn your gran'ma to milk ducks," grinned Brazos Bill, and went on chopping.

But Rusty Strayhorn handed the kid his ax. "Maybe you'd like to show us how it s done, blabber-mouth!"

The Catfish Kid took the ax and spit on his hands. "Cheewah!" he grunted, and swung it.

His scrawny arms lacked power to sink the bit very deep, but in half a dozen swings he trued up Rusty's messy notch.

"Pap learnt me axin' before he taken the lung fever back in Kentucky," he informed them, handing Rusty back his ax. "I got to go see that ol' Cuff ain't pilin' that brush with the ends all one way!"

"You'd think it was his bridge," said Midge Calley as the kid trotted off.

"Why not?" shrugged Brazos Bill. "It was his brushhoppin' that give Cuff the idea."

"A heck of an idea!" grunted Rusty. "If there's two things I hate, it's a stiff-necked trail boss an' a smart-aleck brat!" He threw down his ax, ruefully rubbing a blister puffing up in one palm. "I'm quittin'!"

"Little red bull, when his tail got sore,
Said he wasn't gonna switch flies no more!"

It was a little song Brazos Bill had made up to try to cheer up the Slash

O camp one night after a perilous crossing of the flooded Red nearly two years ago, a crossing during which Brazos Bill had nearly drowned saving two other cowboys who had got knocked off their horses by floating logs. Remembering the occasion, Rusty gave him a queer look.

"Brazos," he said, "Cuff was a purty good feller as a plain cow hand. What's come over him to make him such a rannicky trail boss?"

"He's young," shrugged the big cowboy. "An' two thousand steers is a heap of another man's proputty to be responsible for. I reckon it sobers a man some."

"It don't have to sour him! He can't even grin anymore! I'm gittin' to where I hate the son of a gun's guts!"

"An' I wouldn't blame him for hatin' yours, the way you been giggin' him ever since Doan's Crossing."

"You heard the tongue-whippin' he give me for takin' them few drinks at ol' Doan's Store!"

"You mean for goin' on night guard half drunk," grinned Brazos. "Suppose you'd of belched an' started a stampede?"

"That ain't no reason to keep me ridin' the drag. I'm as good a man on point or swing as ever went up the trail! An' now blisterin' my hands on an ax handle. By glory, Brazos, I'm quittin'!"

"You got trail fever, sorehead!" grinned Brazos Bill. "Let's you an' me go see if Cuff wants to shift you to the draggin' job awhile."

"To heck with you!" growled Rusty, but he went. It is not always easy to refuse a man who has once saved your life.

Up at the bridge site Cuff Howell was dragging the Catfish Kid out of a pothole into which he had tumbled while trying, against orders, to relay some brush the way he thought it ought to be.

"Now you get away from here—and stay away!" Cuff had the kid by the shirt collar, apparently fixing to kick his pants, when Brazos Bill laid a hand on his arm.

"Cuff," he said with that queer, half-clownish hunch of his big shoulders, "I got a man here that ain't worth hog scrapin's with an ax. Whyn't you put him to snakin' brush awhile?"

Howell turned the kid loose. It would have been hard to say whether he looked a little ashamed or only tightlipped from raw-edged nerves.

"Brazos," he said, as if it was an effort to speak quietly, "some of these days you're goin' to use up your credit. All I'm tryin' to do is build a bridge. I don't give a hang who works at what, as long as it keeps the job movin'!"

It would have been a good time for Rusty to keep his mouth shut, but he didn't.

"Mister Howell," he inquired sweetly, "did you ever try pushin' a herd of longhorns onto a fresh-built bridge?"

"I can't say that I have, but—"

"Then you're due to learn somethin'. I'll bet you anything you say that you cain't make 'em cross it!"

"My good Christian friend," said the trail boss, with a challenging gleam in his eye, "if I don't cross the U Bars on this bridge, you'll draw my wages when we get to Montana! If I do cross 'em, you'll stop bellyachin' for the rest of this trip!"

"You've bought you a bet," shrugged Rusty. "What can I lose?"

"Your job if you don't get to work!" snapped Cuff. "I want this bridge done in time for crossin' tomorrow."

The Catfish Kid had not sidled away very far. "You're pilin' them branches crooked agin," he advised with a tentative grin. "Can't I ever learn you Texicans nothin'?"

Piled crooked or not, once there was enough of it, the cottonwood brush ceased to sink, furnishing an adequate though none too steady foundation upon which sweating cow hands grunt-wrestled log after log into place, crowding them close together, plugging cracks full of twig brush, and finally covering the whole works with load after backbusting load of ax-cut sod carried on old scraps of wagon sheet.

What with the difficulty of dropping stringers across the dozen feet of deepwater channel and the time it took to throw up brush wings to funnel an approach to the bridge, it was already dusk on the evening of the second day by the time Cuff Howell took a final walk across the crude, somewhat quivery structure and called it a bridge.

"There she lays, boys," Cuff spoke with some pride. "Dry crossin' for the U Bar heard!"

"In a pig's eye!" said Rusty.

"Purty fair job—for a bunch of Texicans," breezed the Catfish Kid. "I wish some of you ox-wallopers would rustle Josephine outa that herd, so I could git home with her."

"Holy horny toads!" snorted the trail boss. "Don't you never give up?"

It would have been another good time for Rusty to keep his mouth shut.

"Come on, kid," he offered, knowing the trail boss would veto it. "I'll cut that cow for you right now."

Cuff Howell could have said, "Better not, Rusty. I'd rather leave the herd as quiet as possible till we get this crossing made." Instead he said, "You won't do any such of a darn-fool thing, cowboy!"

Even as an order which it was his right to give, he could have spoken less sharply. But there it was again: two good trail men with their neck hair up, touch and go for trouble, for no good reason, as far as Brazos Bill could see, except that once started, friction fed on friction, building up into a kind of trail fever Brazos Bill had more than once seen wind up in a shooting.

"Cuff," said Brazos, "durned if I don't wonder sometimes if it might not have been smarter to let both of you ring-tails drown! We've got our bridge built. Let's go to the wagon. I'm as hungry as an ol' she-wolf with sixteen pups!"

Rusty shrugged. Cuff reached for his horse. Neither one said anything more.

That night, with Brazos Bill and Rusty on fourth guard and dawn not far away, the U Bar herd stampeded. By thin moonlight Brazos saw what spooked them: the Catfish Kid, prowling on foot, probably in search of his cow. It was not a bad run, as stampedes go, but it took till midmorning to get the herd regathered and quieted down enough to try the new bridge. Brazos saw that the boy's speckled cow was still in the herd, but the Catfish Kid seemed to have disappeared. Unless necessary to keep Cuff from blaming Rusty for the stampede, Brazos had meant to hold his tongue about what had caused it. Cuff saved him the trouble.

"I'd like to get my hands on that nester brat!" the trail boss said. "I'd learn him to go prowlin' around a herd when he's been told not to!"

"I seen him steppin' long and foggin' for home," said Tuck Fargus. "I reckon the poor kid savvied you'd be on his tail if you caught him."

"Poor kid, hell!" growled Cuff . . . "All right, let's cross these cattle!"

Experienced cow hands under the orders of a trail boss with cow savvy, the U Bar crew strung the longhorns out, trail style, in a line nearly a mile long and pointed them quietly toward the bridge. A big line-back steer stepped out briskly in the lead, as he had done all the way from Texas. It looked easy.

Fifty yards from the bridge the line-back threw up his head and stopped. So did the dozen secondary leaders close behind him. Quietly, Rusty and three other cowboys eased up from farther back. Cuff rode slowly on ahead. Sometimes cattle will follow a man on horseback. Moving their horses slow and easy, Brazos and Rusty crowded them a little. Heads high, eying the strange structure suspiciously, the leaders moved forward. Slowly Cuff rode onto the bridge. It quivered a little. The big line-back stopped again, snuffing at the freshly placed sod. He hesitated a second, then stepped gingerly onto the bridge, two more steers close behind him. The unsteadiness under their tread was no more than a faint quiver, but it was enough. With a windy snort, they whirled and lunged back off the bridge.

Head high, weaving a little in search of an opening, the line-back leader headed back for what he considered safer territory. Rusty could easily have let him pass, but he didn't. With swift cow-pony zigzags he blocked the steer's flight and turned him. Brazos turned two that came his way, the other cowboys several more.

But it was no use. When a dozen, two dozen, three dozen steers suddenly decided to get out of there, three dozen cowboys could not have held them. All they could do was swing back to mill the herd to keep it from stampeding.

Cuff Howell came riding back from the bridge. "Soon as they settle," he said quietly, "we'll try it again."

Try it again they did, again and many agains. They tried easing them, crowding them, rushing them. They tried driving the remuda across ahead of them in the vain hope of forcing them to follow. They brought the whole herd around in a circle a mile wide, let the usual leaders pass the bridge, then cut off fifty or so of the less alert loiterers that made up the drag and tried to crowd them across. But these also had promised their mammas never to set foot on a fresh-built log bridge.

They tried a flying wedge of a mere dozen steers with all hands whooping at their heels, in the hope that once a few had crossed, the smell of their passing or the sight of them on the far bank would serve to lull longhorn fears. They got ten of these well onto the bridge, but when a sudden balk crowded three off into the mire, they had to give that up too.

At sunset the U Bar crew was a sweat-drained, nerve-frazzled baffled bunch of buckaroos, and not a single U Bar steer had yet crossed Cuff Howell's wonderful bridge.

"Now if—that—don't beat—hell!" By now Cuff had given up the "holy horny toads" and switched to straight swearing. "Rusty, it begins to look like you win your damn bet!"

Rusty went on rolling a smoke and said nothing.

Off to the south a thin dust hazed the air.

"That'll be the Three Bars," said Cuff. "If their steers will cross it, we can't refuse 'em the lead. Maybe ours will follow."

It was, in effect, an admission of defeat.

"Look yonder!" said Rusty suddenly.

Watching the distant dust, they had not noticed the Catfish Kid's approach. Now he came on across the bridge, half leading half driving about a nine-months-old speckled calf.

"Honest, Mister Texican," he addressed the trail boss in a tone of grave anxiety, "I sure never meant to booger your herd last night. If you want to kick my pants, I'll stand for it without hitchin'—only don't kick too durn hard!"

"Forget it," said Cuff shortly. "Brazos, a couple of you boys just as well cut out this kid's cow and let him have her. Maybe he can get her across the bridge, anyhow!"

"Say, by golly!" grinned Brazos Bill suddenly. "Supposin'—"

"What I was figgerin'," broke in the Catfish Kid, "Jasper ain't been weaned so long but what Josephine'll reconnize him. If one of you tucka-hoos'll git a rope on him an' yank him along purty fast, he'll git to bawlin', an' Josephine'll foller him, an' she'll git to bawlin', an' when them Texican steers hear 'em, some of them'll come arunnin', an' they'll git to bawlin', an'—"

"Locate the kid's cow," broke in Cuff Howell. "Shape up the herd, string out a hundred or so of the drag to follow her, and—"

But already he was talking to hoof-dusty air. Well knowing that nothing but the smell of blood could excite range cattle like the distressed beller-ing of a calf, especially with its mother adding her long-tongued vocal anxiety to the din, the U Bar cowboys were already on their way with no need for further orders.

It was Rusty Strayhorn's rope that dragged poor bellering Jasper through a fringe of the herd, out again with Josephine bawling behind him, then on to the bridge and across it, a string-out of excited steers crowding snuffily at her heels, too stirred up even to notice whether they were on a quivering bridge or the good solid earth. Quickly the strange excitement spread through the herd, until it was all the U Bar crew could do to pinch the crowding cattle down to a line thin enough for the nar-row bridge to hold.

Less than an hour later, close behind the last steer across, Brazos Bill let out a wild cowboy yell of triumph, in which even a stiff-necked trail boss and a nester's brat spraddled behind the big cowboy's saddle raucously joined.

Half a mile northward the herd leaders were already spreading out to graze, their excitement all but forgotten. Some distance off to the left, Rusty and Midge were holding the Catfish Kid's now quieted cow and calf out of the herd for him. Giving the drags a parting shove, Brazos Bill rode over there. So did Cuff Howell, still straight, but no longer like a starched ramrod in the saddle.

"Well, Cuff," grinned Rusty, omitting the mock respect of "Mister" for the first time in weeks, "it looks like you win a bet!"

For almost the first time since Doan's Crossing, Cuff Howell's face lost its thin-lipped look in a wide grin.

"I never noticed you sparin' any sweat to keep me from it," he said. "I can make out with a man that don't never forget he's a cowboy."

It was, in the way of the hired men on horseback of that far-gone day, a verbal handshake. It meant, among other things, that tomorrow Rusty Strayhorn would no longer be riding the drag.

The Catfish Kid slid down from behind Brazos Bill's saddle, rubbing his sweaty crotch.

"Well, Josephine," he addressed the speckled cow, "maybe that'll learn you not to run off visitin' with a bunch of longhorns!" He grinned up at the circle of cowboys and began putting his frazzled halter on the now subdued cow.

"Catfish," said Brazos Bill, "we ain't sure which one we ought to kiss, you, the calf or the cow!"

"Don't let him hurraw you, Catfish!" Cuff Howell got off his horse to help the boy halter his cow. "The fact is we're mighty obliged to all three of you. A couple of the boys will help take your cattle home, but meantime—"

"Don't need to help, Mister Texican!"

"I can believe that," Cuff broke in dryly. "But we might, if we hit any more boggy creeks between here and Montana. I'd like mighty well to rustle a horse, saddle, and wages for a cook's helper learnin' to be a cowboy—if you want to go along."

The boy's shrug was elaborately scornful, his tone brash and breezy, his grin wide, but there was a wistful look in his big blue eyes that not a cowboy present could miss.

"Thanks for the free biscuits," he answered, "but not countin' pap's claim to look after, I'd as soon take up with the coyotes as a bunch of Texican ox-wallopers!"

Looking back as they rode on to catch up with the U Bar herd, Brazos Bill saw that the Catfish Kid stood a long time watching them go, and once he waved his old straw hat. Four cowboy sombreros waved in answer.

"Barrin' a sick pap,"—Brazos Bill hunched his big shoulders and chuckled—"he'd have made us a curly wolf, Cuff. I wonder what kind of a fit he'll throw when he finds that ten-dollar gold piece you slipped in his overalls while helpin' him halter ol' Josephine!"

CARRION SPRING

Wallace Stegner

THE MOMENT SHE CAME to the door she could smell it, not really rotten and not coming from any particular direction, but sweetish, faintly sickening, sourceless, filling the whole air the way a river's water can taste of weeds—the carrion smell of a whole country breathing out in the first warmth across hundreds of square miles.

Three days of chinook had uncovered everything that had been under snow since November. The yard lay discolored and ugly, gray ashpile, rusted cans, spilled lignite, bones. The clinkers that had given them winter footing to privy and stable lay in raised gray wavers across the mud; the strung lariats they had used for lifelines in blizzardy weather had dried out and sagged to the ground. Muck was knee deep down in the corrals by the sod-roofed stable; the whitewashed logs were yellowed at the corners from dogs lifting their legs against them. Sunken drifts around the hay yard were a reminder of how many times the boys had had to shovel out there to keep the calves from walking into the stacks across the top of them. Across the wan and disheveled yard the willows were bare, and beyond them the floodplain hill was brown. The sky was roiled with gray cloud.

Matted, filthy, lifeless, littered, the place of her winter imprisonment was exposed, ugly enough to put gooseflesh up her backbone, and with the carrion smell over all of it. It was like a bad and disgusting wound, infected wire cut or proud flesh or the gangrene of frostbite, with the bandage off. With her packed trunk and her telescope bag and two loaded grain sacks behind her, she stood in the door waiting for Ray to come with the buckboard, and she was sick to be gone.

Yet when he did come, with the boys all slopping through the mud behind him, and they threw her trunk and telescope and bags into the buckboard and tied the tarp down and there was nothing left to do but go, she faced them with a sudden, desolating desire to cry. She laughed, and caught her lower lip under her teeth and bit down hard on it, and went around to shake one hooflike hand after the other, staring into each face in turn and seeing in each something that made it all the harder to say something easy: Goodbye. Red-bearded, black-bearded, gray-bristled, clean-shaven (for her?), two of them with puckered sunken scars on the cheekbones, all of them seedy, matted-haired, weathered and cracked as old lumber left out for years, they looked sheepish, or sober, or cheerful, and said things like, "Well, Molly, have you a nice trip, now," or "See you in Malta maybe." They had been her family. She had looked after them, fed them, patched their clothes, unraveled old socks to knit them new ones, cut their hair, lanced their boils, tended their wounds. Now it was like the gathered-in family parting at the graveside after someone's funeral.

She had begun quite openly to cry. She pulled her cheeks down, opened her mouth, dabbed at her eyes with her knuckles, laughed. "Now you take care," she said. "And come see us, you hear?" Jesse? Rusty? Slip? Buck, when you come I'll fix you a better patch on your pants than that one. Goodbye, Panguingue, you were the best man I had on the coal scuttle. Don't you forget me. Little Horn, I'm *sorry* we ran out of pie fixings. When you come to Malta I'll make you a peach pie a yard across."

She could not have helped speaking their names, as if to name them were to insure their permanence. But she knew that though she might see them, or most of them, when Ray brought the drive in to Malta in July, these were friends who would soon be lost for good. They had already got the word: sweep the range and sell everything—steers, bulls, calves, cows—for whatever it would bring. Put a For Sale sign on the ranch, or simply abandon it. The country had rubbed its lesson in. Like half the outfits between the Milk and the CPR, the T-Down was quitting. As for her, she was quitting first.

She saw Ray slumping, glooming down from the buckboard seat with the reins wrapped around one gloved hand. Dude and Dinger were hip-shot in the harness. As Rusty and Little Horn gave Molly a hand up to climb the wheel, Dude raised his tail and dropped an oaty bundle of dung on the singletree, but she did not even bother to make a face or say something provoked and joking. She was watching Ray, looking right into his gray eyes and his somber dark face and seeing all at once what the winter of disaster had done to him. His cheek, like Ed's and Rusty's, was puckered with frost scars; frost had nibbled at the lobes of his ears; she could see the strain of bone-cracking labor, the bitterness of failure, in the lines from his nose to the corners of his mouth. Making room for her, he did not smile. With her back momentarily to the others, speaking only for him, she said through her tight teeth, "Let's git!"

Promptly—he was always prompt and ready—he plucked whip from whipsocket. The tip snagged on Dinger's haunch, the lurch of the buggy threw her so that she could cling and not have to reveal her face. "Good-bye!" she cried, more into the collar of her mackinaw than to them, throwing the words over her shoulder like a flower or a coin, and tossed her left hand in the air and shook it. The single burst of their voices chopped off into silence. She heard only the grate of the tires in gravel; beside her the wheel poured yellow drip. She concentrated on it, fighting her lips that wanted to blubber.

"This could be bad for a minute," Ray said. She looked up. Obediently she clamped thumb and finger over her nose. To their right, filling half of Frying Pan Flat, was the boneyard, two acres of carcasses scattered where the boys had dragged them after skinning them out when they found them dead in the brush. It did not seem that off there they could smell, for the chinook was blowing out in light airs from the west. But when she let go her nose she smelled it rich and rotten, as if rolled upwind the way water runs upstream in an eddy.

Beside her Ray was silent. The horses were trotting now in the soft sand of the patrol trail. On both sides the willows were gnawed down to stubs, broken and mouthed and gummed off by starving cattle. There was floodwater in the low spots, and the sound of running water under the drifts of every coulee.

Once Ray said, "Harry Wills says a railroad survey's coming right up the Whitemud valley this summer. S'pose that'll mean homesteaders in here, maybe a town."

"I s'pose."

"Make it a little easier when you run out of prunes, if there was a store at Whitemud."

"Well," she said, "we won't be here to run out," and then immediately, as she caught a whiff that gagged her, "Pee-you! Hurry up!"

Ray did not touch up the team. "What for?" he said. "To get to the next one quicker?"

She appraised the surliness of his voice, and judged that some of it was general disgust and some of it was aimed at her. But what did he want? Every time she made a suggestion of some outfit around Malta or Chinook where he might get a job he humped his back and looked impenetrable. What *did* he want? To come back here and take another licking? When there wasn't even a cattle outfit left, except maybe the little ones like the Z-X and the Lazy-S? And where one winter could kill you, as it had just killed the T-Down? She felt like yelling at him, "Look at your face. Look at your hands—you can't open them even halfway for calluses. For what? Maybe three thousand cattle left out of ten thousand, and them skin and bone. Why wouldn't I be glad to get out? Who *cares* if there's a store at Whitemud? You're just like an old bulldog with his teethed clinched in somebody's behind, and it'll take a pry-bar to make you unclinch!" She said nothing; she forced herself to breathe evenly the tainted air.

Floodwater forced them out of the bottoms and up onto the second floodplain. Below them Molly saw the river astonishingly wide, pushing across willow bars and pressing deep into the cutbank bends. She could hear it, when the wheels went quietly—a hushed roar like wind. Cattle were balloonily afloat in the brush where they had died. She saw a brindle longhorn waltz around the deep water of a bend with his legs in the air, and farther on a whiteface that stranded momentarily among flooded rosebushes, and rotated free, and stranded again.

Their bench was cut by a side coulee, and they tipped and rocked down, the rumps of the horses back against the dashboard, Ray's hand on the brake, the shoes screeching mud from the tires. There was brush in the bottom, and stained drifts still unmelted. Their wheels sank in slush, she hung to the seat rail, they righted, the lines cracked across the muscling rumps as the team dug in and lifted them out of the cold, snow-bank breath of the draw. Then abruptly, in a hollow on the right, dead eyeballs stared at her from between spraddled legs, horns and tails and legs were tangled in a starved mass of bone and hide not yet, in that cold bottom, puffing with the gases of decay. They must have been three deep—piled on one another, she supposed, while drifting before some one of the winter's blizzards.

A little later, accosted by a stench so overpowering that she breathed it in deeply as if to sample the worst, she looked to the left and saw a long-horn, its belly blown up ready to pop, hanging by neck and horns from a tight clump of alder and black birch where the snow had left him. She saw the wind make catspaws in the heavy winter hair.

"Jesus," Ray said, "when you find 'em in *trees!*"

His boots, worn and whitened by many wettings, were braced against the dash. From the corner of her eye Molly could see his glove, its wrist-lace open. His wrist looked as wide as a doubletree, the sleeve of his Levi jacket was tight with forearm. The very sight of his strength made her hate the tone of defeat and outrage in his voice. Yet she appraised the tone cunningly, for she did not want him somehow butting his bullhead-ed way back into it. There were better things they could do than break their backs and hearts in a hopeless country a hundred miles from any-where.

With narrowed eyes, caught in an instant vision, she saw the lilac bush-es by the front porch of her father's house, heard the screen door bang behind her brother Charley (screen doors!), saw people passing women in dresses, maybe all going to a picnic or a ballgame down in the park by the river. She passed the front of McCabe's General Store and through the window saw the counters and shelves; dried apples, dried peaches, prunes, tapioca, Karo syrup, everything they had done without for six weeks; and new white-stitched overalls, yellow horsehide gloves, var-nished axe handles, barrels of flour and bags of sugar, shiny boots and workshoes, counters full of calico and flowered voile and crepe de chine and curtain net, whole stacks of flypaper stuck sheet to sheet, jars of pep-permints and striped candy and horehound. . . . She giggled.

"What?" Ray's neck and shoulders were so stiff with muscle that he all but creaked when he turned his head.

"I was just thinking. Remember the night I used our last sugar to make that batch of divinity, and dragged all the boys in after bedtime to eat it?"

"Kind of saved the day," Ray said. "Took the edge off ever'body."

"Kind of left us starving for sugar, too. I can still see them picking up those little bitty dabs of fluff with their fingers like tongs, and stuffing them in among their whiskers and making faces, *yum yum,* and wonder-ing what on earth had got into me."

"Nothing got into you. You was just fed up. We all was."

"Remember when Slip picked up that pincushion I was tatting a cover for, and I got sort of hysterical and asked him if he knew what it was? Remember what he said? 'It a doll piller, ain't it, Molly?' I thought I'd die."

She shook her head angrily. Ray was looking sideward at her in alarm.

She turned her face away and stared down across the water that spread nearly a half-mile wide in the bottoms. Dirty foam and brush circled in the eddies. She saw a slab cave from an almost drowned cutbank and sink bubbling. From where they drove, between the water and the outer slope that rolled up to the high prairie, the Cypress Hills made a snow-patched, tree-darkened dome across the west. The wind came off them mild as milk. Poisoned! she told herself, and dragged it deep into her lungs.

She was aware again of Ray's gray eye. "Hard on you," he said. For some reason he made her mad, as if he were accusing her of bellyaching. She felt how all the time they bumped and rolled along the shoulder of the river valley they had this antagonism between them like a snarl of barbed wire. You couldn't reach out anywhere without running into it. Did he blame her for going home, or what? What did he expect her to do, come along with a whole bunch of men on that roundup, spend six or eight weeks in pants out among the carcasses? And then what?

A high, sharp whicker came downwind. The team chuckled and surged into their collars. Looking ahead, she saw a horse—picketed or hobbled—and a man who leaned on something—rifle?—watching them. "Young Schulz," Ray said, and then here came the dogs, four big bony hounds. The team began to dance. Ray held them in tight and whistled the buggy-whip in the air when the hounds got too close.

Young Schulz, Molly saw as they got closer, was leaning on a shovel, not a rifle. He had dug a trench two or three feet deep and ten or twelve long. He dragged a bare forearm across his forehead under a muskrat cap: a sullen-faced boy with eyes like dirty ice. She supposed he had been living all alone since his father had disappeared. Somehow he made her want to turn her lips inside out. A wild man, worse than an Indian. She had not liked his father and she did not like him.

The hounds below her were sniffing at the wheels and testing the air up in her direction, wagging slow tails. "What've you got, wolves?" Ray asked.

"Coyotes."

"Old ones down there?"

"One, anyway. Chased her in."

"Find any escape holes?"

"One. Plugged it."

"You get 'em the hard way," Ray said. "How've you been doing on wolves?"

The boy said a hard four-letter word, slanted his eyes sideward at Molly in something less than apology—acknowledgment, maybe. "The dogs ain't worth a damn without Puma to kill for 'em. Since he got killed they just catch up with a wolf and run alongside him. I dug out a couple dens."

With his thumb and finger he worked at a pimple under his jaw. The soft wind blew over them, the taint of carrion only a suspicion, perhaps imaginary. The roily sky had begun to break up in patches of blue. Beside Molly felt the solid bump of Ray's shoulder as he twisted to cast a weather eye upward. "Going to be a real spring day," he said. To young Schulz he said, "How far in that burrow go, d'you s'pose?"

"Wouldn't ordinarily go more'n twenty feet or so."

"Need any help diggin'?"

The Schulz boy spat. "Never turn it down."

"Ray . . ." Molly said. But she stopped when she saw his face.

"Been a long time since I helped dig out a coyote," he said. He watched her as if waiting for a reaction. "Been a long time since I did anything for *fun*."

"Oh, go ahead!" she said. "Long as we don't miss that train."

"I guess we can make Maple Creek by noon tomorrow. And you ain't in such a hurry you have to be there sooner, are you?"

She had never heard so much edge in his voice. He looked at her as if he hated her. She turned so as to keep the Schulz boy from seeing her face, and for just a second she and Ray were all alone up there, eye to eye. She laid a hand on his knee. "I don't know what it is," she said. "Honestly I don't. But you better work it off."

Young Schulz went back to his digging while Ray unhitched and looped the tugs and tied the horses to the wheels. Then Ray took the shovel and began to fill the air with clods. He moved more dirt than the Fresno scrapers she had seen grading the railroad back home; he worked as if exercising his muscles after a long layoff, as if spring had fired him up and set him to running. The soil was sandy and came out in clean shovelfuls. The hounds lay back out of range and watched. Ray did not look toward Molly, or say anything to Schulz. He just moved dirt as if dirt was his worst enemy. After a few minutes Molly pulled the buffalo robe out of the buckboard and spread it on the drying prairie. By that time it was getting close to noon. The sun was full out; she felt it warm on her face and hands.

The coyote hole ran along about three feet underground. From where she sat she could look right up the trench, and see the black opening at the bottom when the shovel broke into it. She could imagine the coyotes crammed back at the end of their burrow, hearing the noises and seeing the growing light as their death dug toward them, and no way out, nothing to do but wait.

Young Schulz took the shovel and Ray stood out of the trench, blowing. The violent work seemed to have made him more cheerful. He said to Schulz, when the boy stopped and reached a gloved hand up the hole, "She comes out of there in a hurry she'll run right up their sleeve."

Schulz grunted and resumed his digging. The untroubled sun went over, hanging almost overhead, and an untroubled wind stirred the old grass. Over where the last terrace of the floodplain rolled up to the prairie the first gopher of the season sat up and looked them over. A dog moved, and he disappeared with a flirt of his tail. Ray was rolling his sleeves, whistling loosely between his teeth. His forearms were white, his hands blackened and cracked as the charred ends of sticks. His eyes touched her—speculatively, she thought. She smiled, making a forgiving, kissing motion of her mouth, but all he did in reply was work his eyebrows, and she could not tell what he was thinking.

Young Schulz was poking up the hole with the shovel handle. Crouching in the trench in his muskrat cap, he looked like some digging animal; she half expected him to put his nose into the hole and sniff and then start throwing dirt out between his hind legs.

Then in a single convulsion of movement Schulz rolled sideward. A naked gummed thing of teeth and gray fur shot into sight, scrambled at the edge, and disappeared in a pinwheel of dogs. Molly leaped to the heads of the horses, rearing and wall-eyed and yanking the light buckboard sideways, and with a hand in each bridle steadied them down. Schulz, she saw, was circling the dogs with the shotgun, but the dogs had already done it for him. The roaring and snapping tailed off. Schulz kicked the dogs away and with one quick flash and circle and rip tore the scalp and ears off the coyote. It lay there wet, mauled, bloody, with its pink skull bare—a little dog brutally murdered. One of the hounds came up, sniffed with its neck stretched out, sank its teeth in the coyote's shoulder, dragged it a foot or two.

"Ray . . ." Molly said.

He did not hear her; he was blocking the burrow with the shovel blade while Schulz went over to his horse. The boy came back with a red willow stick seven or eight feet long, forked like a small slingshot at the end. Ray pulled away the shovel and Schulz twisted in the hole with the forked end of the stick. A hard grunt came out of him, and he backed up, pulling the stick from the hole. At the last moment he yanked hard, and a squirm of gray broke free and rolled and was pounced on by the hounds.

This time Ray kicked them aside. He picked up the pup by the tail, and it hung down and kicked its hind legs a little. Schulz was down again, probing the burrow, twisting, probing again, twisting hard.

Again he backed up, working the entangled pup out carefully until it was in the open, and then landing it over his head like a sucker from the river. The pup landed within three feet of the buckboard wheel, and floundered, stunned. In an instant Molly dropped down and smothered it in clothes, hands, arms. There was snarling in her very ear, she was bumped hard, she heard Ray yelling, and then he had her on her feet. From his face, she thought he was going to hit her. Against her middle, held by the scruff and grappled with the other arm, the pup snapped and slavered with needle teeth. She felt the sting of bites on her hands and wrists. The dogs ringed her, ready to jump, kept off by Ray's kicking boot.

"God A'mighty," Ray said, "you want to get yourself killed?"

"I didn't want the dogs to get him."

"No. What are you going to do with him? We'll just have to knock him in the head."

"I'm going to keep him."

"In Malta?"

"Why not?"

He let go his clutch on her arm. "He'll be a cute pup for a month and then he'll be a chicken thief and then somebody'll shoot him."

"At least he'll have a little bit of a life. Get *away*, you dirty, murdering . . . !" She cradled the thudding little body along one arm under her mackinaw, keeping her hold in the scruff with her right hand, and turned herself away from the crowding hounds. "I'm going to tame him," she said. "I don't care what you say."

"Scalp's worth three dollars," Schulz said from the edge of the ditch.

Ray kicked the dogs back. His eyes, ordinarily so cool and gray, looked hot. The digging and the excitement did not seem to have taken the edge off whatever was eating him. He said, "Look, maybe you have to go back home to your folks, but you don't have to take a menagerie along. What are you going to do with him on the train?"

But now it was out. He did blame her. "You think I'm running out on you," she said.

"I just said you can't take a menagerie back to town."

"You said *maybe* I had to go home. Where else would I go? You're going to be on roundup till July. The ranch is going to be sold. Where on earth *would* I go but home?"

"You don't have to stay. You don't have to make me go back to ridin' for some outfit for twenty a month a found."

His dark, battered, scarred face told her to be quiet. Dipping far down in the tight pocket of his Levi's he brought up his snap purse and took from it three silver dollars. Young Schulz, who had been probing the den to see if anything else was there, climbed out of the ditch and took the money in his dirty chapped hand. He gave Molly one cool look with his dirty-ice eyes, scalped the dead pup, picked up shotgun and twisting-stick and shovel, tied them behind the saddle, mounted, whistled at the dogs, and with barely a nod rode off toward the northeastern flank of the Hills. The hounds fanned out ahead of him, running loose and easy. In the silence their departure left behind, a clod broke and rolled into the ditch. A gopher piped somewhere. The wind moved quiet as breathing in the grass.

Molly drew a breath that caught a little—a sigh for their quarreling, for whatever bothered him so deeply that he gloomed and grumped and asked something impossible of her—but when she spoke she spoke around it. "No thanks for your digging."

"He don't know much about living with people."

"He's like everything else in this country, wild and dirty and thankless."

In a minute she would really start feeling sorry for herself. But why not? Did it ever occur to him that since November, when they came across the prairie on their honeymoon in this same buckboard, she had seen exactly one woman, for one day and a night? Did he have any idea how she had felt, a bride for three weeks, when he went out with the boys on late fall roundup and was gone two weeks, through three different blizzards, while she stayed home and didn't know whether he was dead or alive?

"If you mean me," Ray said, "I may be wild and I'm probably dirty, but I ain't thankless, honey." Shamed, she opened her mouth to reply, but he was already turning away to rummage up a strap and a piece of whang leather to make a collar and leash for her pup.

"Are you hungry?" she said to his shoulders.

"Any time."

"I put up some sandwiches."

"O.K."

"Oh, Ray," she said, "let's not crab at each other! Sure I'm glad we're getting out. Is that so awful? I hate to see you killing yourself bucking this hopeless country. But does that mean we have to fight? I thought maybe we could have a picnic like we had coming in, back on that slough where the ducks kept coming in and landing on the ice and skidding end over end. I don't know, it don't hardly seem we've laughed since."

"Well," he said, "it ain't been much of a laughing winter, for a fact." He had cut down a cheekstrap and tied a rawhide thong to it. Carefully she brought out the pup and he buckled the collar around its neck, but when she set it on the ground it backed up to the end of the thong, cringing and showing its naked gums, so that she picked it up again and let it dig along her arm, hunting darkness under her mackinaw.

"Shall we eat here?" Ray said. "Kind of a lot of chewed up coyote around."

"Let's go up on the bench."

"Want to tie the pup in the buckboard?"

"O.K.," he said. "You go on. I'll tie a nosebag on these nags and bring the robe and the lunchbox."

She walked slowly, not to scare the pup, until she was up the little bench and onto the prairie. From up there she could see not only the Cypress Hills across the west, but the valley of the Whitemud breaking out of them, and a big slough, spread by floodwater, and watercourses going both ways out of it, marked by thin willows. Just where the Whitemud emerged from the hills were three white dots—the Mountie post, probably, or the Lazy-S, or both. The sun was surprisingly warm, until she counted up and found that it was May 8. It ought to be warm.

Ray brought the buffalo robe and spread it, and she sat down. One-handed because she had the thong of the leash wrapped around her palm, she doled out sandwiches and hard-boiled eggs. Ray popped a whole egg in his mouth and chewing, pointed. "There goes the South Fork of the Swift Current, out of the slough. The one this side, that little scraggle of willows you can see, empties into the Whitemud. That little slough sits right on the divide and runs both ways. You don't see that very often."

She appraised his tone. He was feeling better. For that matter, so was she. It had turned out a beautiful day, with big fair-weather clouds coasting over. She saw the flooded river bottoms below them, on the left, darken to winter and then sweep bright back to spring again while she could have counted no more than ten. As she moved, the coyote pup clawed and scrambled against her side, and she said, wrinkling her nose in her freckleface smile, "If he started eating me, I wonder if I could keep from yelling? Did you ever read that story about the boy that hid the fox under his clothes and the fox started eating a hole in him and the boy never batted an eye, just let himself be chewed?"

"No, I never heard that one," Ray said. "Don't seem very likely, does it?" He lay back and turned his face, shut-eyed, into the sun. Now and then his hand rose to feed bites of sandwich into his mouth.

"The pup's quieter," Molly said. "I bet he'll tame. I wonder if he'd eat a piece of sandwich?"

"Leave him for a while, I would."

"I guess."

His hand reached over blindly and she put another sandwich into its pincer claws. Chewing, he came up on an elbow; his eyes opened, he stared a long time down into the flooded bottoms and then across toward the slough and the hills. "Soon as the sun comes out, she don't look like the same country, does she?"

Molly said nothing. She watched his nostrils fan in and out as he sniffed. "No smell up here, do you think?" he said. But she heard the direction he was groping in, the regret that could lead, if they did not watch out, to some renewed and futile hope, and she said tartly, "I can smell it, all right."

He sighed. He lay back and closed his eyes. After about three minutes he said, "Boy, what a day, though. I won't get through on the patrol trail goin' back. The ice'll be breakin' up before tonight, at this rate. Did you hear it crackin' and poppin' a minute ago?"

"I didn't hear it."

"Listen."

They were still. She heard the soft wind move in the prairie wool, and beyond it, filling the background, the hushed and hollow noise of the floodwater, sigh of drowned willows, suck of whirlpools, splash and guggle as cutbanks caved, and the steady push and swash and ripple of moving water. Into the soft rush of sound came a muffled report like a tree cracking, or a shot a long way off. "Is that it?" she said. "Is that the ice letting loose?"

"Stick around till tomorrow and you'll see that whole damned channel full of ice."

Another shadow from one of the big flat-bottomed clouds chilled across them and passed. Ray said into the air, "Harry Willis said this railroad survey will go right through to Medicine Hat. Open up this whole country."

Now she sat very still, stroking the soft bulge of the pup through the cloth.

"Probably mean a town at Whitemud."

"You told me."

"With a store that close we couldn't get quite so snowed in as we did this winter."

Molly said nothing, because she dared not. They were a couple that, like the slough spread out northwest of them, flowed two ways, he to this wild range, she back to town and friends and family. And yet in the thaw of one bright day, their last together up here north of the Line, she teetered. She feared the softening that could start her draining toward his side.

"Molly," Ray said, and made her look at him. She saw him as the country and the winter had left him, weathered and scarred. His eyes were gray and steady, marksman's eyes.

She made a wordless sound that sounded in her own ears almost a groan. "You want awful bad to stay," she said.

His tong fingers plucked a strand of grass, he bit it between his teeth, his head went slowly up and down.

"But how?" she said. "Do you want to strike the Z-X for a job, or the Lazy-S, or somebody? Do you want to open a store in Whitemud for when the railroad comes through, or what?"

"Haven't you figured that out yet?" he said. "Kept waitin' for you to see it. I want to buy the T-Down."

"You *what*?"

"I want us to buy the T-Down and make her go."

She felt that she went all to pieces. She laughed. She threw her hands around so that the pup scrambled and clawed at her side. "Ray Henry," she said, "you're as crazy as a bedbug. Even if it made any sense, which it doesn't, where'd we get the money?"

"Borrow it."

"Go in debt to stay up *here*?"

"Molly," he said, and she heard the slow gather of determination in his voice, "when else could we pick up cattle for twenty dollars a head with sucking calves thrown in? When else could we get a whole ranch layout for a few hundred bucks? That Goodnight herd we were running was the best herd in Canada, maybe anywhere. This spring roundup we could take our pick of what's left, including bulls, and put our brand on 'em and turn 'em into summer range and drive everything else to Malta. We wouldn't want more than three-four hundred head. We can swing that much, and we can cut enough hay to bring that many through even a winter like this last one."

She watched him; her eyes groped and slipped. He said, "We're never goin' to have another chance like this as long as we live. This country's goin' to change; there'll be homesteaders in here soon as the railroad comes. Towns, stores, what you've been missin'. Women folks. And we can sit out here on the Whitemud with good hay and good range and just make this God darned country holler uncle."

"How long?" she said. "How long have you been thinking this way?"

"Since we got John's letter."

"You never said anything."

"I kept waitin' for you to get the idea yourself. But you were hell bent to get out."

She escaped his eyes, looked down, shifted carefully to accommodate the wild thing snuggled in the darkness at her waist, and as she moved, her foot scuffed up the scalloped felt edge of the buffalo robe. By her toe was a half-crushed crocus, palely lavender, a thing so tender and unbelievable in the waste of brown grass under the great pour of sky that she cried out, "Why, good land, look at that!"—taking advantage of it both as discovery and diversion.

"Crocus?" Ray said, bending. "Don't take long, once the snow goes."

It lay in her palm, a thing lucky as a four-leaf clover, and as if it had had some effect in clearing her sight, Molly looked down the south-facing slope and saw it tinged with faintest green. She put the crocus to her nose, but smelled only a mild freshness, an odor no more showy than that of grass. But maybe enough to cover the scent of carrion.

Her eyes came up and found Ray's watching her steadily. "You think we could do it," she said.

"I know we could."

"It's a funny time to start talking that way, when I'm on my way out."

"You don't have to stay out."

Sniffing the crocus, she put her right hand under the mackinaw until her fingers touched fur. The pup stiffened but did not turn or snap. She moved her fingers softly along his back, willing him tame. For some reason she felt as if she might burst out crying.

"Haven't you got any ambition to be the first white woman in Five hundred miles?" Ray said.

Past and below him, three or four miles off, she saw the great slough darken under a driving cloud shadow and then brighten to a blue that danced with little wind-whipped waves. She wondered what happened to the ice in the slough like that, whether it went on down the little flooded creeks to add to the jams in the Whitemud and Swift Current, or whether it just rose to the surface and gradually melted there. She didn't suppose it would be spectacular like the break-up in the river.

"Mumma and Dad would think we'd lost our minds," she said. "How much would we have to borrow?"

"Maybe six or eight thousand."

"Oh, Lord!" She contemplated the sum, a burden of debt heavy enough to pin them down for life. She remembered the winter, six months of unremitting slavery and imprisonment. She lifted the crocus and laid it against Ray's dark scarred cheek.

"You should never wear lavender," she said, and giggled at the very idea, and let her eyes come up to his and stared at him, sick and scared. "All right," she said. "If that's what you want."

THE GIRL IN THE HUMBERT

Mari Sandoz

I T WAS THE CITY NEPHEWS who first saw smoke in the Humbert. They came galloping home through the oppressive spring heat, bouncing together on the barebacked old pinto, Down's short arms tight around the middle of his nine-year-old brother before him. Together they kicked the old mare at every jump, the reins flapping loose.

When they saw their tall, browned uncle at the ranch-yard gate, the boys let the pinto drop into a walk. Sliding off on the far side, they started reluctantly toward him. But almost at once their eager young legs betrayed them, their legs and the need to tell the news before they were scolded for running the old mare.

"Somebody's—somebody's in the old house!" Down shouted, to beat his brother in the telling.

"There's smoke coming from the chimney in the Humbert," Dickup said, deliberately explicit.

But Jack Pulmer only snapped Down's transparent ear and picked beggar lice from the older boy's tousled hair. So his two young cowpunchers had been seeing a whirlwind and the dust it can raise?

"But there's a car—there is," they cried together.

The uncle nodded a little, and thumbed imperatively toward the lathered old mare, standing head down, sides heaving. So the boys fetched clean corn-cobs from a manger and started to rub her down, one on a side, while they watched their fine big uncle swing his empty car away through the sandpass.

Jack Pulmer hoped that it was only dust and a whirlwind the boys had seen. The Humbert, apparently never Spurwheel ranch property except by claim of occupation, was his best meadow, its hay essential if he was to hold off foreclosure on the ranch another year. Otherwise it would be the last ending of a long descent since Colonel Pulmer, Jack's grandfather, was killed by Frenchy Humbert, over thirty years ago. Families and times both change and the sons of the ruthless old cowman couldn't keep together much of the empire the old colonel cut from the public domain and held against all settlement until Frenchy appeared.

But the free range pinched out, the days of cheap beef and wild cow towns passed. Five years ago, what was left of the Spurwheel and its mortgages fell to young Jack, who had studied voice instead of ranching. In those five years the colonel's grandson learned about cattle markets and stock diseases and that a frozen bit will burn the mouth of a horse. He learned, too, that he couldn't risk a late April prairie fire from any tin-can tourist, particularly not through the Humbert.

By the time the rancher emerged from the pass no smoke darkened the early green of the meadow, the winter-bleached rushes of the swamp, or the high ridge of hills beyond, tawny in the hot sun. But the windmill at the head of the valley was in gear, the wheel turning slowly, lopsided and awkward as a tumbleweed on the prairie, the water gathering in the reservoir Frenchy threw up years ago. There was a car, too, as the boys had said, and new shingle patches shone yellow on the roof of the old sod house.

At the door Jack Pulmer was faced by a cool-eyed young woman in overalls and striped jersey, a worn rifle in her hand. Without greeting, she listened to what he had to say over the gray cowman's hat in his hand.

"No," she told him, when he was done. "I do not think I would be more comfortable at the Spurwheel ranch house."

When he attempted a little firmness, she let her palm slide down to the trigger guard of the rifle and pointed out that she was not trespassing here. She was Arille Hombiert, *h* and *t* silent, please, and she happened to own this place he called the Humbert.

So there was nothing for the young rancher to do but to go, heading away toward the county seat to check up on the claims of this girl with the name something like Frenchy's. She couldn't be much over twenty, slim as September bluestem, with hair bright and free as its ripening seed. And on the sill of the window beside her was a small statuette, a mule-deer doe carved from some light-colored wood, the head delicate and shy, the wide ears alert. Alone, poised for flight, the little animal stood silvery pale against the full-drawn curtain of solid black.

At the courthouse Jack Pulmer discovered that Frenchy's name was really Hombiert and that the girl's title to the deserted meadow was as solid as the earth from which the old sod house grew. So went the Spurwheel's last bit of free grass and left the young rancher owing several thousand dollars in back rent to a cool-eyed girl named Arille, granddaughter of a murderer.

But because he had to know what his chances of leasing this year's hay were, he came back through the low-clouded dusk by way of the Humbert. The soddy was a dark blur beside the road, with no ray of light anywhere. Yet somebody seemed to be working at the old outside chimney, somebody who stood against the blackness of the earthen wall until the car was past.

Around midnight the drizzle turned to a light, rattling sleet. Jack Pulmer drew on his sheepskin and went out to throw the gates of the winter pasture, where a few of the older cows, smelling snow, were already breaking through and bawling for their calves to follow them to the corrals. When he came in, the ground was covered, soft-cushioned and silent under his boots.

By morning the wind was up, the air thick and white and sharp with driving snow that shut in the ranch house all around. The two boys ran for the door, incredulous and excited. But the great-aunt who cared for them was a sister of the old colonel's, and they got no farther than the windows.

Three days later the sun was out, the long drifts mushing under the feet of bawling cattle, just right for snow forts. The old aunt sent the boys out, even though she had brought them West to recover from scarlet fever while their mother, not a Pulmer, got a summer's rest.

On his way back from the north range, his sorrel horse dark with snow water to the flanks, Jack Pulmer cut through the Humbert. But the storm hadn't discouraged the pale-skinned Eastern girl. She was out in sunglasses and boots, shooting at a soup can on a gatepost, the bullets well bunched in the center.

"This snow'll be flooding your hay land," the rancher called from the road.

"I suspect it's been flooded before," the girl replied, her teeth white and derisive in her tanning face.

But the man had to have the hay secure, and so he swung a leg over the horn and dickered. The girl from the Humbert was fair enough:

Standing hay at the going price, to be measured and paid for after stacking. And before the rancher could unlimber his leg from the horn, the girl was gone through the door of the soddy, leaving only her tracks to show that anyone lived there—firm tracks, some large and deep, as though she had worn big overshoes and carried a heavy load.

As soon as the dark velvet of the earth pushed up wet between the shrinking drifts, Dickup and Down got the old pinto out. They had to see what the storm did to their swamp and the open water in its center, where their uncle had a duck boat they might hope to reach along in July. Jack Pulmer knew the boys shouldn't be playing in the Humbert, no matter how much they liked the chattering ducks along the rising water edge, the flooding muskrat houses, the acres of dead rushes still under snow. But the old aunt was down with a bilious attack and so the man slapped the bony hip of the pinto and let them go.

"Tie your horse solid to a hackberry tree on the slope or you'll be a couple cowpunchers hoofing it in. And don't go near the soddy."

Promising everything, the boys got away. They kicked the old mare and yelled, "Yip-pi!" but hung on tight, Dickup holding the reins close, with both hands buried in the mane, Down's arms gripping his brother's middle. They remembered from the day they got their nicknames, the first time they tried the pinto. Dick had pushed Don up and climbed on behind, the reins hanging loose. The old mare dropped her head, kicked up her heels high and both boys slid off over her ears.

"It's Dickup behind and his brother Down in front!" old Pete roared. When the smaller boy began to cry, the chore man stopped. "Why, sa-ay, all a them old-timers had nicknames—like Lame Johnny an' Fly Speck Billy," he complained.

After that it was all right, with Dickup sitting in front, to pull on the reins, Down hanging on behind, the old pinto plodding along with half-closed eyes.

In the Humbert, summer came hard upon the storm, the greening swamp of evening alive with the soft quack of ducks, the late song of blackbirds and the croak of the awakening frogs. As the noise swelled into night, a thin, white old man often slipped out to sit beside the girl. It was old Frenchy, free after ten years of solitary darkness for successive attempts at prison break and twenty years of darkness by choice when his urge to freedom was stilled at last. In those years he went back to the old, old craft of his people, wood carving. With a knife improvised from a broken hinge, and pieces of his plank bunk for material, he formed little wooden statuettes, mostly small, wild, free things—a saucy prairie dog poised at the mouth of his hole, a young gray wolf trying his voice against the sky, the wide-eared doe on the window sill in the Humbert. All this grew up in darkness, by touch, with the simplicity of line that pleased the fingertips, mass that satisfied the palm.

Free now, and back on his homestead, he returned to his earlier craft, the soil, and when powdery dusk filled the valley and the swamp song began he sat upon the doorstep with his rifle beside him. Sometimes he talked a little to his granddaughter, of plants and weather and earth, with slow, spare words, for speech, too, was almost lost to him in those long years of silence.

In the darkness he chopped up the sod of his old garden plot that the girl hired rebroken. With hoe and rake he worked the soil into a fine seed bed, smooth as any done by light of day, and level for irrigation from the old reservoir. Later he crept along the sprouting rows of green, thinning, transplanting, weeding. He did all these things in darkness, in paths his feet remembered, within the bonds of long, long habit.

And in the meantime he taught his granddaughter to shoot the old rifle, for, to his light-blinded eyes, the Spurwheel ranch over the hill was unchanged, and a settler's risk as great as ever.

One cloudy afternoon the boys came riding home just ahead of a rain. They had a little mud turtle, moss-backed, not as big as a saucer, in Dickup's handkerchief, held safely by the corners. They had news too. There had been hammering all day in the Humbert, somebody on the roof, and the house looking different.

Jack Pulmer poked the wet, soiled handkerchief with a finger. "Hadn't you better keep to your livestock, and not be bothering strangers?"

"Yes, uncle," the boys said together, dutifully. Holding the turtle away from them, the claws coming through the cloth like thorns, they went to turn the old mare out to grass. Jack Pulmer watched them go, saw their heads come together, their faces turn slyly back to look at him. Then they started to run, kicking up like colts.

The young rancher knew about the night construction of the extension to the soddy and the buttressing of the four corners of the house like a Southwest 'dobe church, stout and lasting. He had heard the girl shingling the new roof all this cool day and he didn't understand how she could plan and do these things, all the things of the Humbert, this spring. He remembered the time he found her planting late sweet corn across the Spurwheel road to the summer pasture. He stopped the car and went over to the girl.

"It is customary in this country to leave public highways passable," he announced, but smilingly.

"So-o?" she inquired politely, driving her spade into the sod, dropping two kernels in the crevice, stepping on it. "I was informed at the courthouse that this is not a laid-out road."

The way back to the car was a long and awkward one, but the young rancher made himself seem unhurried, flattening an uptilted sod or two with his boot, tossing a clod at a ground squirrel. And when he sneaked a look back, Arille Hombiert was far down the row, wasting no time.

It was after this that Jack Pulmer paid her as much of the back rent as he could, using what he had laid aside for the mortgage. Even if the girl had known about the debts, she could not have forgotten the face of Frenchy Hombiert the day she took him from the prison office, his eyes closed as the dark curtains of the soddy. Only his hands seemed alive at all.

So she took the money and then couldn't tell the old man, afraid he would call it a bribe to forget a great wrong, one miserable thousand dollars for each ten years in a black hole—and a lifetime in the habit of darkness.

The girl still shot target every day, but a little shamefacedly now, putting the rifle away among the flowers about the soddy if she saw the boys come plowing through the rushes, or heard the young rancher's car in the sand pass. But in the evenings old Frenchy still liked to touch his fingers to the centered bullet holes in her target. Yes, this Arille, the only one left to him now, was a true Hombiert, like those old ones who came pushing up the Mississippi two hundred years ago.

It was late in June, when the spiderwort lay blue along the slopes of the Humbert, the yellow currants in the brush sweetening to honey, that Dickup and Down reported seeing a man's foot sticking from behind a curtain at the soddy. Now the uncle discovered, too, that there was lemonade with cookies almost every day, and 'Reel, the girl, waving a dish towel to the boys when it was ready.

The uncle ordered them to stay away from people, and took to watching the Humbert from closer. Finally, one windy night, when the sound of his motor was blown behind him, his unexpected headlight shot through the north pass and cut the figure of an old man from the darkness about the reservoir. Blinded eyes closed, the man waited for the light to pass, motionless, gaunt and white as some lightning-charred tree, long standing. But by then young Jack knew that the girl in the Humbert could sing, too, and once he saw her dance on a knoll in the pale light of a summer moon, a wild, beautiful dance. And finally sink, light as cottonwood down, to the sand where he had killed a rattlesnake the summer before.

Now more and more often the old man stopped between the lush green rows to listen, to move swiftly toward his rifle. Then one Sunday an old open car piled full of ranch hands came through the Humbert. Noisily, with a loud "Whoa-o-o!" they jerked to a stop before the soddy. Hard at one another's heels they trooped up between the flower beds to pound on the old door, pretending a great thirst and wanting to borrow a dipper, please, ma'am.

The girl pointed out that the windmill, in plain sight, was running strong.

"It is quite possible to obtain a good drink from the pipe, you know, by just holding your hand against the flow," she explained carefully, as though they were visiting dudes.

The younger of the hands started to talk up to this pretty girl, but the others nudged their ribs, motioning to Frenchy's old rifle standing in the hollyhocks beside the door, ready at her hand. Silenced, the men fell back and hustled off toward the mill. Pretending to drink, they wiped their mouths and then drove away, the backs of their necks red above the clean work shirts.

When the car was gone, Frenchy began to talk from the darkness of his bunk. "Once more they come," he said slowly, painfully. "Hired men smelling out. We better carry automatics, plenty of shells."

In the dusk of the curtained soddy Arille brought pen and ink, but almost at once the old man started again, weary, defeated. "I don't know— maybe we better get out."

At this his granddaughter stopped, her hands tense. "You mean let them drive us away? No!"

So the guns came. They really sagged the pocket very little and fitted the palm as well as the little wooden statuettes.

Late one evening the Spurwheel hay crew moved into the Humbert, creeping through the pass like a long worm, the tall stacker first, then the mowers, the rakes and the sweeps. It was hard to explain their coming to the old settler, but he knew they must have money, and so he gave in to Arille. For two weeks the humming mowers swung around the meadow, the rakes rolled the new hay into windrows close-ribbed as corduroy and the groaning stacker threw it high. All these days Frenchy sat stiff and awake on his bunk, his rifle across his knees.

But no one came near the soddy, the cold stream of the windmill or the wide patch of watermelons ripening. Not even the two boys, who followed their uncle's sickle bar as he led the mowers, or rode the piles of hay he swept in from the far ends of the meadow.

When the valley was friendly once more, the rancher drew his horse up before the girl, waist deep in her moon poppies, stringing the finest blooms for seed. He had brought the check for the hay, with a notation of his measurements.

"I can't say anything definite about next year," he told her regretfully, "but for this year I'm grateful—"

Without finishing he touched the sorrel into a lope, and for once the girl from the Humbert stood to look after him, the white slip of paper blowing in her hand.

The day of the rodeo and county fair in late August, Arille came into town early to deliver her melons, early cabbage, wild plums and green wild grapes for jelly to the stores. She had hoped to be away before ten and the packing crowd, but at eight the little town was already jammed, its one traffic light and the sweating deputy marshals lost in the honking, the shoutings and the dust. Only the Indians, painted, feathered, in bead-and-scalp-trimmed shirts for the dance in the square, got through the crowd—the Indians and the few grizzled old cowmen, thick-shouldered and heavy-hipped now, driving their cars as they once spurred mustang cow ponies through the border towns on pay day.

When Arille came out of the last store, her errands done, Jack Pulmer stood at her running board, waiting. The girl was in dull blue, soft as fall asters against a far hill. The man had never seen her so fragile and lovely, so far from anything like shingle laying, or target shooting with a rifle that had killed a man. He had never seen her in a dress.

"Not going home so soon?" he asked, making talk.

Yes, she was.

"But it isn't much after noon, and there's the rodeo and—well, I was hoping you'd see it with me," he trailed off, without confidence as the girl turned the car switch and moved her foot toward the starter.

But she really ought to stay, he urged, have a bite at the barbecue pit, see the bronco busting, not like the show business, with chutes and only ten seconds to ride. This was wild horses, eared down, saddled, the blindfold jerked away and the whole world wide open for man and horse to fight it out. He was alone, the boys chasing off after old Pete, who'd bulldogged some mean steers in his day. And besides, it might be hours before she could get her car out.

As he talked the girl considered the young cowman, saw that the sweep of his cheek had gaunted much this summer, his jaw line leaned, his mouth thinned. But his shoulders were still square as good oak beams, his fingers straight-boned and true. And when she finally had to meet the grave brown of his eyes, she jerked the key from the lock.

"For an hour," she agreed.

Together they climbed over bumpers, slipped between running boards and were lost in the packed mass at the intersection. And everywhere around them mouths opened to exclaim above the noise, arms lifted to point them out. A Pulmer and a Humbert together!

"If you want to back out—" the man whispered to the girl. But Arille Hombiert looked straight before her, pushing on as though through a deep tangle of brush or rushes noisy in the wind.

Suddenly the center lane of cars began to move, making way for the high-school band in blue-and-white, marching double file, led by a red-headed girl in a towering white shako. The crowd broke from the street and the barbecue pit, following toward the fairgrounds; past pine booths selling red hamburgers, chances at pillow tops or looks at the headless woman, the petrified man or Popeye; past bingo stands and the agricultural exhibits to the weathered old grandstand. Jack Pulmer stuck a note for Pete in a crack in the Spurwheel section and took Arille away from the gawking crowd toward the grassy oval inside the race track. At the gate they passed a slim-hipped youth twirling a loop about himself, stepping daintily in and out as he sang in a tuneless monotone for the grandstand:

"I'm a kissin', cussin' son of a gun,
I'm the kid from Powder River."

"Face-Powder River, N. Y.," Arille laughed, inanely, and the rancher knew how deep the looks, the pointing out, the talk had gone. He tried to pretend too. Yes, the singing kid was an import all right, but with top contest money only twenty-five dollars, the riders out here in the oval were fresh off the range hereabouts.

They did look authentic, with their wind-burnt faces, their easy levis, standing around licking cigarettes and considering a blindfolded smoke roan. The wild horse was sagging groundward under the saddle leather, puffing himself against the tightening cinch, dust rolling before his stubborn nose.

Now the rider, a lanky, weather-beaten old cow hand from the Spurwheel, tucked in his plaid shirt and climbed awkwardly to the saddle. The hazers pulled in closer, the blind was jerked away and the sky opened.

"Ride 'im, Stovepipe!" somebody yelled from the crowd.

When three or four straight high bucks and stiff-legged landings showed no daylight between the rider and his saddle, the horse stopped. Then suddenly he shot ahead, bucking, swapping ends, spinning, sunfishing, bellowing out over the dusty plain.

The crowd was up. "Whoopee, listen at him bawl!"

The rider's teeth still gleamed in his dark face, his old hat pounding the dusty withers, his spurred heels raking. Finally the smoke roan quieted, hanging his head sullenly, swaying lower and lower, his sunken flanks heaving, his wide nostrils bloody.

"He's done! You got him licked, Stovepipe!" the crowd yelled. But over them all old Pete roared out a warning. "Watch 'im, cowboy, watch 'im!"

Pete was right. Already the horse was gathering himself into a knot. Then his forefeet snapped out, up. The riders stumbled back, their cigarettes slipping from their open lips. The hazers spurred forward. A moment the horse and rider teetered, then, with a whinny wild as a scream, the smoke roan went over backward, shaking the earth.

A groan swept the grandstand. Arille's hand clutched the rancher's arm. But old Stovepipe was free. Coolly he had waited to slide beyond the crushing horn until the last possible moment, ready now to fall back into the saddle as swiftly. But the smoke roan was done. The taut hide rippled a little, a hind foot straightened.

From a gateway a tractor came coughing, swinging around to drag the horse aside. But the girl from the Humbert had seen enough, was hurrying away, the young rancher beside her. On the way out the boys came running, leaving Pete behind. Little Down buried his face in the blue of the girl's dress. "Oh, 'Reel, it's dead! The poor horse is dead!" he sobbed, while Dickup stood close to his uncle's hand, white-faced and silent.

But before the next saddle was on, the boys were impatient to find Pete again, to see the bulldogging, the wild-cow milking, the Indian races. So the girl sent the rancher back with them and went to her car alone.

That night she sat late in the dim light of the new moon, watching her grandfather's bent back among the tomatoes, his head up at the slightest sound that was unusual. Later she listened to his sure hands move over his supper tray in the darkness, stop at the far rise of a little wind and move again when it was past.

The next day the rancher from the Spurwheel found the road past the soddy posted with No Trespassing signs.

Now at last he had to go to the court records of the trial of Frenchy. It was not the story of a lawless invader he had heard from his father, but a story of long persecution of a lone settler, ending in a gate thrown back, a herd of Pulmer cattle eating his corn and garden. When he took them up for damages, men came creeping through the dusk to turn them out. Frenchy, watching, fired over their heads. When a bullet from the buck-brush grazed his arm, he fired point-blank into the stream of red still on his retina and got Colonel Pulmer through the chest. For this he was given ten years for manslaughter and dragged away.

Slowly Jack Pulmer closed the courthouse door and plodded across the street to his car, his boots heavy as iron in the dust.

All through the drought of August, thunderheads had piled high. Lightning flashed rose-red through the clouds; thunder shook the earth, a few drops of rain fell and the wind blew the storm away. In the meantime the prairie was browning, the swamp in the Humbert drying up. The day after the rodeo, Dickup and Down came home shouting they could walk into the very middle, where the boat was, without getting their shoes muddy, hardly. And now their uncle wouldn't let them go back, not with all their pleading that they could be finding a lot of shells for their collection, that next week it would be town and school again.

The rancher was firm until the old aunt had to be taken to the doctor for her gall bladder and he was busy culling stock for shipment. So he let the boys make one more trip to the swamp, just one more, and no going near anybody. The boys nodded and, with their lunch in their pockets, rode away into the hot, quiet morning.

Around noon a little cloud like a fluff of dandelion started at the zenith and spread white and high over the east, dark olive underneath. A bolt or two of lightning fell, thunder rolled. Then the wind came up and blew the smell of ozone away.

Half an hour later a shouting puncher spurred through the dust and bawling cattle to Jack Pulmer. His arm in the air, he pointed off into the east, toward the Humbert, where white smoke billowed up, twisted into yellow, blue and black, and rolled away over the hills.

Letting the cattle spread, the hands whirled their horses toward the Spurwheel. Under pressure of his knee, Jack's sorrel shot ahead for the Humbert, three miles away, while already dark specks moved in over the far hills—fire fighters in answer to the smoke signal of the range country.

At the line fence the rancher found three posts splintered and scorched, the grass blackened and from it a widening tongue of burnt prairie spreading away toward the meadow. He spurred his winded horse on, to see that the farther swamp was a towering mass of smoke, cut by flames leaping high from the piles of dead rushes, the near end only gray ashes, reddening in the wind. The whole meadow was black, the stackyards smoldering piles, the gardens of Frenchy Hombiert cooked dark as by frost, about the sod house and the car. Otherwise there was nothing—nothing except the old pinto tied to a hackberry far up the slope and jerking to get free.

In the dark soddy Jack found only the shadowy figure of an old man, still clutching his rifle against his enemy, but begging him to find Arille, his Arille, who had run out into the smoke and did not return.

Of the boys he knew nothing, nothing at all.

While the Spurwheel outfit drove hard toward the head fire, Pete, in the ranch car, turned off to find his boss.

"The boys?" he yelled from far off. At sight of the rancher's face he jerked a gun from the car pocket and fired three rapid shots into the air—the old, old, distress signal of the hills. Then Jack slid under the wheel and headed for the narrowest strip of rushes between the meadow and the open place in the center, still veiled in curling heat and thin blue smoke.

Here the rancher leaped from the car, began kicking a path into the swamp. Old Pete jerked him back, pounded out the fire in his clothes as two, three, half a dozen cars drew up, the men out before the wheels stopped rolling. In relays of three they shoveled glowing ashes down the wind, running back to soak their burning clothes, shoveling again, driving a path into the swamp.

Jack Pulmer was the first to break through into the little quarter-acre open space, baked hard, drifted white in wind-blown ashes. There was nothing here, nothing except the boat out in the center, turned upside down, the water-logged bottom smoldering.

And face down under it lay the two boys, Arille between them, holding them safe, her own clothing scorched, her overalls burnt off above her knees.

Carefully Jack lifted the girl, brushing the hair from her soil-streaked face. Pete yanked the boys up. They looked with awed faces at the singed, blackened, sweating men about them, over the ruins of their beloved swamp, at the girl limp in their uncle's arms. Quietly Down began to cry, while Dickup ran at the heels of his uncle. "Is 'Reel," he whispered—"is she—dead?"

Pete pulled him back, sent a hand for a telephone and a doctor by plane and got the rest to the soddy. There Jack Pulmer carried the girl away, the boys hanging to Pete, afraid of this silent, terrible man who was their uncle. Inside, old Frenchy peered from the darkness of his room, squinting as the curtains at the windows were jerked back, his tongue as helpless as his eyes. But his hands were swift and sure as he helped the rancher cut away the burnt shoes, the scorched tatters of the overalls, laying bare the flesh, seared as the girl ran through the burning grass to save the boys of the Spurwheel.

The next morning, when the doctor was gone and the girl lay quiet at last, only half awake, the boys were permitted to see her. They forgot the little wooden animals they had to show her, their uncle's careful cautioning, in their excitement to tell their news. That dust cloud 'Reel had seen had been a fire, a terrible fire. "All the swamp burned up while we were hid under the boat," they cried together. "Even the grass."

Then suddenly they saw that the girl's face was very white and drawn, sick-looking, and remembering the plane and the doctor, they were quiet, afraid again. But the old man behind them spoke. Yes, the grass was gone, but it would come again.

"Already it is growing at the roots, finer, greener—"

With the boys pulling at him to show them, he started to the door. A moment he hesitated there, to look back to his Arille and this grandson of Colonel Pulmer. Then, still squinting, old Frenchy stepped out into the sunlight for the first time in thirty years, to show two small boys the grass growing new in the Humbert.

OPEN
WINTER

H. L. Davis

T HE DRYING EAST WIND, which always brought hard luck to Eastern
Oregon at whatever season it blew, had combed down the
plateau grasslands through so much of the winter that it was
hard to see any sign of grass ever having grown on them. Even though
March had come, it still blew, drying the ground deep, shrinking the
watercourses, beating back the clouds that might have delivered rain, and
grinding coarse dust against the fifty-odd head of work horses that Pop
Apling, with young Beech Cartwright helping, had brought down from his
homestead to turn back into their home pasture while there was still
something left of them.

The two men, one past sixty and the other around sixteen, shouldered
the horses through the gate of the home pasture about dark, with lights
beginning to shine out from the little freighting town across Three Notch
Valley, and then they rode for the ranch house, knowing even before they
drew up outside the yard that they had picked the wrong time to come.
The house was too dark, and the corrals and outbuildings too still, for a
place that anybody lived in.

There were sounds, but they were of shingles flapping in the wind, a
windmill running loose and sucking noisily at a well that it had already
pumped empty, a door that kept banging shut and dragging open again.
The haystacks were gone, the stackyard fence had dwindled to a few
naked posts, and the entire pasture was as bare and as hard as a floor all
the way down into the valley.

The prospect looked so hopeless that the herd horses refused even to
explore it, and merely stood with their tails turned to the wind, waiting to
see what was to happen to them next.

Old Apling went poking inside the house, thinking somebody might have left a note or that the men might have run down to the saloon in town for an hour or two. He came back, having used up all his matches and stopped the door from banging, and said the place appeared to have been handed back to the Government, or maybe the mortgage company.

"You can trust old Ream Gervais not to be any place where anybody wants him," Beech said. He had hired out to herd for Ream Gervais over the winter. That entitled him to be more critical than old Apling, who had merely contracted to supply the horse herd with feed and pasture for the season at so much per head. "Well, my job was to help herd these steeds while you had 'em, and to help deliver 'em back when you got through with 'em, and here they are. I've put in a week on 'em that I won't ever git paid for, and it won't help anything to set around and watch 'em try to live on fence pickets. Let's git out."

Old Apling looked at the huddle of horses, at the naked slope with a glimmer of light still on it, and at the lights of the town twinkling in the wind. He said it wasn't his place to tell any man what to do, but that he wouldn't feel quite right to dump the horses and leave.

"I agreed to see that they got delivered back here, and I'd feel better about it if I could locate somebody to deliver 'em to" he said. "I'd like to ride across to town yonder, and see if there ain't somebody that knows something about 'em. You could hold 'em together here till I git back. We ought to look the fences over before we pull out, and you can wait here as well as anywhere else."

"I can't, but go ahead," Beech said. "I don't like to have 'em stand around and look at me when I can't do anything to help 'em out. They'd have been better off if we'd turned 'em out of your homestead and let 'em run loose on the country. There was more grass up there than there is here."

"There wasn't enough to feed 'em, and I'd have had all my neighbors down on me for it," old Apling said. "You'll find out one of these days that if a man aims to live in this world he's got to git along with the people in it. I'd start a fire and thaw out a little and git that pack horse unloaded, if I was you."

He rode down the slope, leaning into the wind to ease the drag of the wind on his tired horse. Beech heard the sound of the road gate being let down and put up again, the beat of hoofs in the hard road, and then nothing but the noises around him as the wind went through its usual process of easing down for the night to make room for the frost. Loose boards settled into place, the windmill clacked to a stop and began to drip water into a puddle, and the herd horses shifted around facing Beech, as if anxious not to miss anything he did.

He pulled off some fence pickets and built a fire, unsaddled his pony and unloaded the pack horse, and got out what was left of a sack of grain and fed them both, standing the herd horses off with a fence picket until they had finished eating.

That was strictly fair, for the pack horse and the saddle pony had worked harder and carried more weight than any of the herd animals, and the grain was little enough to even them up for it. Nevertheless, he felt mean at having to club animals away from food when they were hungry, and they crowded back and eyed the grain sack so wistfully that he carried it inside the yard and stored it down in the root cellar behind the house, so it wouldn't prey on their minds. Then he dumped another armload of fence pickets onto the fire and sat down to wait for old Apling.

The original mistake, he reflected, had been when old Apling took the Gervais horses to feed at the beginning of winter. Contracting to feed them had been well enough, for he had nursed up a stand of bunch grass on his homestead that would have carried an ordinary pack of horses with only a little extra feeding to help out in the roughest weather. But the Gervais horses were all big harness stock, they had pulled in half starved, and they had taken not much over three weeks to clean off the pasture that old Apling had expected would last them at least two months. Nobody would have blamed him for backing out on his agreement then, since he had only undertaken to feed the horses, not to treat them for malnutrition.

Beech wanted him to back out of it, but he refused to, said the stockmen had enough troubles without having that added to them, and started feeding out his hay and insisting that the dry wind couldn't possibly keep up much longer, because it wasn't in Nature.

By the time it became clear that Nature had decided to take in a little extra territory, the hay was all fed out, and, since there couldn't be any accommodation about letting the horses starve to death, he consented to throw the contract over and bring them back where they belonged.

The trouble with most of old Apling's efforts to be accommodating was that they did nobody any good. His neighbors would have been spared all their uneasiness if he had never brought in the horses to begin with. Gervais wouldn't have been any worse off, since he stood to lose them anyway; the horses could have starved to death as gracefully in November as in March, and old Apling would have been ahead a great deal of carefully accumulated bunch grass and two big stacks of extortionately valuable hay. Nobody had gained by his chivalrousness; he had lost by it, and yet he liked it so well that he couldn't stand to leave the horses until he had raked the country for somebody to hand the worthless brutes over to.

Beech fed sticks into the fire and felt out of patience with a man who could stick to his mistakes even after he had been cleaned out by them. He heard the road gate open and shut, and he knew by the draggy-sounding plod of old Apling's horse that the news from town was going to be bad.

Old Apling rode past the fire and over to the picket fence, got off as if he was trying to make it last, tied his horse carefully as if he expected the knot to last a month, and unsaddled and did up his latigo and folded his saddle blanket as if he was fixing them to put in a show window. He remarked that his horse had been given a bait of grain in town and wouldn't need feeding again, and then he began to work down to what he had found out.

"If you think things look bad along this road, you ought to see that town," he said. "All the sheep gone and all the ranches deserted and no trade to run on and their water threatenin' to give out. They've got a little herd of milk cows that they keep up for their children, and to hear 'em talk you'd think it was an ammunition supply that they expected to stand off hostile Indians with. They said Gervais pulled out of here around a month ago. All his men quit him, so he bunched his sheep and took 'em down to the railroad, where he could ship in hay for 'em. Sheep will be a price this year, and you won't be able to buy a lamb for under twelve dollars except at a fire sale. Horses ain't in much demand. There's been a lot of 'em turned out wild, and everybody wants to git rid of 'em."

"I didn't drive this bunch of pelters any eighty miles against the wind to git a market report," Beech said. "You didn't find anybody to turn 'em over to, and Gervais didn't leave any word about what he wanted done with 'em. You've probably got it figured out that you ought to trail 'em a hundred and eighty miles to the railroad, so his feelings won't be hurt, and you're probably tryin' to study how you can work me in on it, and you might as well save your time. I've helped you with your accommoda-

tion jobs long enough. I've quit, and it would have been a whole lot better for you if I'd quit sooner."

Old Apling said he could understand that state of feeling, which didn't
mean that he shared it.

"It wouldn't be as much of a trick to trail down to the railroad as a
man might think," he said, merely to settle a question of fact. "We could-
n't make it by the road in a starve-out year like this, but there's old Indian
trails back on the ridge where any man has got a right to take livestock
whenever he feels like it. Still, as long as you're set against it, I'll meet you
halfway. We'll trail these horses down the ridge to a grass patch where I
used to corral cattle when I was in the business, and we'll leave 'em
there. It'll be enough so they won't starve, and I'll ride on down and noti-
fy Gervais where they are, and you can go where you please. It wouldn't
be fair to do less than that, to my notion."

"Ream Gervais triggered me out of a week's pay," Beech said. "It ain't
much, but he swindled you on that pasture contract too. If you expect me
to trail his broken-down horses ninety miles down this ridge when they
ain't worth anything, you've turned in a poor guess. You'll have to think
of a better argument than that if you aim to gain any ground with me."

"Ream Gervais don't count on this," old Apling said. "What does he
care about these horses, when he ain't even left word what he wants done
with 'em? What counts is you, and I don't have to think up any better
argument, because I've already got one. You may not realize it, but you
and me are responsible for these horses till they're delivered to their
owner, and if we turn 'em loose here to bust fences and overrun that
town and starve to death in the middle of it, we'll land in the pen. It's
against the law to let horses starve to death, did you know that? If you
pull out of here I'll pull out right along with you, and I'll have every man
in that town after you before the week's out. You'll have a chance to git
some action on that pistol of yours, if you're careful."

Beech said he wasn't intimidated by that kind of talk, and threw a couple of handfuls of dirt on the fire, so it wouldn't look so conspicuous. His
pistol was an old single-action relic with its grips tied on with fish line and
no trigger, so that it had to be operated by flipping the hammer. The
spring was weak, so that sometimes it took several flips to get off one shot.
Suggesting that he might use such a thing to stand off any pack of grim-
faced pursuers was about the same as saying that he was simple-minded.
As far as he could see, his stand was entirely sensible, and even humane.

"It ain't that I don't feel sorry for these horses, but they ain't fit to travel," he said. "They wouldn't last twenty miles. I don't see how it's any worse to let 'em stay here than to walk 'em to death down that ridge."

"They make less trouble for people if you keep 'em on the move," old Apling said. "It's something you can't be cinched for in court, and it makes you feel better afterward to know that you tried everything you could. Suit yourself about it, though. I ain't beggin' you to do it. If you'd sooner pull out and stand the consequences, it's you for it. Before you go, what did you do with that grain?"

Beech had half a notion to leave, just to see how much of that dark threatening would come to pass. He decided that it wouldn't be worth it. "I'll help you trail the blamed skates as far as they'll last, if you've got to be childish about it," he said. "I put the grain in a root cellar behind the house, so the rats wouldn't git into it. It looked like the only safe place around here. There was about a half a ton of old sprouted potatoes ricked up in it that didn't look like they'd been bothered for twenty years. They had sprouts on 'em—" He stopped, noticing that old Apling kept staring at him as if something was wrong. "Good Lord, potatoes ain't good for horse feed, are they? They had sprouts on 'em a foot long!"

Old Apling shook his head resignedly and got up. "We wouldn't ever find anything if it wasn't for you," he said. "We wouldn't ever git any good out of it if it wasn't for me, so maybe we make a team. Show me where that root cellar is, and we'll pack them spuds out and spread 'em around so the horses can git started on 'em. We'll git this herd through to grassland yet, and it'll be something you'll never be ashamed of. It ain't everybody your age gits a chance to do a thing like this, and you'll thank me for holdin' you to it before you're through."

II

They climbed up by an Indian trail onto a high stretch of tableland, so stony and scored with rock breaks that nobody had ever tried to cultivate it, but so high that it sometimes caught moisture from the atmosphere that the lower elevations missed. Part of it had been doled out among the Indians as allotment lands, which none of them ever bothered to lay claim to, but the main spread of it belonged to the nation, which was too busy to notice it.

The pasture was thin, though reliable, and it was so scantily watered and so rough and broken that in ordinary years nobody bothered to bring stock onto it. The open winter had spoiled most of that seclusion. There was no part of the trail that didn't have at least a dozen new bed grounds for lambed ewes in plain view, easily picked out of the landscape because of the little white flags stuck up around them to keep sheep from straying out and coyotes from straying in during the night. The sheep were pasturing down the draws out of the wind, where they couldn't be seen. There were no herders visible, not any startling amount of grass, and no water except a mud tank to catch a little spring for one of the camps.

They tried to water the horses in it, but it had taken up the flavor of sheep, so that not a horse in the herd would touch it. It was too near dark to waste time reasoning with them about it, so old Apling headed them down into a long rock break and across it to a tangle of wild cherry and mountain mahogany that lasted for several miles and ended in a grass clearing among some dwarf cottonwoods with a mud puddle in the center of it.

The grass had been grazed over, though not closely, and there were sheep tracks around the puddle that seemed to be fresh, for the horses, after sniffing the water, decided that they could wait a while longer. They spread out to graze, and Beech remarked that he couldn't see where it was any improvement over the ticklegrass homestead.

"The grass may be better, but there ain't as much of it, and the water ain't any good if they won't drink it," he said. "Well, do you intend to leave 'em here, or have you got some wrinkle figured out to make me help trail 'em on down to the railroad?"

Old Apling stood the sarcasm unresistingly. "It would be better to trail 'em to the railroad, now that we've got this far," he said. "I won't ask you to do that much, because it's outside of what you agreed to. This place has changed since I was here last, but we'll make it do, and that water ought to clear up fit to drink before long. You can settle down here for a few days while I ride around and fix it up with the sheep camps to let the horses stay here. We've got to do that, or they're liable to think it's some wild bunch and start shootin' 'em. Somebody's got to stay with 'em, and I can git along with these herders better than you can."

"If you've got any sense, you'll let them sheep outfits alone," Beech said. "They don't like tame horses on this grass any better than they do wild ones, and they won't make any more bones about shootin' 'em if they find out they're in here. It's a hard place to find, and they'll stay close on account of the water, and you'd better pull out and let 'em have it to themselves. That's what I aim to do."

"You've done what you agreed to, and I ain't got any right to hold you any longer," old Apling said. "I wish I could. You're wrong about them sheep outfits. I've got as much right to pasture this ridge as they have, and they know it, and nobody ever lost anything by actin' sociable with people."

"Somebody will before very long," Beech said. "I've got relatives in the sheep business, and I know what they're like. You'll land yourself in trouble, and I don't want to be around when you do it. I'm pullin' out of here in the morning, and if you had any sense you'd pull out along with me."

There were several things that kept Beech from getting much sleep during the night. One was the attachment that the horses showed for his sleeping place; they stuck so close that he could almost feel their breath on him, could hear the soft breaking sound that the grass made as they pulled it, the sound of their swallowing, the jar of the ground under him when one of the horses changed ground, the peaceful regularity of their eating, as if they didn't have to bother about anything so long as they kept old Apling in sight.

Another irritating thing was old Apling's complete freedom from uneasiness. He ought by rights to have felt more worried about the future than Beech did, but he slept, with the hard ground for a bed and his hard saddle for a pillow and the horses almost stepping on him every minute or two, as soundly as if the entire trip had come out exactly to suit him and there was nothing ahead but plain sailing.

His restfulness was so hearty and so unjustifiable that Beech couldn't sleep for feeling indignant about it, and got up and left about daylight to keep from being exposed to any more of it. He left without waking old Apling, because he saw no sense in a leave-taking that would consist merely in repeating his commonsense warnings and having them ignored, and he was so anxious to get clear of the whole layout that he didn't even take along anything to eat. The only thing he took from the pack was his ramshackle old pistol; there was no holster for it, and, in the hope that he might get a chance to use it on a loose quail or prairie chicken, he stowed it in an empty flour sack and hung it on his saddle horn, a good deal like an old squaw heading for the far blue distances with a bundle of diapers.

III

There was never anything recreational about traveling a rock desert at
any season of the year, and the combination of spring gales, winter chilli-
ness and summer drought all striking at once brought it fairly close to
hard punishment. Beech's saddle pony, being jaded at the start with over-
work and underfeeding and no water, broke down in the first couple of
miles, and got so feeble and tottery that Beech had to climb off and lead
him, searching likely-looking thickets all the way down the gully in the
hope of finding some little trickle that he wouldn't be too finicky to drink.

The nearest he came to it was a fair-sized rock sink under some half-
budded cottonwoods that looked, by its dampness and the abundance of
fresh animal tracks around it, as if it might have held water recently, but
of water there was none, and even digging a hole in the center of the
basin failed to fetch a drop.

The work of digging, hill climbing and scrambling through brush piles
raised Beech's appetite so powerfully that he could scarcely hold up, and,
a little above where the gully opened into the flat sagebrush plateau, he
threw away his pride, pistoled himself a jackrabbit, and took it down into
the sagebrush to cook, where his fire wouldn't give away which gully old
Apling was camped in.

Jackrabbit didn't stand high as a food. It was considered an excellent
thing to give men in the last stages of famine, because they weren't likely
to injure themselves by eating too much of it, but for ordinary occasions
it was looked down on, and Beech covered his trail out of the gully and
built his cooking fire in the middle of a high stand of sagebrush, so as not
to be embarrassed by inquisitive visitors.

The meat cooked up strong, as it always did, but he ate what he needed of it, and he was wrapping the remainder in his flour sack to take
along with him when a couple of men rode past, saw his pony, and
turned in to look him over.

They looked him over so closely and with so little concern for his pri-
vacy that he felt insulted before they even spoke.

He studied them less openly, judging by their big gallon canteens that
they were out on some long scout.

One of them was some sort of hired hand, by his looks; he was broad-
faced and gloomy-looking, with a fine white horse, a flower-stamped saddle, an expensive rifle scabbarded under his knee, and a fifteen-dollar

saddle blanket, while his own manly form was set off by a yellow hotel blanket and a ninety-cent pair of overalls.

The other man had on a store suit, a plain black hat, fancy stitched boots, and a white shirt and necktie, and rode a burr-tailed Indian pony and an old wrangling saddle with a loose horn. He carried no weapons in sight, but there was a narrow strap across the lower spread of his necktie which indicated the presence of a shoulder holster somewhere within reach.

He opened the conversation by inquiring where Beech had come from, what his business was, where he was going and why he hadn't taken the county road to go there, and why he had to eat jackrabbit when the country was littered with sheep camps where he could get a decent meal by asking for it?

"I come from the upper country," Beech said, being purposely vague about it. "I'm travelin', and I stopped here because my horse give out. He won't drink out of any place that's had sheep in it, and he's gone short of water till he breaks down easy."

"There's a place corralled in for horses to drink at down at my lower camp," the man said, and studied Beech's pony. "There's no reason for you to bum through the country on jackrabbit in a time like this. My herder can take you down to our water hole and see that you get fed and put to work till you can make a stake for yourself. I'll give you a note. That pony looks like he had Ream Gervais's brand on him. Do you know anything about that herd of old workhorses he's been pasturing around?"

"I don't know anything about him," Beech said, sidestepping the actual question while he thought over the offer of employment. He could have used a stake, but the location didn't strike him favorably. It was too close to old Apling's camp, he could see trouble ahead over the horse herd, and he didn't want to be around when it started. "If you'll direct me how to find your water, I'll ride on down there, but I don't need anybody to go with me, and I don't need any stake. I'm travelin'."

The man said there wasn't anybody so well off that he couldn't use a stake, and that it would be hardly any trouble at all for Beech to get one. "I want you to understand how we're situated around here, so you won't think we're any bunch of stranglers," he said. "You can see what kind of a year this has been, when we have to run lambed ewes in a rock patch like this. We've got five thousand lambs in here that we're trying to bring through, and we've had to fight the blamed wild horses for this pasture since the day we moved in. A horse that ain't worth hell room will eat as much as two dozen sheep worth twenty dollars, with the lambs, so you can see how it figures out. We've got 'em pretty well thinned out, but one of my packers found a trail of a new bunch that came up from around Three Notch within the last day or two, and we don't want them to feel as if we'd neglected them. We'd like to find out where they lit. You wouldn't have any information about 'em?"

"None that would do you any good to know," Beech said. "I know the man with that horse herd, and it ain't any use to let on that I don't, but it wouldn't be any use to try to deal with him. He don't sell out on a man he works for."

"He might be induced to," the man said. "We'll find him anyhow, but I don't like to take too much time to it. Just for instance, now, suppose you knew that pony of yours would have to go thirsty till you gave us a few directions about that horse herd? You'd be stuck here for quite a spell, wouldn't you?"

He was so pleasant about it that it took Beech a full minute to realize that he was being threatened. The heavy-set herder brought that home to him by edging out into a flank position and hoisting his rifle scabbard so it could be reached in a hurry. Beech removed the cooked jackrabbit from his flour sack carefully, a piece at a time, and, with the same mechanical thoughtfulness, brought out his triggerless old pistol, cut down on the pleasant-spoken man, and hauled back on the hammer. He stood there with the pistol poised.

"That herder of yours had better go easy on his rifle," he said, trying to keep his voice from trembling. "This pistol shoots if I don't hold back the hammer, and if he knocks me out I'll have to let go of it. You'd better watch him, if you don't want your tack drove. I won't give you no directions about that horse herd, and this pony of mine won't go thirsty for it, either. Loosen them canteens of yours and let 'em drop on the ground. Drop that rifle scabbard back where it belongs, and unbuckle the straps and let go of it. If either of you tries any funny business, there'll be one of you to pack home, heels first."

The quaver in his voice sounded childish and undignified to him, but it had a more businesslike ring to them than any amount of manly gruffness. The herder unbuckled his rifle scabbard, and they both cast loose their canteen straps, making it last as long as they could while they argued with him, not angrily, but as if he was a dull stripling whom they wanted to save from some foolishness that he was sure to regret. They argued ethics, justice, common sense, his future prospects, and the fact that what he was doing amounted to robbery by force and arms and that it was his first fatal step into a probably unsuccessful career of crime. They worried over him, they explained themselves to him, and they ridiculed him.

They managed to make him feel like several kinds of a fool, and they were so pleasant and concerned about it that they came close to breaking him down. What held him steady was the thought of old Apling waiting up the gully.

"That herder with the horses never sold out on any man, and I won't sell out on him," he said. "You've said your say and I'm tired of holdin' this pistol on cock for you, so move along out of here. Keep to open ground, so I can be sure you're gone, and don't be in too much of a hurry to come back. I've got a lot of things I want to think over, and I want to be let alone while I do it."

IV

He did have some thinking that needed tending to, but he didn't take time for it. When the men were well out of range, he emptied their canteens into his hat and let his pony drink. Then he hung the canteens and the scabbarded rifle on a bush and rode back up the gully where the horse camp was, keeping to shaly ground so as not to leave any tracks. It was harder going up than coming down.

He had turned back from the scene of his run-in with the two sheep-men about noon, and he was still a good two miles from the camp when the sun went down, the wind lulled and the night frost began to bite at him so hard that he dismounted and walked to get warm. That raised his appetite again, and, as if by some special considerateness of Nature, the cottonwoods around him seemed to be alive with jackrabbits heading down into the pitch-dark gully where he had fooled away valuable time trying to find water that morning.

They didn't stimulate his hunger much; for a time they even made him feel less like eating anything. Then his pony gave out and had to rest, and, noticing that the cottonwoods around him were beginning to bud out, he remembered that peeling the bark off in the budding season would fetch out a foamy, sweet-tasting sap which, among children of the plateau country, was considered something of a delicacy.

He cut a blaze on a fair-sized sapling, waited ten minutes or so, and touched his finger to it to see how much sap had accumulated. None had; the blaze was moist to his touch, but scarcely more so than when he had whittled it.

It wasn't important enough to do any bothering about, and yet a whole set of observed things began to draw together in his mind and form themselves into an explanation of something he had puzzled over: the fresh animal tracks he had seen around the rock sink when there wasn't any water; the rabbits going down into the gully; the cotton-woods in which the sap rose enough during the day to produce buds and got driven back at night when the frost set in. During the day, the cottonwoods had drawn the water out of the ground for themselves; at night they stopped drawing it, and it drained out into the rock sink for the rabbits.

It all worked out so simply that he led his pony down into the gully to see how much there was in it, and, losing his footing on the steep slope, coasted down into the rock sink in the dark and landed in water and thin mud up to his knees. He led his pony down into it to drink which seemed little enough to get back for the time he had fooled away on it, and then he headed for the horse camp, which was all too easily discernible by the plume of smoke rising, white and ostentatious, against the dark sky from old Apling's campfire.

He made the same kind of entrance that old Apling usually affected when bringing some important item of news. He rode past the campfire and pulled up at a tree, got off deliberately, knocked an accumulation of dead twigs from his hat, took off his saddle and bridle and balanced them painstakingly in the tree fork, and said it was affecting to see how wide-spread the shortage of pasture was.

"It generally is," old Apling said. "I had a kind of a notion you'd be back after you'd had time to study things over. I suppose you got into some kind of a rumpus with some of them sheep outfits. What was it? Couldn't you git along with them, or couldn't they hit it off with you?"

"There wasn't any trouble between them and me," Beech said. "The only point we had words over was you. They wanted to know where you was camped, so they could shoot you up, and I didn't think it was right to tell 'em. I had to put a gun on a couple of 'em before they'd believe I meant business, and that was all there was to it. They're out after you now, and they can see the smoke of this fire of yours for twenty miles, so they ought to be along any time now. I thought I'd come back and see you work your sociability on 'em."

"You probably kicked up a squabble with 'em yourself," old Apling said. He looked a little uneasy. "You talked right up to 'em, I'll bet, and slapped their noses with your hat to show 'em that they couldn't run over you. Well, what's done is done. You did come back, and maybe they'd have jumped us anyway. There ain't much that we can do. The horses have got to have water before they can travel, and they won't touch that sheep. It ain't cleared up a particle."

"You can put that fire out, not but what the whole country has probably seen the smoke from it already," Beech said. "If you've got to tag after these horses, you can run 'em off down the draw and keep 'em to the brush where they won't leave a trail. There's some young cottonwood bark that they can eat if they have to, and there's water in a rock sink under some big cottonwood trees. I'll stay here and hold off anybody that shows up, so you'll have time to git your tracks covered."

Old Apling went over and untied the flour-sacked pistol from Beech's saddle, rolled it into his blankets, and sat down on it. "If there's any holdin' off to be done, I'll do it," he said. "You're a little too high-spirited to suit me, and a little too hasty about your conclusions. I looked over that rock sink down the draw today, and there wasn't anything in it but mud, and blamed little of that. Somebody had dug for water, and there wasn't none."

"There is now," Beech said, He tugged off one of his wet boots and poured about a pint of the disputed fluid on the ground. "There wasn't any in the daytime because the cottonwoods took it all. They let up when it turns cold, and it runs back in. I waded in it."

He started to put his boot back on. Old Apling reached out and took it, felt of it inside and out, and handed it over as if performing some ceremonial presentation.

"I'd never have figured out a thing like that in this world," he said. "If we git them horses out of here, it'll be you that done it. We'll bunch 'em and work 'em down there. It won't be no picnic, but we'll make out to handle it somehow. We've got to, after a thing like this."

Beech remembered what had occasioned the discovery, and said he would have to have something to eat first. "I want you to keep in mind that it's you I'm doin' this for," he said. "I don't owe that old groundhog of a Ream Gervais anything. The only thing I hate about this is that it'll look like I'd done him a favor."

"He won't take it for one, I guess," old Apling said. "We've got to git these horses out because it'll be a favor to you. You wouldn't want to have it told around that you'd done a thing like findin' that water, and then have to admit that we'd lost all the horses anyhow. We can't lose 'em. You've acted like a man tonight, and I'll be blamed if I'll let you spoil it for any childish spite."

They got the horses out none too soon. Watering them took a long time, and when they finally did consent to call it enough and climb back up the side hill, Beech and old Apling heard a couple of signal shots from the direction of their old camping place, and saw a big glare mount up into the sky from it as the visitors built up their campfire to look the locality over. The sight was almost comforting; if they had to keep away from a pursuit, it was at least something to know where it was.

V

From then on they followed a grab-and-run policy, scouting ahead before they moved, holding to the draws by day and crossing open ground only after dark, never pasturing over a couple of hours in any one place, and discovering food value in outlandish substances—rock lichens, the sprouts of wild plum and serviceberry, the moss of old trees and the bark of some young ones—that neither they nor the horses had ever considered fit to eat before. When they struck Boulder River Canyon they dropped down and toenailed their way along one side of it where they could find grass and water with less likelihood of having trouble about it.

The breaks of the canyon were too rough to run new-lambed sheep in, and they met with so few signs of occupancy that old Apling got overconfident, neglected his scouting to tie back a break they had been obliged to make in a line fence, and ran the horse herd right over the top of a camp where some men were branding calves, tearing down a cook tent and part of a corral and scattering cattle and bedding from the river all the way to the top of the canyon.

By rights, they should have sustained some damage for that piece of carelessness, but they drove through fast, and they were out of sight around a shoulder of rimrock before any of the men could get themselves picked up. Somebody did throw a couple of shots after them as they were pulling into a thicket of mock orange and chokecherry, but it was only with a pistol, and he probably did it more to relieve his feelings than with any hope of hitting anything.

They were so far out of range that they couldn't even hear where the bullets landed.

Neither of them mentioned that unlucky run-in all the rest of that day. They drove hard, punished the horses savagely when they lagged, and kept them at it until, a long time after dark, they struck an old rope ferry that crossed Boulder River at a place called, in memory of its original founders, Robbers' Roost.

The ferry wasn't a public carrier, and there was not even any main road down to it. It was used by the ranches in the neighborhood as the only means of crossing the river for fifty miles in either direction, and it was tied in to a log with a good solid chain and padlock. It was a way to cross, and neither of them could see anything else but to take it.

Beech favored waiting for daylight for it, pointing out that there was a ranch light half a mile up the slope, and that if anybody caught them hustling a private ferry in the dead of night they would probably be taken for criminals on the dodge. Old Apling said it was altogether likely, and drew Beech's pistol and shot the padlock apart with it.

"They could hear that up at that ranch house," Beech said. "What if they come pokin' down here to see what we're up to?"

"Old Apling tossed the fragments of padlock into the river and hung the pistol in the waistband of his trousers. "Let 'em come," he said. "They'll go back again with their fingers in their mouths. This is your trip, and you put in good work on it, and I like to ruined the whole thing stoppin' to patch an eighty-cent fence so some scissorbill wouldn't have his feelings hurt, and that's the last accommodation anybody gits out of me till this is over with. I can take about six horses at a trip, it looks like. Help me to bunch 'em."

Six horses at a trip proved to be an overestimate. The best they could do was five, and the boat rode so deep with them that Beech refused to risk handling it. He stayed with the herd, and old Apling cut it loose, let the current sweep it across into slack water, and hauled it in to the far bank by winding in its cable on an old homemade capstan. Then he turned the horses into a counting pen and came back for another load.

He worked at it fiercely, as if he had a bet up that he could wear the whole ferry rig out, but it went with infernal slowness, and when the wind began to move for daylight there were a dozen horses still to cross and no place to hide them in case the ferry had other customers.

Beech waited and fidgeted over small noises until, hearing voices and the clatter of hoofs on shale far up the canyon behind him, he gave way, drove the remaining horses into the river, and swam them across, letting himself be towed along by his saddle horn and floating his clothes ahead of him on a board.

He paid for that flurry of nervousness before he got out. The water was so cold it paralyzed him, and so swift it whisked him a mile downstream before he could get his pony turned to breast it. He grounded on a gravel bar in a thicket of dwarf willows, with numbness striking clear to the center of his diaphragm and deadening his arms so he couldn't pick his clothes loose from the bundle to put on. He managed it, by using his teeth and elbows, and warmed himself a little by driving the horses afoot through the brush till he struck the ferry landing.

It had got light enough to see things in outline, and old Apling was getting ready to shove off for another crossing when the procession came lumbering at him out of the shadows. He came ashore, counted the horses into the corral to make sure none had drowned, and laid Beech under all the blankets and built up a fire to limber him out by. He got breakfast and got packed to leave, and he did some rapid expounding about the iniquity of risking the whole trip on such a wild piece of foolhardiness.

"That was the reason I wanted you to work this boat," he said. "I could have stood up to anybody that come projectin' around, and if they wanted trouble I could have filled their order for 'em. They won't bother us now, anyhow; it don't matter how bad they want to."

"I could have stood up to 'em if I'd had anything to do it with," Beech said. "You've got that pistol of mine, and I couldn't see to throw rocks. What makes you think they won't bother us? You know it was that brandin' crew comin' after us, don't you?"

"I expect that's who it was," old Apling agreed. "They ought to be out after the cattle we scattered, but you can trust a bunch of cowboys to pick out the most useless things to tend to first. I've got that pistol of yours because I don't aim for you to git in trouble with it while this trip is on. There won't anybody bother us because I've cut all the cables on the ferry, and it's lodged downstream on a gravel spit. If anybody crosses after us within fifty miles of here, he'll swim, and the people around here ain't as reckless around cold water as you are."

Beech sat up. "We got to git out of here," he said. "There's people on this side of the river that use that ferry, you old fool, and they'll have us up before every grand jury in the country from now on. The horses ain't worth it."

"What the horses is worth ain't everything," old Apling said. "There's a part of this trip ahead that you'll be glad you went through. You're entitled to that much out of it, after the work you've put in, and I aim to see that you git it. It ain't any use tryin' to explain to you what it is. You'll notice it when the time comes."

VI

They worked north, following the breaks of the river canyon, finding the rock breaks hard to travel, but easy to avoid observation in, and the grass fair in stand, but so poor and washy in body that the horses had to spend most of their time eating enough to keep up their strength so they could move.

They struck a series of gorges, too deep and precipitous to be crossed at all, and had to edge back into milder country where there were patches of plowed ground, some being harrowed over for summer fallow and others venturing out with a bright new stand of dark-green wheat.

The pasture was patchy and scoured by the wind, and all the best parts of it were under fence, which they didn't dare cut for fear of getting in trouble with the natives. Visibility was high in that section; the ground lay open to the north as far as they could see, the wind kept the air so clear that it hurt to look at the sky, and they were never out of sight of wheat ranchers harrowing down summer fallow.

A good many of the ranchers pulled up and stared after the horse herd as it went past, and two or three times they waved and rode down toward the road, as if they wanted to make it an excuse for stopping work. Old Apling surmised that they had some warning they wanted to deliver against trespassing, and he drove on without waiting to hear it.

They were unable to find a camping place anywhere among those wheat fields, so they drove clear through to open country and spread down for the night alongside a shallow pond in the middle of some new grass not far enough along to be pastured, though the horses made what they could out of it. There were no trees or shrubs anywhere around, not even sagebrush. Lacking fuel for a fire, they camped without one, and since there was no grass anywhere except around the pond, they left the horses unguarded, rolled in to catch up sleep, and were awakened about daylight by the whole herd stampeding past them at a gallop.

They both got up and moved fast. Beech ran for his pony, which was trying to pull loose from its picket rope to go with the bunch. Old Apling ran out into the dust afoot, waggling the triggerless old pistol and trying to make out objects in the half-light by hard squinting. The herd horses fetched a long circle and came back past him, with a couple of riders clouting along behind trying to turn them back into open country. One of the riders opened up a rope and swung it, the other turned in and slapped the inside flankers with his hat, and old Apling hauled up the old pistol, flipped the hammer a couple of rounds to get it warmed up, and let go at them twice.

The half darkness held noise as if it had been a cellar. The two shots banged monstrously. Beech yelled to old Apling to be careful who he shot at, and the two men shied off sideways and rode away into the open country. One of them yelled something that sounded threatening in tone as they went out of sight, but neither of them seemed in the least inclined to bring on any general engagement. The dust blew clear, the herd horses came back to grass, old Apling looked at the pistol and punched the two exploded shells out of it, and Beech ordered him to hand it over before he got in trouble.

"How do you know but what them men had a right here?" he demanded sternly. "We'd be in a fine jackpot if you'd shot one of 'em and it turned out he owned this land we're on, wouldn't we?"

Old Apling looked at him, holding the old pistol poised as if he was getting ready to lead a band with it. The light strengthened and shed a rose-colored radiance over him, so he looked flushed and joyous and lifted up. With some of the dust knocked off him, he could have filled in easily as a day star and a son of the morning, whiskers and all.

"I wouldn't have shot them men for anything you could buy me!" he said, and faced north to a blue line of bluffs that came up out of the shadows, a blue gleam of water that moved under them, a white steamboat that moved upstream, glittering as the first light struck it. "Them men wasn't here because we was trespassers. Them was horse thieves, boy! We've brought these horses to a place where they're worth stealin', and we've brought 'em through! The railroad is under them bluffs, and that water down there is the old Columbia River!"

They might have made it down to the river that day, but having it in sight and knowing that nothing could stop them from reaching it, there no longer seemed any object in driving so unsparingly. They ate breakfast and talked about starting, and they even got partly packed up for it. Then they got occupied with talking to a couple of wheat ranchers who pulled in to inquire about buying some of the horse herd; the drought had run up wheat prices at a time when the country's livestock had been allowed to run down, and so many horses had been shot and starved out that they were having to take pretty much anything they could get.

Old Apling swapped them a couple of the most jaded herd horses for part of a haystack, referred other applicants to Gervais down at the railroad, and spent the remainder of the day washing, patching clothes and saddlery, and watching the horses get acquainted once more with a conventional diet.

The next morning a rancher dropped off a note from Gervais urging them to come right on down, and adding a kind but firm admonition against running up any feed bills without his express permission. He made it sound as if there might be some hurry about catching the horse market on the rise, so they got ready to leave, and Beech looked back over the road they had come, thinking of all that had happened on it.

"I'd like it better if old Gervais didn't have to work himself in on the end of it," he said. "I'd like to step out on the whole business right now."

"You'd be a fool to do that," old Apling said. "This is outside your work contract, so we can make the old gopher pay you what it's worth. I'll want to go in ahead and see about that and about the money that he owes me and about corral space and feed and one thing and another, so I'll want you to bring 'em in alone. You ain't seen everything there is to a trip like this, and you won't unless you stay with it."

VII

There would be no ending to this story without an understanding of what that little river town looked like at the hour, a little before sundown of a windy spring day, when Beech brought the desert horse herd down into it. On the wharf below town, some men were unloading baled hay from a steamboat, with some passengers watching from the saloon deck, and the river beyond them hoisting into whitecapped peaks that shone and shed dazzling spray over the darkening water.

A switch engine was handling stock cars on a spur track, and the brakeman flagged it to a stop and stood watching the horses, leaning into

the wind to keep his balance while the engineer climbed out on the tender to see what was going on.

The street of the town was lined with big leafless poplars that looked
as if they hadn't gone short of moisture a day of their lives; the grass
under them was bright green, and there were women working around
flower beds and pulling up weeds, enough of them so that a horse could
have lived on them for two days.

There was a Chinaman clipping grass with a pair of sheep shears to
keep it from growing too tall, and there were lawn sprinklers running
clean water on the ground in streams. There were stores with windows
full of new clothes, and stores with bright hardware, and stores with
strings of bananas and piles of oranges, bread and crackers and candy and
rows of hams, and there were groups of anxious-faced men sitting around
stoves inside who came out to watch Beech pass and told one another
hopefully that the back country might make a good year out of it yet, if a
youngster could bring that herd of horses through it.

There were women who hauled back their children and cautioned
them not to get in the man's way, and there were boys and girls, some
near Beech's own age, who watched him and stood looking after him,
knowing that he had been through more than they had ever seen and not
suspecting that it had taught him something that they didn't know about
the things they saw every day. None of them knew what it meant to be in
a place where there were delicacies to eat and new clothes to wear and
look at, what it meant to be warm and out of the wind for a change, what
it could mean merely to have water enough to pour on the ground and
grass enough to cut down and throw away.

For the first time, seeing how the youngsters looked at him, he understood what that amounted to. There wasn't a one of them who wouldn't
have traded places with him. There wasn't one that he would have traded
places with, for all the haberdashery and fancy groceries in town. He
turned down to the corrals, and old Apling held the gate open for him
and remarked that he hadn't taken much time to it.

"You're sure you had enough of that ridin' through town?" he said. "It
ain't the same when you do it a second time, remember."

"It'll last me," Beech said. "I wouldn't have missed it, and I wouldn't
want it to be the same again. I'd sooner have things the way they run with
us out in the high country. I'd sooner not have anything be the same a
second time."

A DAY WITH A DEER, A BEAR AND NORAH SMITH

Paul St. Pierre

O N A JUNE MORNING which sang of summer with golden throat, Norah Smith and a roan gelding named Tackatoolie were churning up dust and turds in the horse corral. It was a half stampede. Tackatoolie was a tall horse. Norah was short and two months pregnant besides. Each time she tried to slip on the hackamore he tossed his big head, which was shaped exactly like a claw hammer and contained about the same amount of brains. This would bunt Norah a couple of feet and permit him to run to another corner of the corral. She would follow, saying sweet things and sometimes swear words through her white, even teeth.

She was making her fifth or sixth try when she saw that her husband had been watching the performance through the bars of the corral gate.

"Damit," shouted Smith, "stop lettin' him push you around. You're spoilin' that horse."

While her attention was thus distracted, Tackatoolie butted her with his head and she fell into a pile of fresh horse turds and dirtied her one good pair of slacks. She threw the hackamore on the ground and walked out past Smith with tears in her eyes. He noticed that. He followed her back to the house and upstairs, where she was taking her old, faded blue jeans off a peg and snuffing back tears. Smith never claimed to be a man who understood women well. He knew that under usual circumstances they were unpredictable, and when pregnant, damn near impossible. Nevertheless, he tried to cheer her up as best he could. He spoke to her in the friendliest way imaginable, pointing out that all her troubles were in her head, but that did no good. She started to bawl and after a while he left her to get over whatever it was.

It was a day that had begun badly for Norah hours before her encounter with Tackatoolie. Bearing the third Smith, she was still subject to morning sickness and had puked in the yard before setting about shaving feather-sticks from jack-pine kindling to start the morning fire in the kitchen stove. As was expected in the Smith house, she was first up. When she brought out the castiron skillet for hot cakes and saw the dawn reflected in its greasy face, she was sick a second time. When she came back, Smith had arisen. There was an absence of comfort in the sight of him. He had not shaved for two days. He wore Stanfield's button-ups and jeans with a boot on one foot and a sock on the other. Smith was never bothered that he could not find both boots when he woke of a morning. He would pull on whichever he found and then make his morning perambulations around the downstairs floors drinking coffee and talking, from time to time, about some obscure subject which had seized his attention upon waking.

Even in winter his bootless foot never seemed to chill although the temperature at floor level might be an even thirty two degrees Fahrenheit. From time to time, he would observe that, by God, one of his boots seemed to have gone missing. She would answer that it was under the bed, upstairs, as always. That he would accept as being just another contribution to the great national debate about the twentieth century belonging to Canada, giving her no more serious attention than reasonable men give to high-priced teams of economists. Often as not, should he choose to go outdoors, he would pull an overshoe or some other mismatched boot over the other foot and walk gimpy for half a day.

He was leaning on the counter by the sink, sipping his second cup of coffee and looking at his favorite mountain, when she first spoke to him.

"Do you know what day it is today, Smith?" she asked.

He thought for a moment. "Monday?" he said. He was not sure. Mondays on a ranch are pretty much like Tuesdays.

"No, I mean another kind of day."

A ripple of uneasiness spread on the calm surface of his mind. He thought quite a long time. "Mother's Day?" he said.

"That was a month ago."

"Oh."

"It's our wedding anniversary," she said.

"Oh. So it is. I'd forgot."

"You also forgot to bring Roosevelt home from the Larsens' yesterday."

"Well," he said, "I didn't exactly forget. I remembered when I got there but when it was time to leave I had sort of lost track of him." He sucked up some more coffee. "It is alright anyhow Norah," he said. "I figure Roosevelt wanted to stay over with them for another day or two anyhow. Otherwise he would have been at the truck when I pulled out."

"That's not for him to decide, he's only a kid. He should be here for his school lessons this morning."

"Margaret Larsen will probably give him some lessons. You can have a sort of holiday. You will only have Sherwood to teach today."

"I will not, because we are all going out to the McQuarries' today."

"Oh."

"Will you stop saying 'oh.' You have known for two weeks that we were goin' to the McQuarries' today."

"I might have known it but my mind never got really roped into it. It sort of caught me by one hind leg and I shook off the lassrope. I have been spending my mind more on the national debt and things like that. I have gone on to bigger things."

"You bloody well do remember. You promised to show him the old survey stake. The one he can't find."

"McQuarrie couldn't find his own bellybutton using both hands and holding a flashlight in his teeth."

"Why do you dislike the McQuarries?"

"I don't dislike them. Damit, why can't you get that in your headbone. I do not dislike the McQuarries."

In honesty, of which she carried the share of ten ordinary Canadians, Norah had to admit, however privately, the truth of that statement. Nobody disliked the McQuarries, who were honest, charming, gentle, mild, well-bred, well-educated and naturally intelligent. It was just that people would not take them seriously.

The Smiths had been the first to meet Colin McQuarrie who came into the country having read many books including *Swiss Family Robinson* and the *RCAF Survival Manual*. Norah, who liked him, quickly perceived that his failing was that he could not help believing what people told him. Smith, if he perceived that fault, was less forgiving.

On his first morning at the Smith ranch, McQuarrie had politely requested a horse with Arab blood, but not too hot-blooded. They ran in a wise, patient and notoriously lazy gelding named Stanley Steamer, from the dude string. That was only polite. Then McQuarrie insisted on saddling his own horse.

Smith came out to inspect the job, closely followed by Norah, whose instincts urged her to do that.

Stanley Steamer was all right in the saddle, as Smith tested by shoving four fingers under the cinch to check the tightness. His bridle, however, had been, with much lacing and unlacing and turning of buckles, installed upside down. Stanley Steamer was restive, but he accepted it as one of those things. He had known many dudes.

"Yep," said Smith. "Just right." He checked the cinch again. "You had to let some air out of him before cinching up, I guess."

McQuarrie, who had read about that too, admitted modestly that he had performed the knee trick.

"There is just one small thing," said Smith.

"Oh?"

"Yeah. That is, if you don't mind my mentioning it."

"What's that?"

"Well, just a small thing. That there bridle."

"Something wrong about the bridle?" said McQuarrie.

"No. Nothing wrong. Nothing wrong at all. A perfect job. On the right horse. On a stud horse that would be exactly right. However, this here horse is a gelding. With a gelding or a mare, you put the bridle exactly the opposite."

"Sorry," said McQuarrie. "My mistake."

"An easy mistake to make," said Smith. "Made it many times myself. The simple rule is, don't never bridle a horse without you look under the tail first."

"Let me get that bridle, Colin," said Norah. "They're tricky." She re-jigged the buckles and the lines, hearing over the shoulder McQuarrie trying to make conversation.

"Would there be some Percheron in that horse?" asked McQuarrie.

"Exactly right. We breed into the Percheron for big bone, so they can pack. Then we cross with shithouse rat, for the smarts. In Stanley Steamer the rat strain seems to be plumb wore out."

Norah led Steamer over. "He's ready to travel, Colin," she said.

Colin thanked her. He was a man who said thank you most of the day. A bread-and-butter man, Smith called him.

Despite such puzzling introductions to the ways of the Namko Country, McQuarrie and his wife had moved there and bought the old Soap Lake Place. It had been abandoned by the first settler whose bowels were unequal to dissolved sodas. Almost all the Soap Lake range rights had been acquired by neighboring ranches and little remained of the ranch but a grey, two-storied square log cabin, a log barn which was sounder, a mile of fence, a horse corral and a piece of bottom land beside Soap Lake Creek, which was big enough to nourish a Nubian goat and a Newfoundland dog but not much more. It suited them perfectly because of the view of Kappan Mountain, an asset most settlers thought came for free. McQuarrie graveled the road to the old house. He had a bridge built across the creek, restored the house and installed running water, a septic tank and twin kitchen sinks. He got a tractor, a diesel electric light plant, a matched pair of Bouvier Flanders dogs, twelve Mongolian pheasants that died, one goat which didn't and a sincere, enduring relationship with his banker.

For horses, he bought two golden-coin palominos. Namko never had parades, only stampedes. He bought palominos anyway.

His wife was a woman with a voice like silver bells and her thoughts were gold, twenty-four carat. She hired Indian girls, from the Reserve, to serve as housemaids. Three left, without notice, so she hired a fourth. How else, she said, could the McQuarries learn to speak Chilcotin, the original language of the land and a bounden duty upon the whites that they should speak it? None of the local Indians had ever had that idea. She brought it into the country fresh and they were, a year later, still examining the idea thoughtfully. Chilcotin is one of the dialects of the Athapaskan language and foreigners who understand it, and they number below six, say it is more impressive, more precise and far less bastardized than English. However, verb tenses alter in every context and there is also a requirement for inflection, as in Cantonese, to provide full meaning to what is being said. At the end of ten months the McQuarries had a grasp of about seventeen words and didn't know how to say any of them.

Their favorite was the Chilcotin world for 'hello' but they pronounced it like the word for 'drunk' and quite misunderstood the response it brought.

"It would be awful if we didn't show up today," Norah said to Smith that morning. "She's getting up dinner for us at twelve o'clock."

"Don't she normally cook dinner? What do the McQuarries do about eating if there is no visitors? Don't they eat when they're by themselves?"

"That's what I mean. You don't like the McQuarries."

He sighed. "I have never known anybody with logic like yours," he said. "All I said was that I figured she would cook dinner at her house whether there was any Smiths in it or not. Somehow that turned into me not liking the McQuarries. How do you arrive at conclusions like that? There should be some sort of a prize for thinking of that kind."

"Well anyway, we have got to go."

"As for my logic," he said, "it works in an entirely different track. Now, in my logic, if you and me and Sherwood are goin' to the McQuarries' today, then Sherwood ain't goin' to get any school anyhow. And neither would Roosevelt, if he was here. So Roosevelt stayin' over a day or two at the Larsens' don't make the slightest difference to him or you or me or anybody in the world."

"You can always twist things somehow."

"You didn't see my other boot any place, did you?" he said.

"It's under the bed."

"Are you sure?"

"Yes. I saw it there when I got up."

"I looked, but I never saw it there."

"It's there."

"Well, I will look again then. Maybe it was lyin' underneath something else."

He went upstairs. Sherwood, their oldest boy, came down.

"We're going over to the McQuarries' today, Sherwood."

"Ugh," he said.

"Why are you making that face?"

"She always talks to me so much."

"Sherwood. Mrs. McQuarrie is a very nice lady."

He answered in calm, conversational tones much like Smith's. "Oh, yes," he said, "she's nice. But she's an awful talker. Is breakfast ready?"

She cooked Sherwood's hot cakes soggy, the way he liked them, and had Smith's turning from brown to black, the way he liked his, and then she noticed they were both missing. She found them monkey wrenching some equipment in the toolshed. She noticed the truck was missing.

"Where's the truck?"

"I loaned it to Frenchie for a couple of days."

"What'd you do that for?"

"I didn't figure we had any use for it and he needed it."

"How do we get to the McQuarries'?"

"Well, we will just saddle horses. It is almost as quick, going over the jack-pine ridge."

"Oh, hell."

"And a nice morning to travel saddle horse, too," he said, casting his eyes over the June morning which was, in fact, one of the better mornings of that year.

When it was time to go to the McQuarries', Smith had gone missing.

"We gonna go without Smith?" said Sherwood.

"Too bloody true. He can find his own way over."

"Smith can find his way anyplace," said Sherwood.

"When he chooses. Come on, Sherwood, we'll trot."

Knowing as he did that there was far more time in this world than was known to wives, Smith had saddled up and ridden to the draw on Oregon Jim Creek. He had cut deer sign there a few days before. An hour's hunt, he thought, would soothe his mind, which was getting heavy with domestic disputes.

Deer on Smith's range had faded away after the huge influx of moose during the thirties and sometimes a year or more would pass without them shooting one on the Home Place. He missed them, both because they were not ugly and stupid as were the moose and because in the hot weather the family could eat almost a whole deer before it spoiled. Much moose meat spoiled in summer unless made into jerky. Of late it had been difficult to coax Norah into making jerky.

The deer in the draw were probably a bunch moving late toward the beautiful meadows above timberline and by today might be gone, but it was a worth a ride to see if perhaps they had hung up there. Anyway, the air was good this morning, the ground was dry, the meadows were green and the snows on the mountain reminded him of newly starched white sheets. He loved to get between white sheets occasionally, sheets starched so hard that they almost crackled. Particularly when dirty, and before bothering to take a bath. When a man came home dog-tired and smelling like a bush-tail rat and dove straight into starched white sheets for sleep it made him appreciate the joys of married life.

He tied the horses in a poplar grove at the edge of the meadow and walked the side of the draw on a dusty path made by the feet of his horses and cattle. There, among the prints of the domestic stock, were the neater prints of deer.

Canada geese in a nearby pond began to raise a kalakalowa. They were talking to a pair which was circling to his right. He squatted in the track and watched the two flying birds swing in a broad turn. They came past him up the draw, not a hundred feet from him. Because he was still, they had not noticed him but in passing one turned his head and looked him straight in the eye.

A quarter of a mile further, he spotted the ears of a deer which had bedded down beside a deadfall on the creekside. He stopped, but the deer had seen him first. When the doe stood, he saw that her coat was dull, her flanks thin, and he guessed that she had a fawn hidden in the grass near her feet. She was not worth shooting but she was company of sorts. Smith stood, unmoving, watching her calmly and she, as calmly, watched him. In an instant there passed between those two living creatures the agreement to truce, that no man has ever explained, the silent compact that there was, at this particular time, at this particular place, no hunter and no hunted. She paced, a few steps right, a few steps left, of the hidden fawn.

"Now mama," he said. "Why don't you pick up that little guy and move along?" She stood, fanned her ears toward the easy sound of his voice, but did not go. "It's a dry doe I'm looking for," he explained.

Then the buck stood. He had been sleeping at the creek's bank. His antlers did not yet have their full season's growth but in their heavy velvet, which was lustrous in the new sun of the day, they were a glowing crown.

The buck had not been startled into wakefulness. He seemed to have risen, fresh, clean and brisk, for no purpose except to enjoy the new breeze which had begun to walk down the draw. He was a perfect animal enjoying a perfect morning.

Slowly, so slowly that the doe did not spook, Smith drew down the rifle on the buck. He brought the bead of the front sight flush to top of the notch in the backsight and centered it just back of the shoulder. This was where he almost always took his shots. It spoiled some meat, but the country had much free meat in it. When he was younger he used to take head shots and being a good shot, usually connected and spoke of it later in a modest way. However, he had once taken a shot at a perfect four point which ran. He thought he had missed it until, weeks later, he found the carcass of the starved animal with the lower jaw all shot away. He had never spoken of this to anybody and he had never taken a head shot again.

This time, however, he didn't want to shoot into the chest cavity so he shifted the sight to the neck. If a bullet didn't snap the neck or cut the main artery, the deer could keep going and good luck to him. He held his breath to squeeze off and the world stopped turning for him. When a shot is good, a man knows it before the last of the pressure is off the trigger. This was that kind of shot.

When the buck went down Smith didn't bother to jack a second shell into the chamber. He walked forward slowly and waved again at the racing doe and her fawn, who did not look back at him. He stepped across the creek, moving deftly from one boulder to the next, scarcely wetting his boots.

He found the buck as he knew he would find him, stone dead. The deer had dropped in a little heap, his proud head falling back over his body.

Smith knew that the buck had died full of the joy of life and believing the terrible lie that he would live forever. It had been quick. The deer had known no pain, no fear, had not had even one instant for the immense regret of things in this life which he might have done and hadn't.

From full life into eternal death the translation had been instantaneous, like somebody switching off an electric light. It was a wonderful way to go and Smith hoped to God that somebody would do as much for him when the time came, although he surer than hell wasn't ready to go yet.

Smith took great care in gutting out the animal. He rolled his sleeves to his elbow. He worked slowly, pausing once to put a new edge on his knife. He hung the four clean quarters from poplar branches. He would bring a pack horse over tomorrow for them. He washed his hands and arms in the sands of the cold creek. There was scarcely a drop of blood on his shirt.

In a small pouch made from a piece of the hide he carried away the fresh liver and presented it to Mrs. McQuarrie when he rode into the Soap Lake Place an hour later to join Norah and Sherwood. Mrs. McQuarrie remarked on the lovely brown eyes of a deer she had never met, but she accepted the liver.

Smith and Colin McQuarrie rode for an hour to look for survey stakes. Smith could not find one. The trees, he said, were creeping down on the grass and had been doing so for ten years or more. Unless they had a damn good twenty-mile forest fire pretty soon, and threw the Crown's minister for grazing permits into the middle of it, the whole country was damn near ruined.

"I guess I'll have to bring in a surveyor from Williams Lake," said Mc-Quarrie as they sat at the dinner table, eating roast beef proudly flavored with wild garlic which Mrs. McQuarrie had plucked in their horse pasture.

"Expense for nothing," said Smith. "You can see your meadow. If you want to throw up a fence, just build her wide."

"Everybody's fences get wide in this country," said Norah. "Just build along the nearest jack-pine ridge at the edge of your meadow."

"That might make for trouble in later years, mightn't it?" said McQuarrie to Smith. "I would feel uneasy about doing that."

"Hire a surveyor then," said Smith. "At least he'll feel easier about his business."

McQuarrie talked about his breeding stock which, along with grass, is the second of two essential items for ranching. He had none yet but had been reading much literature about the Hereford, the Charolais, the Sementhal and the other strains of beef cattle. What did Smith think of them?

"Did you ever think of keeping sheep?" asked Smith, mildly.

Norah was reminded that at times she hated this man she married and never more so than when he said such things in sweet deception. McQuarrie didn't know and couldn't see where sheep men ranked in Smith's estimation. She knew well Smith's sure order of priorities. The only truly good men were those who kept horses, although it was understood that they also had to keep some beef cattle because you couldn't make any money with horses and you could, some of the time, with beef.

Men of the next rank admitted dairy cows to their herd and the class below that raised pigs as well and had a lettuce garden. Sheep men were far down the list, being little better than farmers who wore overalls and had shoes with laces. Smith recognized that below the farmer class there were other trades in the world, carpentering and logging and school teaching and politics, but these were so far beneath his field of vision as to be not worth dividing into classes.

"Do you think sheep would do well here?" said McQuarrie.

"Who can say," said Smith. "It suits for some people."

Norah left and began rattling dishes in Mrs. McQuarrie's sinks.

The McQuarrie kitchen was a magnificent place and Norah was soothed by standing in the midst of it.

Norah had her share of the moral flaws common to the human character, but of one particularly corrosive sin she was free. On that imperfect and imperfectible little soul there was not a single strain of covetousness. She could enjoy other people's good fortune almost as much as her own.

In the McQuarrie kitchen there was running water, both hot and cold, cupboards with birch paneling, an Osterizer, and a pop-up toaster, which operated from a gasoline-fired, 110-volt system. There was a propane stove, which had all the knobs and a pilot light that worked.

Her hostess joined her and they began to clatter dishes together.

Mrs. McQuarrie, for all the china hands and voice of violets, had depths of thought too.

"I don't think Smith likes sheep," she said.

"Why do you say that?"

"I just got that impression."

Norah washed and Mrs. McQuarrie dried.

"Norah, will you tell me something?"

"Sure, if I can."

"Tell me what a rancher is."

Norah laughed. "Anybody who will catch a horse to ride rather than walk to his front gate."

Mrs. McQuarrie's voice was fainter, tighter.

"But we're not ranchers, are we?"

"Why sure. Everybody here is a rancher."

"We are strangers."

"You are not. Everybody likes you. You're some of the most popular people in the whole country."

"Popular strangers," said Mrs. McQuarrie.

They changed the subject.

From the living room came Smith's voice.

"My old dad had sheep once."

"Did he have trouble with foot rot?"

"Not a bit. They all died first winter before the foot rot could start."

"Too bad. Did he run out of feed?"

"No. There was lots of feed. What happened is he went to Oregon to buy a stud horse and got on a real bat. By the time he got home the sheep was all gone to the wolves and the weather. I always remember after he come home somebody asked him how his sheep were doing. He said, 'I never had fewer and I never felt better about it.'"

"I suppose when a man has nothing he must gain a certain sense of freedom," said McQuarrie.

"If we didn't have to keep horses and cows on these ranches we would all be free and happy men," said Smith.

Norah came into the living room. "It's time we started home," she said, shortly.

Sherwood, who had been studying the ads in a *Western Horseman* magazine, stood up and shook his pantlegs over the tops of his tiny riding boots. He was quiet like Smith, but neater. "I guess it's about time I pulled out," he said.

"Pull out where?" said Norah.

"He is taking a message to Frenchie for me," said Smith. "I'm going to meet Frenchie to pick up the truck at the store tomorrow. There's some stuff I got to cart back home from there."

"Why can't you go over to Frenchie's?"

"Because I am expecting Narcisse Peter to buy a horse from me today at our place."

She said no more. They went out to their horses. McQuarrie's wife, who felt the loneliness of the range pressing in on her again, was offering up little trills and cheeps of polite dismay that they were going so soon.

Sherwood was riding a big bay. It was tall. So tall, Smith sometimes said, that the connection between its brain and feet was too distant. Sherwood had to lead it to the side of the corral and climb up one log in order to get his foot into the stirrup. "See you later," he said, and trotted off.

Norah called after him.

"Sherwood. You come home right after supper at Frenchie's. You hear me?"

"Sure," said the boy, tossing the word over his shoulder.

"I bet he don't get home till pretty near dark," she said to Smith.

"Probly."

She watched the big horse and the tiny boy, going into the wide and empty that would soon swallow them silently.

"Gee. He seems so young, to be off all by himself on a ten-mile ride."

"He's small for his age," said Smith. He got into his own saddle. "How old is he now anyhow?" he asked.

"Ten."

"Oh, ten is he? I had forgot." Smith waved a hand casually at the Mc-Quarries, and went away at a fast trot. He was almost into the timber on the edge of the Davie Allen Meadow before Norah caught up to him.

When they were walking their horses, side by side, she said, "Why did you say that about sheep to McQuarrie?"

"I was just keeping conversation going."

"But you despise sheep and you know it."

"What difference does that make? If he likes them why should I try to make him sensible?"

"You were making fun of him."

"I was only keeping conversation goin'. I was participating."

She grunted. Ten minutes later she said, "What's a rancher, Smith?"

"Now what kind of question is that?"

"Well, Mrs. McQuarrie asked me and I couldn't tell her. So you tell me. What is a rancher?"

"Mort Dilloughboy's got it best, I guess. He says ranch country is where the places are far enough apart that every man has got to keep his own tomcat."

"So Morton is a rancher, then."

"Oh, sure he is."

"Morton has never raised anything on his place except mortgages. Every year he loses more cows than he gets calves."

"I never said he was successful. I said he was a rancher. Morton is a failed rancher but he is a rancher anyhow. Anybody in the country will tell you that."

"But they won't tell me why," she said.

"Because if you have to ask why about a man, then he is not a rancher," said Smith. "It is a question that just answers itself without being asked. The very best kind of question there is."

"And Colin McQuarrie is not a rancher."

"Well, what do you think?" said Smith. "As I say, it answers itself."

Yes, she thought, Morton, who did everything wrong, was a rancher, because he was a good old boy, a delightful drinker, a teller of fine stories and a horseman. He was one of the brotherhood. So was Stettler, sour, dour, Stettler, a mean, cold man whose smile was like a ripple on a slop pail. Stettler, too, was one of them. And Colin McQuarrie, successful or unsuccessful, drunk or sober, helpful or helpless, was not. Like Arch McGregor at the store, like almost everybody on the face of this great earth, he was not and, almost certainly, he would never be.

Two miles from their home place they came upon the bear.

"Look at that dirty scut," shouted Smith. He jumped off his horse and threw its reins to Norah. "I am goin' to civilize that bastard," he said. "Right here and now." He reached out a hand for the gun, forgetting that he'd dropped it off at the house after shooting the deer.

"Give me a gun," he said.

"There's no gun on this saddle."

"Well why not, damit, why not?"

"Don't blame me. Why did you leave it home."

"Damn. Damn, damn, damn. Look at that black bastard eating my cow."

"That's the carcass of that old cow that aborted. That bear didn't kill her. Leave him alone, Smith."

"Eatin' one of my cows. Son of a bitch."

"Leave him alone."

Smith took a few steps away from the horse and toward the bear. The black bear looked up at him from the ripe carcass of the cow and then returned to his feeding.

"Look at him," said Smith, "won't even stop eatin' when we're here. Dirty, greedy bastard."

"What are you so mad about? It's only an old rotten carcass. He never killed that cow."

Smith looked around for a rock. There were none handy so he tore up a clod of earth and, running a few steps toward the bear, threw the clod at it. The bear had not had clods of earth thrown at it before. It was a simple, unsophisticated bear from the mountains who had never made the acquaintance of any ranchers. It looked at the flying clod of earth and batted at it with its paw.

"Stop it, Smith," she said. "These horses are getting excited."

"Ride back to the house and get my gun," he said.

"I will not."

"Hurry. Go back and get the gun. It's only a couple of miles. I'll keep teasing him here until you get back." He threw another clod of dirt at the bear.

The bear stood up and took its first good look at a rancher.

The horses, now with a good sniff of the bear's scent, snorted and danced.

"Get on your horse, you damn fool," she said.

Smith threw another clod at the bear. "You miserable, dirty black bastard," he said, "if I had an axe I'd go after you right here and now. Go on back to the house, Norah. Get my gun." The bear pushed its head forward and moved it, snakelike, from one side to the other.

Norah brought her own horse and Smith's under control to ride toward her husband. The lines of her bridle were long. She used the free end to lash Smith across the shoulders.

"Ouch," he said.

"Get on that horse," she said.

"Oh alright," he said, "alright. I s'pose he wouldn't stay until you got a gun anyhow."

He mounted and they rode off, leaving the most puzzled bear in Namko Country still standing. When some distance from it they saw it drop back to its front legs and waddle off into the jack pines. Smith shook his fist at it. "Next time," he shouted, "I will have a gun and you will become a Christian in one hell of a hurry."

There still being daylight, he considered taking a pack horse over to the draw to pick up the deer quarters but instead he took the gun and went back to look for the bear.

"What if Narcisse comes?" said Norah.

"I have waited for him three days, he can wait for me three hours."

"I thought that was the reason we had to send Sherwood down to Frenchie's, because you had to meet Narcisse."

"Talk about twisting words. Jesus. You should be in Parliament. Just make sure if Narcisse comes, don't let him go. I want to sell him a horse. We can use the money."

The bear scooted for the timber as soon as Smith appeared the second time. Smith tried to track him, but the ground was dry and he had no dog so he rode over to one meadow to look for horses and to another to look for cows. He found none. It didn't matter. It was a good day for riding.

Spring was Smith's favorite season. In spring a man looked forward to two summers and only one winter. People said the fall was cleaner and prettier, but in fall you faced two winters and only one summer. The range was preparing for sleep in russet twilight when he got back and Norah, whose clothesline had broken again, had not started supper because she had been obliged to do the wash a second time.

Narcisse was there however. Narcisse had spoken little to Norah. He liked Smith but could barely tolerate his woman whom he found a noisy, clattering creature. It was a pity, Narcisse thought, that Smith couldn't have found himself an Indian woman or, failing that, have taken a stick to the white woman whom he'd picked. However, being Indian, Narcisse was polite and he forebore from ever indicating his feelings about Norah. "I figured Sherwood might get home before dark," she said to Smith.

"Oh, he would hardly have made it by now," he said. "You better throw something on for Narcisse and me. I guess the last of the meat is gone, en't it."

"I thought you were gonna bring that deer in."

"Oh, it would be too fresh anyhow. Throw on a lot of macaroni and cheese. If there is enough of it, maybe Narcisse and me will not notice that there is no meat in it. You'll eat, Narcisse?"

"I got to go real quick," said Narcisse.

"Nobody has got to go real quick until they're killed," said Smith.

"I'm s'posed to be in that place Pella Coola."

"Bella Colla. What are you doin' there?"

"I'm lokkin'."

"Ah. So you're a logger now, Narcisse. Well, that is probably smarter than bein' a cowboy. But I tell you Narcisse, you will not like it for long."

"How much money do you make, Narcisse?" asked Norah.

Narcisse, who knew exactly, said he guessed it was about twenty dollars a day.

"Twenty dollars a day," she said. "Imagine. What would it be like to have twenty dollars cash money comin' into the house every working day?"

She was talking to herself. They realized this, so paid no attention.

"I tried logging for a few months after the war," said Smith. "It is a poor kind of life. Whistles blowin'. Everybody hollering. And nothing but goddamed trees around you. How do you like the Bella Coola yourself?"

"It's OK, I guess."

"A dark, wet stinkin' place," said Smith. "It is no place for people like you and me, Narcisse."

"Sure lots money," said Narcisse.

"You will get over that feeling," said Smith.

"Just like Smith, you'll get over being interested in money," said Norah.

"Surely there is some coffee," said Smith to her.

She brought them coffee.

"You didn't happen to spot Sherwood when you came across, did you?" she said. Narcisse agreed. He had not spotted Sherwood.

"Narcisse," said Smith. "How'd you like to buy that little buckskin mare, the one I call Dancer."

"I don't think I know that horse."

"Great horse for kids," said Smith. "Put one of your kids aboard Dancer and he will really get smartened up in a hurry."

Narcisse sipped his coffee with pleasure and lit a tailor-made cigarette. He enjoyed conversation with a smart man.

"Maybe I come back for her in ten years," he said.

"She might be past her peak then," said Smith.

"Maybe I do like Ken Larsen says about his wife. He keeps her until she's forty and trades her in on two twenties."

"Ken will find out he ain't wired for two-twenty," said Smith, but that went past Narcisse; there was no electricity on the Namko Reserve.

"Then there is that young stud I got," said Smith. "He is just like his father. I don't want two studs, I might as well sell one of them."

"S'pose I had two studs like that," said Narcisse, "I would sell two of them."

Nicely done, Narcisse, said Smith to himself.

They amiably exchanged stories and insults about their horses and other people's horses for twenty minutes, sometimes becoming grave while they spoke respectfully about Namko horses long dead. It was the accepted wisdom that all the best horses were the horses of memory, not those now living.

They both smoked and sucked up coffee.

"Well," said Smith. "Have you found a horse you do want?"

"Yeah. I find him."

"What one?"

"It's that horse got that funny brand."

"You mean he ain't got my brand."

"No, that funny brand."

"You don't mean that old Lazy Z Bar horse I got years ago? Two white stockings, bay? White star on his face?"

There was no answer.

"That is the only horse I remember that I never got around to branding. Except young stuff, of course. A brand like this?" Smith went to the counter and found a pencil and discarded cigarette paper package. On it he drew the brand.

"I guess," said Narcisse.

"Well," said Smith. "Who would have believed it? I thought old Lightning Rod was dead three years ago. Wherever did you find him?"

"He hangs around that Happy Ann Meadow," said Narcisse.

"Still alive!" said Smith. "Imagine. Twenty or twenty-two years old at the least, and he toughed out three winters alone. By jing, I think we could all learn something from that old horse. In fact, I plan to think about him when I am ninety-three years old myself.

"Think of that, Norah. Old Lightning Rod is still around."

"I am thinking of it," she said.

"I guess he ain't worth much that horse," said Narcisse.

"Worth much! Worth much? Why, he ain't worth nothin'. Nothin'."

"He's good enough, I guess."

"He is not good enough." Smith leaned forward in his chair toward Narcisse. "Let me tell you about that horse. For one thing, he is so old that you will not get any use out of him."

"That's OK. I go to Bella Coola anyhow. I don't use him much."

"Then why do you want to buy the horse?" asked Norah.

"I ain't got no horse now," said Narcisse.

"That's a good answer," said Smith. "But you interrupted me. I want to tell you some of the things that are wrong with Old Lightning Rod. I won't be able to tell them all, because I can't remember them all, but I will scrape together as many as I can in the next half hour . . . "

"I am going to ride out and meet Sherwood," said Norah.

"When it's near dark? Why?"

"He'll be on the trail, won't he?"

"Anyway, your horse isn't in the corral."

"Did you turn him out?"

"Yes I did."

"Why'd you do that?"

"I didn't expect you would take a notion to go riding saddle horse tonight. All is well, Norah. He will be home as soon as he gets here. Have you got enough supper on for him too?"

"I opened three big tins of beans and there is bannock from this morning."

"Good. Then all is well. Now, Narcisse, one thing above all else about that horse. He is lazy. Rustling his own grass for three winters is the most ambitious thing that horse ever did in his lifetime. Also, in case you didn't notice, he has a bog spavin."

"I don't want to pay much money for a horse," said Narcisse.

"Did I say one bog spavin? I meant to say two. Two bog spavins. And as I remember it, a split hoof."

Norah went out. The evening star glowed. She made her way to the horse pasture, stumbling in the hummocks made at the creekside by the animals' hooves. She thrust through the heavy willows that tried to switch her face and claw her. Neither seeing nor hearing any horses, she came back across the creek, losing one boot in the mud and fishing it out only by feeling around in the slop. She walked to the gate and peered into the dark trees out of which Sherwood should come. Only the darkness of the night rode silently in from the eastern horizon.

When she came back to the house the kitchen was empty, the pot of beans boiling over. She set the beans at the back of the stove and covered them with a plate. She wasn't hungry. She made a cup of tea, turned on the radio and tuned in a children's choir on one of the evangelical radio stations broadcasting from the United States.

At eleven o'clock she thought she heard a halloo and went to the door, but it was a coyote yelling up by the draw. At eleven-thirty she heard another. This time it was Smith and Narcisse, driving a dozen horses to the corral, a plunging dark mass tearing the creek waters apart and cracking the rocks with their sparking hoofs at the shoreline. Smith was hazing them with his high, artificial yell. Half an hour later there was more racket when they turned them out again to the horse pasture. She ran to the door as the horses went past.

"Did you keep my horse in the corral?" she said.

Smith trotted his horse over to her. "Yeah, he is there. Not that there is any point riding him, but he is there."

"Sherwood isn't home yet."

"Well, maybe he is staying over at Frenchie's for the night."

"He should be home long ago."

"Not if he is stayin' at Frenchie's, he shouldn't. He can't sleep at Frenchie's and be at home here at the same time."

"I'm worried, Smith."

"All is well, Norah," he said.

"You always say all is well."

"And you always say all is not well. It is just the difference of our temperaments."

"Well, I am going to ride to Frenchie's right now."

"Leave it, leave it be, will you. I will ride over, since you insist."

He started for the door.

"Are you going now?"

"In a minute or two. Give him twenty minutes more. If he ain't here, I will ride over. Both Sherwood and me can spend the night at Frenchie's, if that's the way it's got to be."

Half an hour later he came back to report that Narcisse had gone with a horse. Narcisse had taken old Lightning Rod after all. Smith would have felt badly had the rest of the country learned of him selling such crowbait but he had resolved the problem by making a gift of the horse. This preserved his reputation. People said that there were times that Smith would not sell you a horse, but he might give you one.

"You are no businessman," Norah said.

"I never claimed I was. I am a rancher, not a businessman. Sherwood is back?"

"No."

"Alright then, I'll go."

"I am going to ride with you."

"Go to bed and stop worrying."

She looked at him, silent. He fidgeted. "Oh alright. We will both go. There is no need for it, but we will both go."

"You got your horse in the corral too?"

"Yeah."

"Why'd you keep him in, if you wasn't worrying yourself?"

"I am not worried. I do not worry. You can do enough worrying for any two normal people. There is no worrying left for me to do around this place. Now, just so I don't fall in a fainting fit, I am gonna eat one plate of beans and then we will go, OK?"

She went out, and was back in the kitchen before he'd taken a bite. "You better come out, Smith," she said.

Sherwood's horse was in the yard, the saddle empty. It had stepped on one line and broken it off; the other was trailing. "Oho," said Smith. He spoke gently to the horse. "Now boy, now boy, now boy." He walked slowly toward it.

It backed away, trod on the remaining rein and he grasped the bridle. "Now boy," he said. "Now boy." He looked at the shoulders. The horse had been lathered up; the hair was stiff with dried sweat. He examined the saddle and walked around the horse while Norah held its head.

"He ain't scarred up and there is no mud on the saddle," he said. "No doubt all that has happened is that Sherwood got off him for a minute and then couldn't get back on again. He's a tall horse. Sherwood has to make quite a jump to get into that first stirrup."

Norah made no answer.

"Put a new bridle on him," said Smith. "We will lead him back over the trail. Sherwood will be a little tired of walking when we get to him. I think he will be pleased to have a horse to come back on."

Before she found the other bridle, however, Sherwood walked into the yard with his chaps slung over his thin shoulders. He was whistling. She reached the kitchen door almost as quickly as he did. Smith was inside.

"Well, Sherwood," Smith said. "You are late for supper."

"I'm sure hungry," said Sherwood, and slung his chaps on the peg. Norah followed, a step or two behind the boy, as he walked to the stove and slid the plate aside on the bean pot.

"Only beans?" he said.

"There will be meat tomorrow," said Smith. "Let us eat. You had better have something too, Norah." He sat in the chair at the head of the kitchen counter and Sherwood sat on the bench at one side.

"We've been worried, Sherwood," she said.

"What about?"

"Yes," said Smith. "That is what I have been saying. What about? Let us have the beans, Norah. They are not the finest food on earth, but we can think about oatmeal mush while we are eating them and feel lucky.

"Mind you, Sherwood," he continued, "I was surprised when your saddle horse came home before you did."

"Oh, that was just a couple of miles up the road," said Sherwood. "He startled and I went over his head."

"Oh yes . . . ?"

Smith wanted to hear more. Sherwood, sensing this, took his time in answering.

Norah brought the bean pot over and filled their plates and stood waiting, as Smith was waiting, for the answer. Smith pretended not to be waiting, but he was, she knew.

"There was a bear come right up the path toward us."

"Ah. That bear. I imagine that would be the bear that I was educating this afternoon."

"I was trottin' old Bud and he never saw the bear until we was almost on top of him. So when he stopped, I kept goin', right over his head."

" . . . Yeah . . . "

Old Bud, he went one way. The bear went 'woof' and he went the other way."

"What did you do, Sherwood?" said Norah.

Sherwood considered his answer before delivering it. "I just sat there in the trail feelin' lonely," he said.

When she looked at Smith, he was laughing, silently, bubbles of amusement rising from his thin gut but making no pop when they came out his mouth. He spoke to her. "I like that," he said. "Feelin' awful lonely. I like that."

These words he spoke to Norah, but he went further. He turned to the boy and paid him the highest compliment it was within his power to utter. "I admire your style, Sherwood," he said.

"We are lucky Sherwood is alive." said Norah, but Smith paid her no heed and continued an amiable conversation with Sherwood.

"Sherwood," he said. "You know, it wouldn't surprise me if you was to make a rancher some day."

Norah, who was still holding the pot, said, "Yes, Sherwood, you will be a rancher some day."

They both looked up at her. Up to this point, they had been paying her little attention.

"You will be poor and you won't know the difference," she said. "Your house won't ever have a flush toilet and you will dress like a bum."

"But, then," she continued, dropping her voice, "that won't matter, will it? Because you will be a rancher, like your father. And no matter how tough things are, you will always have the satisfaction of knowing that you are superior to all the poor, non-ranchers who infest the rest of this world. You will be like Smith. Smug." She repeated, in even softer tones, "Smug." She said it a third time. "Smug."

She carried the bean pot toward Smith but instead of pouring it on his plate she poured the whole steaming mess into his lap, and once more, sweetly, she said, "Smug."

Smith tore open his belt and slapped the pants to his knees to avoid scorching the family jewels. Sherwood, too, was on his feet.

"Holy God Smith!" said Sherwood.

Norah smiled again. "Good night, gentlemen," she said, and went upstairs to the bedroom.

"Smith," said Sherwood. "Smith. What did she do that to you for?"

Smith looked at the hole in the air left by his wife. "She must be mad about something," he said.

Taking a table knife, he began to scrape the beans from his pants to the floor. "Your mother should have been a gunfighter. She has the fastest draw in the west. You better hunt another can of beans from the cupboard."

Thus the day ended, shortly after midnight.

It had been a good day for the deer, although short, and a confusing one for the bear. Norah's day had been poor. Smith's day had been, as usual, not bad.

But for Sherwood the day had been immense, grand, huge beyond his imagination. He knew that even when he was an old, old man, he would still remember this day, the day his mother dumped the plateful of beans into Smith's lap, on purpose.

THE HORSEBREAKER

Max Schott

SOME PEOPLE JUST GET OLD, but Clyde got old and rich. And he was pretty old, too, before he took it into his head to get rich. Not only that, if he wanted to brag on himself, but he'd gone to a new town and entered a new business to do it. And there was no reason it had to be chalked up to luck, either, unless he wanted to call just being himself lucky. It was no fluke: when he got too old to do anything else, or to feel much like doing anything else, he just naturally began to make money. It seemed to him now that he always half knew that's how it would be.

Even so, there was too little to it. Selling real estate made and kept him rich, but it wasn't really what he did: he didn't really do anything. He was a has-been—and a has-been is better than a never-was, but not much. The stories he told about himself began to ring false even to his own not unsympathetic ear. They were true, those stories: in case anyone doubted it, his brother could always be called in for a verification. But no one seemed to want to call his brother in, nor was his brother very accommodating.

Clyde had an endless number of true and astounding tales to tell about himself: horses and mules he'd broken and shod, miraculous operations he'd performed on the eyes of cows (cutting cancers off them) after the vets had given up; and there were even people, especially in cold weather, willing to sit in his office and listen. There was a big number of stories, but still some were better than others, and Clyde tended to repeat those.

It wasn't senility. For one thing, he wasn't so old, less than sixty; and as his brother Ben would tell you, he'd always been like that. Only when Clyde called him up one night and announced that he was breaking a horse did Ben begin to wonder about him.

There was not much use arguing with the old fellow, but Ben tried it anyway.

"You say you have a horse you want someone to break?" Ben said. "Talk louder!"

"Try the other ear," Clyde said. (Ben was a little deaf in one ear.)

"What do you want a horse broke for?" Ben said. "You're too lazy to ride one. There's a boy right next door to you who breaks them—at least he has a sign up that says so."

"I know he does," Clyde said. "I don't want one broke—I aim to break one."

"Why mess your nest?" Ben said. "Don't be stunting around—a man of your age. What horse?"

"Little horse belongs to Sterling Green—had his ears stung off."

"Why you know the story on that horse—you're crazier than you act."

"He's never been soft," Clyde said. "Never been properly softened up, that little horse, not till I got ahold of him."

"You'll think soft," Ben said. "I sat in my truck and watched him put two better men than you where it's soft, right in one day."

"I doubt that," Clyde said.

"Doubt it?—doubt what?"

"I doubt two better men. Hey you, don't you remember that pinto mule in Bakersfield? That one who they claimed he—"

"Yes, I have a long memory. I want to talk to you, old son," Ben said.

"How's that skim-milk pig doing?" Clyde said.

"I want to talk horses," Ben said.

"I've got him half soft and soaking tonight. His neck needed pounding. Tomorrow I'll have him in the sack. I'll have him in the sack tomorrow. They don't buck with their head up. You know that. Anybody knows it. What's unknown is how to keep it up. They've got to be soft and you've got to have quick hands. Say, my hands are still fast, you know that? Damn right!"

"You're fast all over," Ben said. "I want to see you in the morning."

"All tied up," Clyde said. "Down to my office at two, be down to my office at two and I'll talk to you then. Squeeze you in. On the instant—whereby all expectorations remaining unramified I'll perpetrate."

"Don't real estate me," Ben said. "You just tell me now that—"

Hey, let's go to Reno tomorrow night," Clyde said, "what do you say? We'll get this young horsefighter next door to go with us and we'll all get drunk together and puke in each other's hair. He can't do his wife because she's eight months along and out of town. We're sick of this town, all of us. I feel revigorated. How about yourself?"

"I feel as if I shoveled ditch all day on a sour stomach," Ben said. He'd have to try to remember to go to his brother's office the next day at two, and see if he was still alive.

Earlier in the day the young horsefighter next door had lost a fight with a horse, and that was how Clyde got into it.

First of all, weeks ago, he'd seen the boy move in, and he'd gone over and introduced himself. The boy didn't seem big on talking about himself, but that was all right with Clyde. Then from his porch Clyde had off and on watched as the fellow built himself a round corral that could only be a horsebreaking corral. Worked kind of slow but didn't do a half bad job: big juniper posts set *deep* in the ground—judging by the length of time it took him to dig the holes in that easy sandy ground—and then circles of cables in which were inserted a great number of vertical pickets and brushy branches, so that you could hardly even see through it when he was done.

Then he'd hung out a shingle, just a few days ago:

HORSES BROKE, TRAINED AND SHOD
Guaranteed

Clyde figured that the word "guaranteed" gave him away: he wasn't familiar with breaking horses for the public. Most people couldn't stay on top of a sawhorse, and there was no use promising they could.

Then Clyde, sitting by his stove in the morning, had heard a truck gearing down. He went onto the porch and saw Sterling's outfit come by, carrying a lone horse whose head was stuck up as high as possible over the racks, looking out. It was the little horse Sterling called Hornet, who'd been into a bee's nest as a colt and lost the tips of his ears. And Clyde said to himself that wasn't the only story he knew on the horse.

He watched the truck turn into his neighbor's lane and back up to the loading chute. He told his wife to go down to the office and open up; he wouldn't be down. Don't call him unless there was something so live it just couldn't wait. Sterling left, and his wife left, and Clyde wandered around the house. It was midmorning before Wesley finally led the horse out to the wicker corral. None of my business, Clyde thought, but the boy gets to his work kind of late in the day.

Clyde drove over, sneaked up, and peeked through the pickets. It wasn't polite, but what else could he do? The horse was saddled and ready. The horsebreaker was adjusting himself. Clyde counted the times he pulled down his hat and rearranged his chaps. The horse appeared calm, acted gentle to handle, quiet.

Suddenly he wanted to yell through the fence, "Jesus Christ get a short hold on the reins and pull his head around *to* you!" But what did he care? It wasn't him in the corral. The boot went in the stirrup and without so much as an eyeball flicker Hornet jumped ahead and stuck a hind foot in the horsebreaker's belly.

The stirruped boot jammed against the horse's heart; the rest of the horsebreaker's body flew back and his head struck the ground. The horse snorted a little and jumped sideways. The boy was jerked a few inches when the boot came off and hung alone in the stirrup. There it was, stuck, an empty boot, and for the first time the horse seemed really scared. He ran to the fence, hit it, and spun, whistling through his nose and rolling his left eye and all the ears he had toward the boot. With the accuracy of one who had been desperate before, the horse cow-kicked the boot from the stirrup and sent it spinning across the corral. Immediately he subsided and stood where he was.

Clyde looked at the horsebreaker. His hat was off. Stretched out there, he looked still younger. Hardly twenty, and there was a hole in his sock. The horsebreaker had told Clyde his wife would be arriving in a few days, and that she was going to have a baby. Clyde imagined her unable to darn a sock, potbellied and popping with milk, legs like an antelope: delicate! *that* was what he liked. He wondered if they'd been married long enough . . . then he began to wonder if the boy was ever going to get up.

The horsebreaker did sit up then, and began making sure all his parts were operating. Work down from top to bottom, Clyde thought. The best thing for him to do was to sneak away and come back and announce himself. He walked off among the barn and the sheds, turned, and slowly came back.

Clyde yelled. The gate rattled and swung. "Good morning," Clyde said. "Or is it still morning? How are you and Bee-ears getting along?"

"I'm not so sure," the horsebreaker said, blinking. "I haven't been on him yet."

"You haven't, huh? Let me put it to you this way," Clyde said. "How much do you know about this horse?"

The horsebreaker was blinking rapidly, then succeeded in stopping. "Sterling said he was well started."

"He told you the truth then," Clyde said. He laughed, eyes aglitter. "He's been started more than any horse around and by more different men. You don't mind if I sit on the fence and watch?"

"Do whatever you want," the horsebreaker said.

"I like to ask. Some don't want anyone around. To tell the truth, I never did myself. I never liked anyone around." Clyde waited for the horsebreaker to draw him out about his past. "When I was breaking horses," he added. At last he broke silence again himself: "Have you rode many colts?"

"My share of saddlebroncs."

"Rodeos," Clyde said. "Ah now, that's another business altogether now isn't it?"

Whatever you say."

The horsebreaker caught the horse and led him to the middle of the corral. This time he did try to pull the head around, but the horse's neck was no more pliable than Clyde's stiff old boar's-dick quirt. You never thought of softening him up a little? Clyde said to himself.

He started up the fence. He picked the biggest post. When he grabbed hold of it he felt it was broken off at the bottom, hanging from the cables now instead of supporting them. Could that horse have broken it? Surely Wesley must have backed into it with a pickup. Clyde crawled up the fence and got on top of the post anyway. If they'd gone a little farther out in the hills, he thought, and cut down a little bigger tree, the post would never have broken, would have been stronger in the ground and broader on the top and a little more comfortable sitting.

At least this time the boy was taking a short hold on the reins, and he kept his back near the horse's front end and got a deathhold on the horn before he put his foot in the stirrup. When the horse threw his wingding, the horsebreaker went right on up into the saddle. Clyde was elated. Of course with the horse's head free, the horsebreaker never got seated, nor even a foot in the right stirrup. Down again, soft this time, carefully brushing the shit out of his hat.

Clyde could see that Hornet did only what needed to be done. Like a mule, saving himself. Better and harder things ahead. The boy would never get settled on him the way he was going at it, that was plain. It was a disappointment. He would like to see the horsebreaker get a good seat, just once. He wanted to see if the horse would walk astraddle of his own neck and squeal like a dog, at least for a jump or two, or throw himself on the ground. No, he doubted that last. It was a puzzle, curious, the end predictable but not the action. He himself was shivering; he crossed his arms and wished for his coat.

Up again, the horsebreaker said, "Hornet, he's further along in his education than l am."

"Lookit here, son, maybe it's not mine to say," Clyde said, "but if I was you I believe what I'd do is to—"

The horsebreaker turned on him, cocked his head up to Clyde sitting on the high post like God. "Lookit here yourself. If you were me and I were you, you'd be down here and I'd be up there, but if I was you I'd keep more quiet. I've had all the big-hatted advisers I need."

Clyde was calm. "What would you give a man to start this horse?" he said.

"You'd better watch yourself," the horsebreaker said, and turned away.

Face blanched, Clyde stood, boot-balanced on the highest cable, poised like an eagle. He started to jump, cast his weight forward nimbly as any man, one boot heel jamming between two pickets where they met the cable, the rotted-off post lurching, and he swung forcibly like a hinged board, face first.

"Man overboard," the horsebreaker said.

Clyde dragged himself up, red-faced and spitting sand, and turned to inspect the part of his boot heel that remained in the fence. He dug it out with his knife and put it in his pants pocket. "Two dollars to get it fixed back on," he mumbled.

Yet before the horsebreaker was through smiling Clyde pried him again. "What would you give a man to start this horse for you?"

"Why just what I'd give to see a piss-ant eat a bale of hay. All l have. Which is nothing. At least you couldn't further spoil him."

"What's Sterling paying you?" Clyde said. "No, never mind. You feed him and keep him and let me use your place and I'll start him for you. It won't take long. Five dollars a day and you pay me when Sterling pays you."

"Well I'm not your daddy," the horsebreaker said. "You be the fool and I'll be the audience."

Without unsaddling the horse, the horsebreaker climbed onto Clyde's post. Clyde drove home, lifted *his* saddle from a hook in the barn, opened the old war chest: took out his quirt, a snaffle-bit bridle with soft rope reins, a hobble made of a split and twisted tow sack, a soft cotton rope an inch and a half thick, and a lariat a little mashed by storage. He cut the wires from a bale of hay and twisted them into a slender baling-wire bat.

When he faced the horse, he noticed that even the air in the bottom of the corral was considerably different from that on the post. The horse flicked his foot at a fly and Clyde felt a twitch in his own thigh, like the reflex from a blow. When he bent over to sort his equipment his face got red, and when he stood up it got white—he had that kind of face. Too much pork and chair, he thought. For a moment he felt as if he'd gone by a gully with something dead in it. Then he was all right. He felt good. He disregarded his audience.

With one hand he took hold of the rein up close to the bit and with the other threw the cotton rope over the horse's head and tied a knot in it around the base of the neck. He wondered if the horsebreaker had ever seen anyone tie a bowline with one hand. If he had an eye in his head he'd notice. Clyde flicked the slack of the rope between the hind legs. A foot raised to kick was hooked. The horse didn't throw a fit: apparently this had been done before too, and done well enough so that he was afraid to fight it. Clyde drew the leg up high under the belly, twisted the escape out of the rope, and tied it off. He pulled the saddle and bridle from the fouled horse and went to throw them up on the fence, swinging them neatly off his hip. To his surprise the saddle fell back into his arms. It was too high, he couldn't make it. "Here," said the horsebreaker, and in some embarrassment Clyde handed them up.

Clyde changed his rope. For the horse, then, to jump would be to fall. Hornet wouldn't make the move and Clyde couldn't pull down the braced weight. Facing the horse to the fence, Clyde tied the foot ropes forward to a post and suddenly struck the horse in the face with the heel of the quirt. Hornet in terror jumped backwards, hind legs snatched forward, falling. Clyde was fast: jerked the knot loose from the fence and fell on the falling animal's head. He lay down alongside Hornet, one knee plunged against throat, other knee hooked around muzzle, locked his legs together and twisted the head as hard as he could. He reached up and tightened the leg ropes with his hands.

He was a little surprised the horse didn't thrash his head, even when it was released, or strain against the ropes. This had most likely all been done to him before, yet it must have been a while ago. The horse began to sweat. Clyde noticed it first at the flanks—just a dark turn to the hair. Then all the body oozed at once, or so it seemed. There was water in the crease below the chopped ears; it rolled in and out of the eye sockets and trickled from the nostrils.

With the baling-wire bat Clyde struck the supple part of the neck. The horse curled from the ground, face wet and slick, wet ears pinned flat, mouth striking. Clyde mashed his heel into it, stood on the horse's mouth and continued pounding with a rapid stroke.

Noon, and no one to cook. He fried him some sausage. For business purposes he had a sticker on his car: "Eat beef for health." But pork was really his meat and sausage his cut. "I like the grease off the meat," he was fond of saying. After lunch he hated to leave the shade of his porch. Yet at one sharp he was back in the corral. He rolled the horse over and began pounding the other side of the neck. The horse had turned black and settled the dust around him. Apparently there was no end to the water he could put out. The boy was there on the post. Was he there again or there still? Surely *again,* Clyde thought. Who would sit staring at a tied-down horse for an hour, without even a speck of shade? With veterinary curiosity Clyde reached between the hind legs and stroked the hairless chocolate-colored skin where the testicles had been cut out three or four years ago.

The horse needed hind shoes. Clyde hated the thought. Yet now while he had him down was the time. Rather than build a fire and shape some shoes to fit properly, he drove down to the hardware and bought some pre-shaped and -sized "cowboy" shoes. He asked the horsebreaker to lend him some tools. They included a pair of fine hand-forged nippers that had been worn out once and repinned. He wondered if the boy didn't shoe horses better than he broke them. It was true that his knuckles were scarred and he had a proper curl to his shoulders.

"Don't you tell anyone who shod this horse," Clyde said. "I guessed his size: he only takes an aught shoe and's got a six-year-old mouth. Nice small feet." Clyde unbent his back and glanced down at his own feet, which were also small (the horsebreaker's weren't), proving that he, Clyde, was a rider, not a plodder.

He clinched the shoes on to stay, if not to fit. It seemed his back would never be half straight again—and here he used to shoe sometimes eight or nine head in a day. An idiot's life! Though maybe he hadn't thought so then. . . .

Clyde untied the ropes, hit the horse with the sack hobble; Hornet scrambled up, shook, staggered, planted his feet squarely and stood blinking. With a rope Clyde jacked up a hind leg as before. He hobbled the front legs together and jumped and struggled onto Hornet's back. The horse stood a second, then, even fouled as he was, snorted and erupted, sprang in the air, and fell on his ribs. Clyde was thrown clear on hands and knees, perfectly clear yet arms and legs churning like a pig on ice. He got on his feet and whipped the horse up quickly. When he got on again, Hornet stood. Clyde moved around over the back, petting and massaging for what seemed endless minutes, but the horse never stopped shaking.

Clyde brushed the horse's back and belly with his hand and saddled him. "Let's tie him in your barn," he said. "When he cools off, you can feed him and pack him some water."

"I'll take him," the horsebreaker said. "You're not going to unsaddle him?"

"Uh-uh, I want to see what he does. I don't want to tell you your business, but if you're going to lead him you better get a hold close to his face."

The horsebreaker opened the gate, holding the exhausted horse on twelve inches of slack. Hornet bogged his head and took it. Hind feet crossed the boy's face, hit the brim of his hat.

"I'll get your hat for you," Clyde said. "Rope burn you?"

The horsebreaker flapped his hands and stared fascinated: "Pootah la Maggie, look at him fire."

The horse was mopping the barnyard with his nose on the ground, breath shooting gravel at their knees. Stiff-kneed landings drove the stirrups straight in the air where they clashed repeatedly over the saddle, the stirrup leathers snapping like whips. A fog of dust obscured him and when they saw him again he was running.

"Could you ride your pony if you ever got seated on him?" Clyde said.

"I don't imagine, but that's for me to ask you."

The horse ran down the lane, slid up to the gate, spun and came galloping back. Clyde stood ready in the end of the lane with a loop hidden behind him. He would have liked to turn him a flip, and as the horse shied by he did forefoot him neatly. But the instant the loop enveloped his legs, Hornet planted himself and slid to a stop. They anchored him for the night.

"You're not going to unsaddle him now?" the horsebreaker said.

Clyde said he wasn't. He drove home, wandered out to find his cow, who was waiting for him near the barn, tight-bagged, and he milked her crudely with stiff fingers.

The evening was unpleasant. His wife didn't like what he was up to and said nothing to him except that he must call Ben. No business would be talked tonight. When he'd finished supper and watched television a bit, he did get up and call. But Ben's words and her silences had equally little effect on Clyde.

The next day the horsebreaker limped out of the barn. "I led him to water and tied him back up," he said.

"Uh-huh. How'd he lead this morning?" Clyde said.

"Sudden."

"Huh. You kept ahold of him though, right? You reached and got him and snatched him back. You're waking up. To tell the truth, I saw you from the porch." Clyde untied the horse and led him to the corral. The neck was swollen, a small ridge on each side, but the real soreness would be underneath, in the muscles. Clyde was satisfied. He thought, Bee-ears, you're tender and bendable as a flower. There were mouth corners yet to be done.

He tied the left rein to a ring in the left saddle skirt and had the horse chasing himself, whirling from the pressure and from him—Clyde—who stood there snapping hobbles and kicking dirt. This was done on the other side too, and the skin where the black lips met was peeled down to pink by the bit rings. Clyde tied long ropes to both bit rings, ran the ropes back through the stirrups, and began driving the horse from behind like a plowman.

He jumped the horse into a trot, stayed well back himself, and made the inside circles. Still he had to open his mouth to get enough air, and what he got seemed straight dust.

"Can you open the gate?" he said. Hornet spurted through the opening. Clyde let him run the length of the lines, threw his weight onto one. He had the leverage. The head whipped around, the body flew on, circling the head, unfooted, helpless, ungainly, crashing. It was a while before Clyde could get the horse up. After that he had him turning every which way and stopping, hooves sliding, making short figure elevens in the gravel. He had a good natural stop, Clyde thought. Wasn't it time to quit? He had almost run out of air himself. And if he went too far the horse would be immune to feeling. Soft and watching—and if he was any judge the horse was at that point. Though you never knew if a little less or a little more would do better. Who could say? He looked at his watch: ten-thirty. He'd rest until one, maybe even go without dinner.

At one Clyde brought back a short leather strap with snaps on each end. With this he hobbled the stirrups together, passing the strap across under the horse's belly.

Holding the reins short, and getting the cheek of the bridle tight in his hand, Clyde pulled the horse's head around and made him whirl in a circle. He was at the center, and he kept the horse spinning even after he was in the saddle, until he had the seat he wanted. The horse was grabbing himself, tail clamped, back humped, trying to buck with his head up. Clyde suddenly drove a spur in him, snatched him to the left again, driving the right spur. Pulled him back and forth then and into the fence, loping finally, Clyde's feet driving him on. The horse had a right to scotch, for every time Clyde suspected him of getting wits and balance together he slid a hand down one rein and pulled the horse hard into the fence.

The head busy, the head busy, Clyde thought, soft as butter. The horse lathered white between the legs and specks of blood showed at the mouth corners. They never slowed up. "Swing the gate once more for me, son, if you would," and out they shot.

Clyde let him run halfway across the barnyard, spurs gigging him on, then he set down so hard on one rein that he was afraid the horse would turn another squawdeedo, this time land on him. Hornet did start to fall sideways, stumbling, and Clyde threw the reins to him, let him gather his feet, and then snatched him again, this time the other side, whirled him both directions and off they went right down the center of the highway, Clyde still jerking the horse in circles first one way then the other and gigging him with both spurs, sparks flying off the asphalt, Hornet given no chance to forget he was being used.

The skidding shod and unshod hooves rang on varying pavement. Their tracks would be there in the tarry patches, Clyde thought. Immortal! Or at least until the first hard freeze this fall. For a minute he was afraid the streets would be deserted. Then he straightened his back in the saddle, swelling like an old boar, the bull of the woods, drawing in his belly, increasing by inches. The horse seemed to dwindle.

A motorcycle passed: Hornet rolled an eye, leaped, was pulled easily around, stumbling. Clyde imagined what they'd say tonight in the Frontier Club. . . .

Someone stepped into the street, hailing him. Clyde said, "Is this the horse you think it is? I expect it is. Only horse around's had both ears stung off. . . ." He went on, stopped again: "Uh-huh, I brought him in right off to get used to the boogers. He's never been uptown before, do you imagine? 'Cept just passing through, trying to stare the slats out of a truck. What do you say?"

Ben was standing in front of the office. Faces of children were pressed to the window of one of Clyde's duplexes across the street He heard the excited hum of voices coming through the walls, though he finally realized this was a television.

Ben bowed and took off his hat, a wild head of hair springing out like the white beard on a goat.

"Yessir!" Clyde said "Do you want to talk to me?"

"I did but I don't," Ben said. "I changed my mind. You'd best go on before she decides to come out of the office "

"She won't," Clyde said. Yet she might, and he rode on.

Heading out the other side of town he was light-headed. I should have eaten a little, he thought, a piece of bread and honey or some plum jam by itself. He turned across the canal. When the hooves rattled the bridge boards, Hornet snorted and tried halfheartedly to bolt. Clyde pulled him around. "Ante," he said. "If you've got to be a nigger, be a good one." You're in the sack now, he thought.

They jogged on across the juniper flat, skirting town and heading home. He put his reins in one hand now. Something gray appeared at the edge of vision: "Coyote," Clyde said, and lifted his free hand. Hornet jumped sideways and landed stiff-kneed, an ear cocked at Clyde who'd been snapped off center. A hair off, but Hornet took it. Mouth open, Clyde's teeth smashing tongue, Hornet's head gone out of sight and the noise coming up, like a stuck pig or a dog in the mower blades, continuous.

It was this squealing that terrified Clyde. He got his seat back, as good a deep socked-in seat as anyone ever had. Boots jammed to the heels down the hobbled stirrups, spurs jobbed into the cinch and through the cinch to the hide and through the hide, an arch thrown into his back and his weight against the reins trying to control the head, drawing mouth blood too, all he could, though that wouldn't help now.

Clyde grunted. The horse too, whose body couldn't stand its own lock-kneed hitting. Hornet's mouth showering back a bloody salt into Clyde's eyes and he himself spitting air. He refixed the jumping desert each time they landed. Forced himself not to be confused by the sky, to keep refocusing the horse's neck against the ground. His eyes were gauging accurate, but beginning to lag, lagging, falling behind like the bubble on a spinning level. He was being moved, knew he was, crotch drifting, will couldn't stop it. Off center, a hump jerked into his back, the left leg taking too much shock, the right one spinning loose, spur popped from the cinch.

He lost the stirrup, felt it go, and only hoped then to lose the left one too. Mane glimpsed against the sky, track all lost of where he was, while he felt it there solid, his foot stirruped, hobbled, spur spurred into the cinch and through it, twisting now like a hook; he the fish now, a whole new set of things to think about, too fast, rising changing sand bushes. Clyde's face passing Hornets mouth, open, blood on the bit rings, eye glazed visionless. Bucking blind, then quit and ran.

For fifty yards Hornet tried to kick him loose. Clyde dragging. His eye buried in the crook of one arm and the other arm enfolding his head. Even during this he imagined the luck of the foot breaking, getting sluffed out of his boot. The horse hit the badger hole, folded down upon Clyde's leg. He thought this was salvation and spun over onto his back, watched the horse pawing up again, saw himself still hooked, suspended, moving off, face slapped by branches, and discovered his hands lacing around juniper trunk. And him knowing he could pull his leg off if he had to. An explosion in his knee, vision of juniper roots bursting, fibers flayed out like the nerve ends on a lighted chart. The saddle fell on his feet, the horse tangled in bridle reins, stepping on them and brutally stabbing his own mouth. Hornet stopped, tied to his own legs.

Clyde discovered that he was still squeezing his juniper. He let go. Who saw? He turned slowly. She would be there, arms across chest; Ben quizzical, hat off, head at an angle; the boy who wanted to break horses; behind them a great vague crowd of townspeople. No, he saw the buildings of town, that was all, and farther west the ridge of his own canal bank.

He fished up his knife, leaned forward and cut a few strands of cinch away from his spur. If the latigo on the saddle hadn't broken, the strands would have, he thought. He pulled his boot from the stirrup and got up. As far as he could tell, nothing was broken, and neither back nor knee would be impossible until tomorrow. All the rest was skin, the knees and elbows ripped out of his clothes, bruises, teeth. He must have hit his mouth. Where was his hat? There. Way back there. Well, he'd gone a long while with his own teeth, hadn't he? Way longer than Ben.

His inclination was to pull the bridle off Hornet and start walking. But if he left the horse here, this whole story was going to be out an hour after feeding time. And what if he led him in? If he walked alone he could wade the canal anywhere, but the horse wouldn't follow him through the water. He'd have to go to the bridge, which was right by the highway and visible from the horsebreaker's house too. It wouldn't do to be seen leading the horse in, and if he waited till dark, his wife would have the whole town out after him. There was nothing to be done but to mend his latigo and be seen riding in, if he was to be seen at all.

Clyde threw his stirrup hobbles away and hid the spurs in the badger hole. He couldn't control his knee and didn't want to be spurring the horse by accident. This was one ride he wanted to sneak. He hobbled Hornet with a rein, saddled him, and when he went to get on cheeked him tight as the mouth could stand—not much now.

The horse dragged his toes, even over the rattling crossboards of the bridge. But Clyde wasn't taking any chances: he kept his eyes on the horse's head. If he'd dared to look around, he might have seen the listless dragging tracks Hornet was making in the sand, and been less nervous.

Clyde was a couple of days in the house recuperating, and when he did go back to the office he looked pretty bunged up. The horse was loping along like a good one and stuck his foot in a badger hole and took a tumble: that was the story Clyde thought of telling, but he was afraid it wouldn't be believed and changed his mind. Besides the episode as it really was was good enough.

And it was lucky for him that he didn't try to lie. That darned Sterling, the first day Clyde was back at the office, knocked on the door of Clyde's house and asked his wife if it wasn't okay to borrow something out of the tackroom. She told him to go ahead, and under pretense of borrowing something (though he really did borrow something), he looked at Clyde's saddle and found the track of the right spur rowel where it had crossed the seat of the saddle on Clyde's way off—and Sterling told everyone about it.

Ben stopped in at the office a week later, to say the pig he was fattening for Clyde was ready (he also wanted to have a look at him). Once there, he regretted it, and could hardly wait to make his escape.

"You saw yourself," Clyde said to him, "I had him between my two hands. Soft as butter, don't you doubt it."

"I don't doubt it," Ben said wearily. "I saw it myself."

"Only I ought to have kept both hands on the reins at all times. Darned if a man no matter how much he knows and how well he knows it won't always lose his wherewithal at the sight of a coyote or some silly thing."

"Now there's a bit of first-class wisdom for you," Ben said. Clyde was having some teeth made, but right now he was missing some out of his mouth like an old cow. It didn't make him look younger. And he had a new cane—Ben saw it leaning up against the desk—to help him out with his knee. But for all that, he appeared to be in a lively enough mood. Ben thought he'd bait him a little. "How long again you say you rode that horse?"

"Two days, so far."

"Two. . . . Pay you, did they?"

"Five a saddle."

"Uh-huh—ten dollars. That pay those dentist bills pretty well, will it?"

"I've just about got that dentist sold a piece of property," Clyde said. Anyway he's easy money from now on, that horse—you could sit on him backwards. "Not me," said Ben.

COWBOYS ARE MY WEAKNESS

Pam Houston

I HAVE A PICTURE IN MY MIND of a tiny ranch on the edge of a stand of pine trees with some horses in the yard. There's a woman standing in the doorway in cutoffs and a blue chambray work shirt and she's just kissed her tall, bearded, and soft-spoken husband goodbye. There's laundry hanging outside and the morning sun is filtering through the tree branches like spiderwebs. It's the morning after a full moon, and behind the house the deer have eaten everything that was left in the garden.

If I were a painter, I'd paint that picture just to see if the girl in the doorway would turn out to be me. I've been out west ten years now, long enough to call it my home, long enough to know I'll be here forever, but I still don't know where that ranch is. And even though I've had plenty of men here, some of them tall and nearly all of them bearded, I still haven't met the man who has just walked out of the painting, who has just started his pickup truck, whose tire marks I can still see in the sandy soil of the drive.

The west isn't a place that gives itself up easily. Newcomers have to sink into it slowly, to descend through its layers, and I'm still descending. Like most easterners, I started out in the transitional zones, the big cities and the ski towns that outsiders have set up for their own comfort, the places so often referred to as "the best of both worlds." But I was bound to work my way back, through the land, into the small towns and beyond them. That's half the reason I wound up on a ranch near Grass Range, Montana; the other half is Homer.

I've always had this thing about cowboys, maybe because I was born in New Jersey. But a real cowboy is hard to find these days, even in the west. I thought I'd found one on several occasions, I even at one time thought Homer was a cowboy, and though I loved him like crazy for a while and in some ways always will, somewhere along the line I had to face the fact that even though Homer looked like a cowboy, he was just a capitalist with a Texas accent who owned a horse.

Homer's a wildlife specialist in charge of a whitetail deer management project on the ranch. He goes there every year to observe the deer from the start of the mating season in late October until its peak in mid-November. It's the time when the deer are most visible, when the bucks get so lusty they lose their normal caution, when the does run around in the middle of the day with their white tails in the air. When Homer talked me into coming with him, he said I'd love the ranch, and I did. It was sixty miles from the nearest paved road. All of the buildings were whitewashed and plain. One of them had been ordered from a 1916 Sears catalogue. The ranch hands still rode horses, and when the late-afternoon light swept the grainfields across from headquarters, I would watch them move the cattle in rows that looked like waves. There was a peace about the ranch that was uncanny and might have been complete if not for the eight or nine hungry barn cats that crawled up your legs if you even smelled like food, and the exotic chickens of almost every color that fought all day in their pens.

Homer has gone to the ranch every year for the last six, and he has a long history of stirring up trouble there. The ranch hands watch him sit on the hillside and hate him for the money he makes. He's slept with more than one or two of their wives and girlfriends. There was even some talk that he was the reason the ranch owner got divorced.

When he asked me to come with him I knew it would be me or somebody else and I'd heard good things about Montana so I went. There was a time when I was sure Homer was the man who belonged in my painting and I would have sold my soul to be his wife, or even his only girlfriend. I'd come close, in the spring, to losing my mind because of it, but I had finally learned that Homer would always be separate, even from himself, and by the time we got to Montana I was almost immune to him.

Homer and I live in Fort Collins, Colorado, most of the year, in houses that are exactly one mile apart. He's out of town as often as not, keeping track of fifteen whitetail deer herds all across the West. I go with him when he lets me, which is lately more and more. The herds Homer studies are isolated by geography, given plenty of food in bad winters, and protected from hunters and wolves. Homer is working on reproduction and genetics, trying to create, in the wild, super-bucks bigger and tougher than elk. The Montana herd has been his most successful, so he spends the long mating season there. Under his care the bucks have shown incredible increases in antler mass, in body weight, and in fertility.

The other scientists at the university that sponsors Homer respect him, not only for his success with the deer, but for his commitment to observation, for his relentless dedication to his hours in the field. They also think he is eccentric and a bit overzealous.

At first I thought he just liked to be outdoors, but when we got to the ranch his obsession with the deer made him even more like a stranger. He was gone every day from way before sunrise till long after dark. He would dress all in camouflage, even his gloves and socks, and sit on the hillsides above where the deer fed and watch, making notes a few times an hour, changing position every hour or two. If I went with him I wasn't allowed to move except when he did, and I was never allowed to talk. I'd try to save things up for later that I thought of during the day, but by the time we got back to our cabin they seemed unimportant and Homer liked to eat his dinner in front of the TV. By the time we got the dishes done it was way past Homer's bedtime. We were making love less and less, and when we did, it was always from behind.

The ranch owner's name was David, and he wasn't what you'd think a Montana ranch owner would be. He was a poet, and a vegetarian. He listened to Andreas Vollenweider and drank hot beverages with names like Suma and Morning Rain. He wouldn't let the ranch hands use pesticides or chemicals, he wouldn't hire them if they smoked cigarettes. He undergrazed the ranch by about fifty percent, so the organic grain was belly-high to a horse almost everywhere.

David had an idea about recreating on his forty thousand acres the Great Plains that only the Indians and the first settlers had seen. He wasn't making a lot of money ranching, but he was producing the fattest, healthiest, most organic Black Angus cattle in North America. He was sensitive, thoughtful, and kind. He was the kind of man I always knew I should fall in love with, but never did.

Homer and David ate exactly one dinner a week together, which I always volunteered to cook. Homer was always polite and full of incidental conversation and much too quick to laugh. David was quiet and sullen and so restrained that he was hard to recognize.

The irreconcilable differences between Homer and me had been revealing themselves one at a time since late summer. In early November

I asked him what he wanted to do on Thanksgiving, and he said he'd like most of all to stay on the ranch and watch the does in heat.

Homer was only contracted to work on the ranch until the Sunday before Thanksgiving. When he asked me to come with him he told me we would leave the ranch in plenty of time to have the holidays at home.

I was the only child in a family that never did a lot of celebrating because my parents couldn't plan ahead. They were sun worshipers, and we spent every Thanksgiving in a plane on the way to Puerto Rico, every Christmas in a car on Highway 95, heading for Florida. What I remember most from those days is Casey Kasem's Christmas shows, the long-distance dedications, "I'll be home for Christmas" from Bobby D. in Spokane to Linda S. in Decatur. We never had hotel reservations and the places we wound up in had no phones and plastic mattress covers and triple locks on the doors. Once we spent Christmas night parked under a fluorescent streetlight, sleeping in the car.

I've spent most of the holidays in my adult life making up for those road trips. I spend lots of money on hand-painted ornaments. I always cook a roast ten pounds bigger than anything we could possibly eat.

Homer thinks my enthusiasm about holidays is childish and self-serving. To prove it to me, last Christmas morning he set the alarm for six-thirty and went back to his house to stain a door. This year I wanted Thanksgiving in my own house. I wanted to cook a turkey we'd be eating for weeks.

I said, "Homer, you've been watching the deer for five weeks now. What else do you think they're gonna do?"

"You don't know anything about it," he said. "Thanksgiving is the premium time. Thanksgiving," he shook one finger in the air, "is the height of the rut."

David and I drank tea together, and every day took walks up into the canyon behind ranch headquarters. He talked about his ex-wife, Carmen, about the red flowers that covered the canyon walls in June, about imaging away nuclear weapons. He told me about the woman Homer was sleeping with on the ranch the year before, when I was back in Colorado counting days till he got home. She was the woman who took care of the chickens, and David said that when Homer left the ranch she wrote a hundred love songs and made David listen while she sang them all.

"She sent them on a tape to Homer," David said, "and when he didn't call or write, she went a little nuts. I finally told her to leave the ranch. I'm not a doctor, and we're a long way from anywhere out here."

From the top of the canyon we could see Homer's form blending with the trees on the ridge above the garden, where the deer ate organic potatoes by the hundreds of pounds.

"I understand if he wasn't interested anymore," David said. "But I can't believe even he could ignore a gesture that huge."

We watched Homer crawl along the ridge from tree to tree. I could barely distinguish his movements from what the wind did to the tall grass. None of the deer below him even turned their heads.

"What is it about him?" David said, and I knew he was looking for an explanation about Carmen, but I'd never even met her and I didn't want to talk about myself.

"Homer's always wearing camouflage," I said. "Even when he's not."

The wind went suddenly still and we could hear, from headquarters, the sounds of cats fighting, a hen's frantic scream, and then, again, the cats.

David put his arm around me. "We're such good people," he said. "Why aren't we happy?"

One day when I got back from my walk with David, Homer was in the cabin in the middle of the day. He had on normal clothes and I could tell he'd shaved and showered. He took me into the bedroom and climbed on top of me frontwards, the way he did when we first met and I didn't even know what he did for a living.

Afterwards he said, "We didn't need a condom, did we?" I counted the days forward and backward and forward again. Homer always kept track of birth control and groceries and gas mileage and all the other things I couldn't keep my mind on. Still, it appeared to be exactly ten days before my next period.

"Yes," I said, "I think we did."

Homer has never done an uncalculated thing in his life, and for a moment I let myself entertain the possibility that his mistake meant that somewhere inside he wanted to have a baby with me, that he really wanted a family and love and security and the things I thought everybody wanted before I met Homer. On the other hand, I knew that one of the ways I had gotten in trouble with Homer, and with other men before him, was by inventing thoughts for them that they'd never had.

"Well," he said. "In that case we better get back to Colorado before they change the abortion laws."

Sometimes the most significant moments of your life reveal themselves to you even as they are happening, and I knew in that moment that I would never love Homer the same way again. It wasn't so much that not six months before, when I had asked Homer what we'd do if I got pregnant, he said we'd get married and have a family, It wasn't even that I was sure I wanted a baby. It wasn't even that I thought there was going to be a baby to want.

It all went back to the girl in the log cabin, and how the soft-spoken man would react if she thought she was going to have a baby. It would be winter now, and snowing outside the windows warm with yellow light. He might dance with the sheepdog on the living-room floor, he might sing the theme song from *Father Knows Best*, he might go out and do a swan dive into the snow.

I've been to a lot of school and read a lot of thick books, but at my very core there's a made-for-TV-movie mentality I don't think I'll ever shake. And although there's a lot of doubt in my mind about whether or not an ending as simple and happy as I want is possible anyone in the world, it was clear to me that afternoon that it wasn't possible with Homer.

Five o'clock the next morning was the first time I saw the real cowboy. He was sitting in the cookhouse eating cereal and I couldn't make myself sleep next to Homer so I'd been up all night wandering around.

He was tall and thin and bearded. His hat was white and ratty and you could tell by looking at his stampede strap that it had been made around a campfire after lots of Jack Daniel's. I'd had my fingers in my hair for twelve hours and my face was breaking out from too much stress and too little sleep and I felt like such a greaseball that I didn't say hello. I poured myself some orange juice, drank it, rinsed the glass, and put it in the dish drainer. I took one more look at the cowboy, and walked back out the door, and went to find Homer in the field.

Homer's truck was parked by a culvert on the South Fork road, which meant he was walking the brush line below the cliffs that used to be the Blackfeet buffalo jumps. It was a boneyard down there, the place where hundreds of buffalo, chased by the Indians, had jumped five hundred feet to their death, and the soil was extremely fertile. The grass was thicker and sweeter there than anywhere on the ranch, and Homer said the deer sucked calcium out of the buffalo bones. I saw Homer crouched at the edge of a meadow I couldn't get to without being seen, so I went back and fell asleep in the bed of his truck.

It was hunting season, and later that morning Homer and I found a deer by the side of the road that had been poached but not taken. The poacher must have seen headlights or heard a truck engine and gotten scared.

I lifted the back end of the animal into the truck while Homer picked up the antlers. It was a young buck, two and a half at the oldest, but it would have been a monster in a few years, and I knew Homer was taking the loss pretty hard.

We took it down to the performance center, where they weigh the organic calves. Homer attached a meat hook to its antlers and hauled it into the air above the pickup.

"Try and keep it from swinging," he said. And I did my best, considering I wasn't quite tall enough to get a good hold, and its blood was bubbling out of the bullet hole and dripping down on me.

That's when the tall cowboy, the one from that morning, walked out of the holding pen behind me, took a long slow look at me trying to steady the back end of the dead deer, and settled himself against the fence across the driveway. I stepped back from the deer and pushed the hair out of my eyes. He raised one finger to call me over. I walked slow and didn't look back at Homer.

"Nice buck," he said. "Did you shoot it?"

"It's a baby," I said. "I don't shoot animals. A poacher got it last night."

"Who was the poacher?" he said, and tipped his hat just past my shoulder toward Homer.

"You're wrong," I said. "You can say a lot of things about him, but he wouldn't poach a deer."

"My name's Montrose T. Coty," he said. "Everyone calls me Monte."

I shook his hand. "Everyone calls you Homer's girlfriend," he said, "but I bet that's not your name."

"You're right," I said, "it's not."

I turned to look at Homer. He was taking measurements off the hanging deer: antler length, body length, width at its girth.

"Tonight's the Stockgrowers' Ball in Grass Range," Monte said. "I thought you might want to go with me."

Homer was looking into the deer's hardened eyeballs. He had its mouth open, and was pulling on its tongue.

"I have to cook dinner for Homer and David," I said. "I'm sorry. It sounds like fun."

In the car on the way back to the cabin, Homer said, "What was that all about?"

I said, "Nothing," and then I said, "Monte asked me to the Stockgrowers' Ball."

"The Stockgrowers' Ball?" he said. "Sounds like a great time. What do stockgrowers do at a ball?" he said. "Do they dance?"

I almost laughed with him until I remembered how much I loved to dance. I'd been with Homer chasing whitetail so long that I'd forgotten that dancing, like holidays, was something I loved. And I started to wonder just then what else being with Homer had made me forget. Hadn't I, at one time, spent whole days listening to music? Wasn't there a time when I wanted, more than anything, to buy a sailboat? And didn't I love to be able to go outdoors and walk anywhere I wanted, and to make, if I wanted, all kinds of noise?

I wanted to blame Homer, but I realized then it was more my fault than his. Because even though I'd never let the woman in the chambray work shirt out of my mind I'd let her, in the last few years, become someone different, and she wasn't living, anymore, in my painting. The painting she was living in, I saw, belonged to somebody else.

"So what did you tell him?" Homer said.

"I told him I'd see if you'd cook dinner," I said.

I tried to talk to Homer before I left. First I told him that it wasn't a real date, that I didn't even know Monte, and really I was only going because I didn't know if I'd ever have another chance to go to a Stockgrowers' Ball. When he didn't answer at all I worked up to saying that maybe it was a good idea for me to start seeing other people. That maybe we'd had two different ideas all along and we needed to find two other people who would better meet our needs. I told him that if he had any opinions I wished he'd express them to me, and he thought for a few minutes and then he said,

"Well, I guess we have Jimmy Carter to thank for all the trouble in Panama."

I spent the rest of the day getting ready for the Stockgrowers' Ball. All

I'd brought with me was some of Homer's camouflage and blue jeans, so I wound up borrowing a skirt that David's ex-wife had left behind, some of the chicken woman's dress shoes that looked ridiculous and made my feet huge, and a vest that David's grandfather had been shot at in by the Plains Indians.

Monte had to go into town early to pick up ranch supplies, so I rode in with his friends Buck and Dawn, who spent the whole drive telling me what a great guy Monte was, how he quit the rodeo circuit to make a decent living for himself and his wife, how she'd left without saying good-bye not six months before.

They told me that he'd made two thousand dollars in one afternoon doing a Wrangler commercial. That he'd been in a laundromat on his day off and the director had seen him through the window, had gone in and said, "Hey, cowboy, you got an hour? You want to make two thousand bucks?"

"Ole Monte," Buck said. "He's the real thing."

After an hour and a half of washboard road we pulled into the dance hall just on our edge of town. I had debated about wearing the cowboy hat I'd bought especially for my trip to Montana, and was thankful I'd decided against it. It was clear, once inside, that only the men wore hats, and only dress hats at that. The women wore high heels and stockings and in almost every case hair curled away from their faces in great airy rolls.

We found Monte at a table in the corner, and the first thing he did was give me a corsage, a pink one, mostly roses that couldn't have clashed more with my rust-colored blouse. Dawn pinned it on me, and I blushed, I suppose, over my first corsage in ten years, and a little old woman in spike heels leaned over and said, "Somebody loves you!" just loud enough for Monte and Buck and Dawn to hear.

During dinner they showed a movie about a cattle drive. After dinner a young enthusiastic couple danced and sang for over an hour about cattle and ranch life and the Big Sky, a phrase which since I'd been in Montana had seemed perpetually on the tip of everybody's tongue.

After dinner the dancing started, and Monte asked me if I knew how to do the Montana two-step. He was more than a foot taller than me, and his hat added another several inches to that. When we stood on the dance floor my eyes came right to the place where his silk scarf disappeared into the shirt buttons on his chest. His big hands were strangely light on me and my feet went the right direction even though my mind couldn't remember the two-step's simple form.

"That's it," he said into the part in my hair. "Don't think. Just let yourself move with me."

And we were moving together, in turns that got tighter and tighter each time we circled the dance floor. The songs got faster and so did our motion until there wasn't time for anything but the picking up and putting down of feet, for the swirling colors of Carmen's ugly skirt, for breath and sweat and rhythm.

I was farther west than I'd ever imagined, and in the strange, nearly flawless synchronization on the dance floor I knew I could be a Montana ranch woman, and I knew I could make Monte my man. It had taken me ten years, and an incredible sequence of accidents, but that night I thought I'd finally gotten where I'd set out to go.

The band played till two and we danced till three to the jukebox. Then there was nothing left to do but get in the car and begin the two-hour drive home.

First we talked about our horses. It was the logical choice, the only thing we really had in common, but it only lasted twenty minutes.

I tried to get his opinion on music and sailing, but just like a cowboy, he was too polite for me to tell anything for sure.

Then we talked about the hole in my vest that the Indians shot, which I was counting on, and half the reason I wore it.

The rest of the time we just looked at the stars.

I had spent a good portion of the night worrying about what I was going to say when Monte asked me to go to bed with him. When he pulled up between our two cabins he looked at me sideways and said,

"I'd love to give you a great big kiss, but I've got a mouthful of chew."

I could hear Homer snoring before I got past the kitchen.

Partly because I didn't like the way Monte and Homer eyed each other, but mostly because I couldn't bear to spend Thanksgiving watching does in heat, I loaded my gear in my truck and got ready to go back to Colorado.

On the morning I left, Homer told me that he had decided that I was the woman he wanted to spend the rest of his life with after all, and that he planned to go to town and buy a ring just as soon as the rut ended.

He was sweet on my last morning on the ranch, generous and atten-
tive in a way I'd never seen. He packed me a sack lunch of chicken salad
he mixed himself, and he went out to my car and dusted off the inch of
snow that had fallen in our first brush with winter, overnight. He told me
to call when I got to Fort Collins, he even said to call collect, but I suppose one of life's big tricks is to give us precisely the thing we want, two
weeks after we've stopped wanting it, and I couldn't take Homer seriously, even when I tried.

When I went to say good-bye to David he hugged me hard, said I was
welcome back on the ranch anytime. He said he enjoyed my company
and appreciated my insight. Then he said he liked my perfume and I wondered where my taste in men had come from, I wondered whoever taught
me to be so stupid about men.

I knew Monte was out riding the range, so I left a note on his car
thanking him again for the dancing and saying I'd be back one day and we
could dance again. I put my hat on, that Monte had never got to see, and
rolled out of headquarters. It was the middle of the day, but I saw seven
bucks in the first five miles, a couple of them giants, and when I slowed
down they just stood and stared at the truck. It was the height of the rut
and Homer said that's how they'd be, love-crazed and fearless as bears.

About a mile before the edge of ranch property, I saw something that
looked like a lone antelope running across the skyline, but antelope are
almost never alone, so I stopped the car to watch. As the figure came closer I saw it was a horse, a big chestnut, and it was carrying a rider at a full
gallop, and it was coming right for the car.

I knew it could have been any one of fifty cowboys employed on the
ranch, and yet I've learned to expect more from life than that, and so in
my heart I knew it was Monte. I got out of the car and waited, pleased
that he'd see my hat most of all, wondering what he'd say when I said I
was leaving.

He didn't get off his horse, which was sweating and shaking so hard I
thought it might die while we talked.

"You on your way?" he said.

I smiled and nodded. His chaps were sweat-soaked, his leather gloves
worn white.

"Will you write me a letter?" he said.

"Sure," I said.

"Think you'll be back this way?" he asked.

"If I come back," I said, "will you take me dancing?"

"Damn right," he said, and a smile that seemed like the smile I'd been waiting for my whole life spread wide across his face.

"Then it'll be sooner than later," I said.

He winked and touched the horse's flank with his spurs and it hopped a little on the takeoff and then there was just dirt flying while the high grass swallowed the horse's legs. I leaned against the door of my pickup truck watching my new cowboy riding off toward where the sun was already low in the sky and the grass shimmering like nothing I'd ever seen in the mountains. And for a minute I thought we were living inside my painting, but he was riding away too fast to tell. And I wondered then why I had always imagined my cowboy's truck as it was leaving. I wondered why I hadn't turned the truck around and painted my cowboy coming home.

There's a story—that isn't true—that I tell about myself when I first meet someone, about riding a mechanical bull in a bar. In the story, I stay on through the first eight levels of difficulty, getting thrown on level nine only after dislocating my thumb and winning my boyfriend, who was betting on me, a big pile of money. It was something I said in a bar one night, and I liked the way it sounded so much I kept telling it. I've been telling it for so many years now, and in such scrupulous detail, that it has become a memory and it's hard for me to remember that it isn't true. I can smell the smoke and beersoaked carpets, I can hear the cheers of all the men. I can see the bar lights blur and spin, and I can feel the cold iron buck between my thighs, the painted saddle slam against my tailbone, the surprise and pain when my thumb extends too far and I let go. It's a good story, a story that holds my listeners' attention, and although I consider myself almost pathologically honest, I have somehow allowed myself this one small lie.

And watching Monte ride off through the long grains, I thought about the way we invent ourselves through our stories, and in a similar way, how the stories we tell put walls around our lives. And I think that may be true about cowboys. That there really isn't much truth in my saying cowboys are my weakness; maybe, after all this time, it's just something I've learned how to say.

I felt the hoofbeats in the ground long after Monte's white shirt and ratty hat melded with the sun. When I couldn't even pretend to feel them anymore, I got in the car and headed for the hard road.

I listened to country music the whole way to Cody, Wyoming. The men in the songs were all either brutal or inexpressive and always sorry later. The women were victims, every one. I started to think about coming back to the ranch to visit Monte, about another night dancing, about another night wanting the impossible love of a country song, and I thought:

This is not my happy ending.

This is not my story.